NEW PATHS TO URBANIZATION IN CHINA:
SEEKING MORE BALANCED PATTERNS

NEW PATHS TO URBANIZATION IN CHINA:
SEEKING MORE BALANCED PATTERNS

YU ZHU

Nova Science Publications, Inc.
Commack, New York

Editorial Production:	Susan Boriotti
Office Manager:	Annette Hellinger
Graphics:	Frank Grucci and Jennifer Lucas
Information Editor:	Tatiana Shohov
Book Production:	Donna Dennis, Patrick Davin, Christine Mathosian, Tammy Sauter and Lynette Van Helden
Circulation:	Maryanne Schmidt
Marketing/Sales:	Cathy DeGregory

Library of Congress Cataloging-in-Publication Data

Zhu, Yu.
New Paths to Urbanization in China: Seeking More Balanced Patterns / by Yu Zhu.
     p.   cm.
Includes bibliographical references and index.
ISBN 1-56072-681-4
1. Urbanization--China. 2. Urban policy--China. 3. China--Rural conditions.
4. China--Economic Condition--1976-- I. Title.
HT384.C6Z485   1999   99-22770
307.76'0951—dc21   CIP

Copyright © 1999 by Nova Science Publishers, Inc.
       6080 Jericho Turnpike, Suite 207
       Commack, New York 11725
       Tele. 516-499-3103   Fax 516-499-3146
       e-mail: Novascience@earthlink.net
       e-mail: Novascil@aol.com
       Web Site: http://www.nexusworld.com/nova

Printed in the United States of America

CONTENTS

LIST OF TABLES AND FIGURES

LIST OF TABLES

LIST OF FIGURES

ACKNOWLEDGMENTS

This book is a revised version of my Ph.D. thesis. I would like to thank the Demography Program of the Australian National University for admitting me as a Ph.D. candidate in July 1995, and Professor Peter McDonald for inviting me as a program visitor to complete this book after I submitted the thesis in September 1998. I am grateful to the Australian Government and the Australian National University for providing me with the scholarships. I also wish to express my thanks to all the staff in the Demography Program for their teaching, supervising and all kinds of assistance.

I am particularly indebted to the chair of my supervision panel, Professor Gavin W. Jones; my supervisors Dr. Zhongwei Zhao and Dr. Chris Wilson; and my advisers, Dr. David Lucas and Professor Dean Forbes for their intellectual stimulation, guidance, and constructive comments. My great thanks also go to Mrs. Wendy Cosford for her careful reading of my draft and skilful editing, and Mr. Keith Mitchell for drawing the maps. I would also like to acknowledge with gratitude the helpful comments and suggestions from Professor Michael Douglass at the Department of Urban and Regional Planning of the University of Hawaii Manoa; Professor Graeme Hugo at the Department of Geography of the University of Adelaide; Professor Zeng Yi at the Institute of Population Research of Peking University; Professor G. J. R. Linge at the Department of Human Geography of the ANU; Professor Jamie Mackie at the Department of Economics of the ANU; Ms. Marian May at the Demography Program of the ANU; Dr. Alaric Maude, Dr. Ross Steele, and Mr. Noel Tracy of Flinders University; and editors and the anonymous referees for my papers derived from my Ph.D thesis and published in the journals *Third World Planning Review* and *Asia-Pacific Population Journal*. Most of the material in Chapter 3 was published as "'Formal' and 'informal urbanisation' in China: trends in Fujian Province" in *Third World Planning Review* 20(3):267-284. Most of the material in section 4.3 of Chapter 4 was published as "Spatial effects of 'informal urbanization' in China: the case of Fujian Province" in *Asia-Pacific Population Journal* 13(1):25-44. I would like to acknowledge both *Third World Planning Review* and *Asia-Pacific Population Journal* for permitting me to include these materials in this book.

I wish to extend my thanks to my old colleagues at the Institute of Geography in Fujian Normal University, especially Professors Jiayuan Chen, Daxian Zheng, Yougong Wu, and Zhong Lin for their helpful suggestions and for sharing their material about Fujian. I would also like to give many thanks to the relevant provincial and local government departments in Fuzhou, Fuqing, and Jinjiang for their kind assistance and for providing invaluable data during my fieldwork. My special thanks go to my fellow residents at 20 Balmain Crescent, especially Thomas Schindlmayr.

Finally, I express my deep appreciation and love for my wife Kunmei Huang, my parents Liyao Zhu and Ruilan Yang, and my son Chuanshi Zhu, for their understanding and full support.

CHAPTER 1

INTRODUCTION

1.1 RATIONALE FOR THE STUDY

1.1.1 THE SIGNIFICANCE OF STUDIES ON URBANIZATION AND ITS PATTERNS IN DEVELOPING COUNTRIES

The accelerating pace of world urbanization has been one of the most significant developments of the twentieth century. This development has had great effects on almost all aspects of our lives. It is vital for economic growth, diversification and development. It transforms people's values, attitudes, behavior, and life styles in general. In fact, "during the twentieth century, increasing urbanization has probably generated greater social and economic change than occurred in the preceding millennium" (Hauser 1987:xv). Urbanization and its implications are so profound that it is termed "urban transition" (Kelley and Williamson 1984). It is not surprising that urbanization attracts much research attention from various disciplines.

While most developed countries were urbanized in the nineteenth and early-twentieth centuries, urbanization in developing countries is mainly a late-twentieth century and early-twenty-first century process. Because "contemporary patterns of urbanization in much of the developing world depart substantially from those that would have been expected on the past experience of industrialized countries or of stereotypical models of urban industrialization" (Hackenberg 1980:391), it is of great scholastic interest to examine the urbanization patterns in developing countries. Given the great effects of urbanization on social and economic development, this kind of study also has great practical significance in developing countries. In addition, many problems arising in the process of urbanization are related to its pattern (Rondinelli 1980:332). Therefore studies on urbanization patterns in developing countries can provide an important base of information and analysis for solving their urban problems.

1.1.2 THE DILEMMA OF URBANIZATION IN DEVELOPING COUNTRIES: THE NEED TO SEEK NEW URBANIZATION PATTERNS

As mentioned above, urbanization patterns in many developing countries are quite different from those of currently developed countries in their industrialization period. In fact, developing countries are facing a dilemma in their urbanization processes (Jones 1983:3-4). On the one hand, the rate of urbanization in developing countries is not unusual by historical standards (Preston 1979:196; United Nations 1995:23). Given their low levels of urbanization, an increase in the level of urbanization in developing countries is inevitable. On the other hand, because of the much faster natural population growth in these countries, the rise in urbanization levels requires an unprecedentedly higher urban population growth rate. As Preston pointed out in 1979,

Urbanization in developing countries did not proceed with unusual speed in the quarter-century from 1950 to 1975. In this period the percentage urban grew from 16.7 to 28.0 in developing countries. While this is a rapid increase, it is very similar to the one that occurred in more developed countries during the last quarter of the nineteenth century. Between 1875 and 1900 the percentage urban of countries now more developed grew from 17.2 to 26.1 (Preston 1979:196).

Nevertheless,

Between 1875 and 1900, urban populations in now-developed countries grew by 100 percent and rural populations by 18 percent. While developing countries were traversing roughly the same range in proportions urban between 1950 and 1975, their urban populations grew by 188 percent and their rural ones by 49 percent (Preston 1979:198).

The new UN estimate and projection show that developing countries will again traverse roughly the same range in proportions urban between 1975 and 2000 as now-developed countries did between 1900 and 1925 (from 26 percent to 40 percent), but urban population in less developed countries will increase by 145 percent in the period 1975-2000, still much faster than in now-developed countries between 1900 and 1925 (90 percent) (United Nations 1980:7; 1998:88-89, 96-7). Thus rapid urbanization is needed in developing countries, but Western levels of urbanization, if they are to be achieved, "imply increases in urban population so massive that they are almost impossible to conceive" (Jones 1983:3-4). This kind of dilemma is an important characteristic of the urbanization patterns in many developing countries. It suggests that developing countries need to seek a pattern which can best keep the balance between the desirable level of urbanization and the appropriate pace of urban growth.

The necessity of seeking new patterns of urbanization is further emphasized by another important characteristic of urbanization in developing countries: its highly concentrated spatial pattern. From 1950 to 1990 the percentage of urban population living in million-plus cities increased from 22.5 to 35.0 in less developed countries. The most striking manifestation of this pattern is the emergence of more and more mega-cities. In 1950, only New York and London had a population of 8 million or more. But in mid-1994, there were 22 cities with a population of 8 million or more in the world, and 16 of them were in the less developed regions (United Nations 1995:6-10). These large cities have significant proportions of their country's urban population. In Asia for example, more than one-half of Thailand's urban population lives in Bangkok, and one-third of the urban population of the Republic of Korea, Bangladesh and the Philippines live in Seoul, Dhaka and Metro Manila, respectively. The populations of Jakarta, Karachi, Istanbul and Teheran account for almost 20 percent of their nations' urban population. In these Asian cities a population growth rate of 3 percent per annum was quite common in the period 1970-1990 (United Nations 1993:2-8). Again the rapid growth of mega-cities occurred in settings of low levels of urbanization and development, and there is urgent need for developing countries to develop policies to cope with this process (United Nations 1993:2-22).

Furthermore, two difficulties arising in the process of urbanization in developing countries confirm the concern about the above-mentioned urbanization patterns with unprecedented and highly-concentrated urban population growth. One difficulty is that developing countries' cities face serious urban problems with which they do not have the resources to cope. In Asia for example, cities of developing countries have the most serious shortages of land, shelter, and infrastructure services as well as environmental deterioration. Large segments of urban population living below the poverty line and without productive employment are also obvious and visible manifestations of urban problems (United Nations 1993:2-39—2-55). In Latin America, the largest cities are also experiencing serious housing, transport, pollution, employment, and service supply problems (Rondinelli 1983:31-2). Another difficulty is that the expansion of metropolitan cities is often directly and causally connected with regional disparities. This is a major feature of the spatial structure in developing countries and causes serious development problems (Bronger 1993:35). Rondinelli (1980:331) analyzed urbanization and development problems in Asian nations. He pointed out that the goals of modernization sought in the development plans for more than a quarter of a century were largely achieved in the major urban centers. Cities are growing and prospering, but at the same time great disparities remain between industrializing economies and agricultural economies; between urban wealthy elites and the poor masses that live in rural areas and the urban fringes; among geographic regions; and between different people with different access to productive resources and employment opportunities. These problems offset or reduce the benefits of urbanization in developing countries. Facing these problems we have to answer such questions as: are these patterns of urbanization our only choices? If not, what are the alternative patterns of urbanization that would ensure the largest benefits while reducing the costs to the utmost extent? To answer these questions extensive country case studies are obviously needed.

1.1.3 THE UNKNOWN EXPERIENCES OF CHINA: NEW PATHS TO URBANIZATION?

Until recently studies on urbanization in developing countries have focused almost exclusively on large metropolitan areas and primate cities (Rondinelli 1983:12). More and more problems relating to over-concentrated urbanization have been revealed, but less attention has been given to the possible alternative patterns of urbanization which exist outside the big cities (Jones 1991:22). In this regard studies on China's urbanization patterns could have significant importance. First, China's patterns of urbanization are remarkably different from those in other nations (Ebanks and Cheng 1990; Ma and Lin 1993:583). As it has not been long since China adopted reform and open door policies, not enough attention has been paid to these patterns, and their characteristics and effects on socioeconomic development have not been fully examined. Secondly, since 1978 new patterns of "urbanization from below" (Ma and Lin 1993:584) have been emerging in the Chinese countryside. One of the major effects of these urbanization patterns has been the decline in the degree of primacy in the city system. This trend is in sharp contrast with the experience of most developing countries where urbanization has been dominated by the growth of the primate cities, as mentioned above; and it is at odds with conventional theories (Xu and Li 1990:67) which will be reviewed later. It seems that China's urbanization patterns provide alternatives to those prevailing in other developing countries (Chang and Kwok 1990:141), and studies on them would not only be helpful in answering the questions posed above, but also enrich our understanding of urbanization in developing countries in general. Besides, as Chang, Douglass and Kim (1989:11) point out, "the present choice of which path to be pursued along China's urbanization road will be of importance for decades to come". There have been major differences and heated discussions on this matter in China (Gu 1991:187; S. Z. Liao 1992; Zhu 1992; D. Q. Liao 1995). Because of this a study on the new urbanization patterns in China would have important policy implications.

The research project regarding China's new urbanization patterns presented in this book is proposed on the basis of the aforementioned considerations. These new urbanization patterns first emerged in some coastal provinces pioneering in China's reform and open-door processes, and are still in the process of further development and diffusion to other provinces in China. China's conventional official data on urbanization are far from adequate for examining these new patterns. So this project is not intended to give a general description of urbanization patterns in China as a whole. Rather it tries to explore the causes, effects and implications of these new urbanization patterns through case studies in areas where these patterns are most developed. To serve this purpose I chose Fujian Province to conduct this project. As described in detail in Chapter 2, this area is one of the regions with the fastest economic growth in China. It is also one of the trial bases of China's reform and open door policies and has been at the forefront of social and economic development, including urbanization. Nevertheless, most of these changes have been happening in the rural areas, taking the form of rural industrialization and town development. Furthermore, there has been no massive migration to the major cities in this region; on the contrary many new small urban places have emerged on a widespread regional basis, and many migrants have been attracted to the areas where township and village enterprises[1] have been developing very quickly. The proportion of urban population living in the major cities of this area has declined (Zhu 1994a, b). Thus the new patterns of urbanization in China after 1978 can be explored through the case studies in this area. Furthermore, although Fujian is becoming an increasingly important coastal province, it has attracted far less attention in academic circles than its coastal

---

[1] "Township and village enterprises" (TVEs) is actually not a perfect translation of the corresponding Chinese term, because it does not cover towns, which have been important in China's rural industrialization. But as it is a widely used term, I also use it.

counterparts like Guangdong, Zhejiang, Jiangsu, let alone Shanghai. In fact urbanization in Fujian since 1978 has been basically unknown to the Western world (Tang 1995:1), and thus deserves more exploration.

1.2 RESEARCH BACKGROUND

Existing theories and empirical studies regarding urbanization patterns can be divided into two distinct foci: one relates to the causes of urbanization in general, and the other to the causes of polarization in large urban centers. A literature review on both aspects confirms the possibility of seeking new urbanization patterns, and shows that although there are many existing theories providing a framework for analysis of urbanization patterns, more and more new questions about actual situations have been emerging, and further research is needed to articulate new situations, and enable revision and expansion of existing theories. Some studies on China's urbanization since the 1980s have already contributed to our understanding in this aspect, but much remains to be done.

1.2.1 PREVIOUS RESEARCH ON THE CAUSES OF URBANIZATION IN GENERAL

Theories regarding the causes of urbanization can be traced back to the classical "push-pull" model in nineteenth-century writings. As reviewed by Williamson (1988:426), while Engels thought it was the rapid development of industrialization that led to Manchester's booming growth, Ravenstein maintained that rural-urban migration was caused by Malthusian forces, agricultural land scarcity, and enclosure. Here Engels explained urbanization by "pull" factors, whereas Ravenstein explained it by "push" factors. Meanwhile, as early as in 1861 Mayhew already referred to the low-wage ("informal sector") labor in London, stressing the role of informal sectors in the employment of rural-urban migrants. All three arguments are still present in explaining urbanization in developing countries today. Although they exist in different, more advanced forms, they have the same characteristics that economic factors and employment opportunities occupy pride of place among reasons for urbanization. These arguments have profoundly influenced later economists' thinking about development and urbanization.

In the 1950s Lewis (1954) set forth the "dual economy" model of economic development; later this model was modified and extended by Ranis and Fei (1961). The dual economy model views the economy of developing countries as consisting of two sectors: the traditional, agricultural sector characterized by low productivity and surplus labor and the modern, non-agricultural sector characterized by high productivity and higher wages. With economic development, labor would be gradually transferred from the traditional agricultural to the modern non-agricultural sector. Such transfer has obvious spatial implications, the notable example being urbanization (Williamson 1988:449). It is assumed that rational economic choices are involved in labor transfer: migrants move because they expect to find better jobs and higher wages in the urban non-agricultural sector. The model also suggests that the level of wages in the urban non-agricultural sector will be constant while surplus labor persists, and will be determined in the long run by labor supply from rural areas.

Later Todaro (1969) developed a new model known as the "expected income" model. In this model migration proceeds in response to urban-rural differences in expected, rather than actual income. The decision to move is a function of two variables: the gap in income between the rural and urban populations, and the possibility of finding employment in the cities. Migration takes place until the expected urban wage is equated to the rural wage, although migrants are aware of the possibility of being underemployed in the "informal sector" or even totally unemployed for substantial periods of time. In this way, Todaro tried to explain the paradox of long-lasting unemployment along with massive rural-urban migration, which generated long-lasting debate on this issue.

These theories explain the functions of structural changes in the economy in the process of urbanization; but they still do not fully reveal the mechanism of urbanization, because "agglomeration economies can provide an endogenous explanation for the rate of urban productivity growth and on this basis alone deserve investigation" (Montgomery 1988:692). So the full explanation of urbanization has to incorporate the phenomenon of agglomeration economies, and the mechanisms whereby these translate into faster and more concentrated urbanization than would otherwise be the case.

Agglomeration economies are connected with the minimization of transport, information, and communication costs. They can take two forms: localization economies and urbanization economies. Localization economies reflect possibilities for greater specialization among an industry's firms with increasing industry size in an area, reduced cost in matching job categories for workers specializing in that industry, and more rapid transmission of new technology. Urbanization economies are the result of the overall level of economic activity in a city. They reflect the effect of such factors as a large labor market, a large business service sector, and economies associated with large-scale provision of public infrastructure (Friedmann 1966:29; Hamer 1987:196-7). Obviously to achieve agglomeration economies the spatial clustering of firms, workers, and consumers is necessary. That is why structural economic change is accompanied by spatial transformation, which normally takes the form of urbanization.

The above theories reveal that structural economic changes and the corresponding spatial clustering are the major mechanisms of urbanization. They will be important components of the analytical framework of the urbanization study in China; but it should be noted that these theories are only valid at a certain level of generality. They only reflect the general trends of urbanization and development and cannot explain the concrete relationships between urbanization and economic development, especially under changing social and economic conditions in developing countries. Besides China's experiences mentioned above, several studies have produced evidence indicating this problem. The most apparent evidence is that "the relationship between structural economic change and urbanization....is not as tight as it is often imagined" (Jones 1991:12). A major indication of the flexibility in this relationship is that there is a wide range of both industry-urban ratios and non-agricultural employment-urban ratios in developing countries (Jones 1983:9-21). In fact during the course of economic development the rural labor force does not simply passively release agricultural workers for non-agricultural employment in the cities; indeed in the rural area itself, more and more people engage in non-agricultural activities (Jones 1983:18-21; 1991:11-2). Hackenberg also notes the evidence in developing countries that rural areas are being penetrated by urban-like forms of production, infrastructure, and administration—a process of "diffuse urbanization" that is introducing new possibilities for dispersed economic growth and new patterns of spatial and social mobility (Hackenberg 1980:391).

McGee and Ginsburg also provide evidence of a "settlement transition", which involves "the urbanization of the countryside without massive rural-urban migration", in "the extended metropolis" in Asia (Ginsburg 1991). They argue that in the Asian context the conventional view of the urban transition, which assumes that the widely accepted distinction between rural and urban will persist as the urbanization process advances, needs to be re-evaluated (McGee 1991:4).

Taiwan's experience shows that the highly concentrated distribution of population can be prevented by adopting certain social and economic policies and programs without slowing down the rapid economic development and urbanization (Tsai 1987). All these are indications that structural change in employment and economic development can be achieved under new patterns that are at odds with the conventional wisdom, which suggests a rigid correspondence between structural economic change and spatial clustering. But despite all these indications there are still few studies that examine systematically what characteristics these new patterns have and how they work. The existing theories need to be revised or extended on the basis of this kind of study in order to articulate the new realities. China's new experiences in this aspect make this kind of study even more necessary.

1.2.2 PREVIOUS RESEARCH ON THE CAUSES OF POLARIZATION IN LARGE CITIES

In consideration of the striking increase in the percentage of urban population living in large cities, the aforementioned theoretical framework seems inadequate to cover the whole range of issues. There are obviously other forces besides structural changes of economy and agglomeration economies which influence the urbanization process in developing countries, especially the growth of metropolitan areas. So we need to go further into the causes of polarization in the large cities in developing countries.

Theories and evidence regarding this problem are both various and controversial (Jones 1991:19-21, 23-5). Many relevant existing theories, such as the classical location theory and the spatial organization theory, are deficient in dealing with the problems relating to the regional (or spatial) system and its evolution in the development process (Friedmann 1972:82-5). The most famous theoretical approach regarding the process of urban and spatial concentration is Friedmann's "center-periphery" model, which incorporated the ideas of Myrdal and Hirchmann about how market forces accentuated regional inequalities, general models of economic development, and regional planning strategies (Friedmann 1966; Gilbert and Gugler 1982:31-5; Xu and Li 1990:49). In this model the center-periphery dichotomy characterizes the urbanization process. In the early stages of development urban centers appear for service and administrative purposes. Then as industrialization proceeds, people, capital, technology, innovation and power are concentrated in one or two urban centers with higher productivity.

Gradually a dualistic spatial structure emerges with the largest urban center forming the core, smaller towns and the countryside forming the periphery. Disparities increase as resources continue to flow to the core away from the periphery. At some point when industrialization becomes mature the process of development begins to trickle down, allowing the periphery to develop. The combined effects of national government intervention, provincial initiative, and rising national income reduce regional disparities and bring about greater spatial balance. Finally a fully integrated space economy will emerge with minimum essential inter-regional imbalance. The corollary of this model is that polarization is a natural process in the pace of national development, and the emergence of the metropolis is rational, because it is the most efficient way to increase production. Some evidence seems to support this view (Jones 1991:24).

However, there is much evidence which casts doubt on the necessity and effect of polarization in the process of industrialization, especially when the polarization is so extreme. The experience of currently developed countries in their industrialization period does not seem to support this model unanimously. In that period cities with populations of 100,000 or more were already referred to as large cities, many of which would be classified only as small- or medium-sized cities in today's developing countries. The relative growth rates of these large cities with relation to other cities were much more complicated than the model would suggest[2]. In fact the highly concentrated pattern of urban growth now seen in many developing countries did not appear until the early twentieth century (Rondinelli 1983:86).

World system theory (Wallerstein 1974; 1976) and its earlier form dependency theory (Frank 1969) provide another major perspective from which to examine the primacy issues in developing countries. According to these theories, the internal spatial structure of developing countries should be viewed as part of the world system of production and consumption, which is characterized by the exploitation of periphery states by core states (Gilbert and Gugler 1982:34-5; Shannon 1989:28-32). The emergence of metropolitan cities in developing countries is not purely the result of industrial growth; in fact many large cities in developing countries are the legacy of colonial penetration. For example the emergence of many large cities in both Asia and Latin America resulted from the trade relationship with and natural resource exploitation by colonial powers. This spatial pattern continues in the post-colonial phases because of the difficulties of

---

[2] For more detailed discussion see Chapter 6.

overcoming the early effects of concentrated investment and primacy. It is even enhanced by the location of government and the paraphernalia of modernization (Rondinelli 1978:15-6, 1983:86-7; Gilbert and Gugler 1982:38-48; Brohman 1996:227).

As to the effect of polarization, Jones (1991:25) warns that "it may be naive to expect polarization reversal to happen automatically in most developing countries". There are several reasons for this: developing countries today may never reach the development stage at which regional disparities begin to narrow; regional disparities in these countries are much more serious; and convergence needs effective government intervention, but many governments show little interest or ability to intervene. There are also reasons to doubt the efficiency of large cities. The high productivity in the large cities should not necessarily be attributed only to agglomeration economies, for it could also be attributed to the better urban infrastructure or higher-quality labor. Therefore the urban primacy in developing countries can be seen as a distorted and undesirable manifestation (Gilbert and Gugler 1982:177-9).

This debate suggests new research needs, one of which is: what would happen to the spatial pattern of development if there were no influence of colonization, and post-colonial concentration of administration and investment in the major cities in developing countries? New insights into the issue of polarization in developing countries can be gained through such studies.

1.2.3 PREVIOUS RESEARCH ON CHINA'S URBANIZATION SINCE THE 1980S

As alternatives to the prevailing urbanization patterns in developing countries, China's new urbanization patterns have attracted some scholars' attention. Their preliminary studies have already been beneficial to our understanding not only about China, but also about the theoretical and empirical problems reviewed in the preceding two sections.

First, scholars from both China and abroad recognized the unusualness of China's urbanization patterns since the 1980s. One of the major characteristics of those patterns is rapid industrialization with a lag in urbanization[3], which is char-

---

[3] This has been the case if only the conventionally understood urbanization is concerned. Nevertheless, things will be different if "spontaneous urbanization" is taken into account, as can be seen in the following chapters.

acterized furthermore by the development of small cities and towns (Ma and Lin 1993; Liao 1995). As already pointed out, this kind of urbanization challenged the traditional models of urbanization and the conventional theories with regard to both the relationship between structural change of the economy and spatial clustering and the polarization process in regional development (Ebanks and Cheng 1990; Xu and Li 1990; Ma and Lin 1993).

Secondly, much work has been done to reveal China's urbanization level and examine the proximate causes of urbanization at the national level, focusing on the influence of China's confusing urban definitions (Goldstein 1990; Gu 1991; Chan 1994). This kind of work made clearer the real trend of urbanization in China, and to some extent revealed the mechanism of China's urbanization with regard to "floating population" and reclassification. This is certainly a necessary step towards a deeper understanding of China's urbanization.

Thirdly, some studies have been conducted to reveal the underlying causes of the urbanization patterns in China. For example, in their study about the urbanization experience in Guangdong Province since the 1980s, Xu and Li (1990) identified more balanced spatial development and explored the reasons for this, most of them concerning broad macro factors such as economic and administrative reforms and Guangdong's relationship to Hong Kong.

Despite all those achievements much more remains unclear. First, while there is consensus that China's urbanization patterns are unusual, it is still controversial whether those patterns are desirable and feasible (Chang and Kwok 1990:140). There have been major differences and heated discussions on this matter in China (Gu 1991:187; Zhu 1992; S. Z. Liao 1992; D. Q. Liao 1995). Secondly, there is the need to examine China's urbanization trends and patterns from a new perspective. For example, while there has been much discussion on China's urban definitions and their influence on China's urbanization levels, rural urbanization, which is largely driven by township and village enterprises and often not covered by the official definitions of urban population, has been neglected. The conclusion that China's urbanization lags behind industrialization is actually established on such a basis and needs further examination. In addition, the significance of reclassification and migration is far beyond the problem of urban definition and urbanization level. More research needs to be done to reveal their spatial implications for China's urbanization. Thirdly, the urbanization process in China has rarely been analyzed in an international and historical perspective. Some disputes on the desirability of China's urbanization patterns arise from this problem. A common assertion in these disputes is that the rapid growth of large cities is a "rule" confirmed by the experience of various countries in the world, especially that of developed countries. This rule is taken as the evidence supporting large cities as the key of urban development strategy (Liao 1995). As can be seen in Chapter 6, such a "rule" is oversimplified, resulting from the lack of complete understanding of other countries' urbanization experience. Fourthly, as China is so big and different regions have different experiences, more case studies should be undertaken and more factors, especially those at a micro-level, should be articulated into the macro-analysis to gain full understanding of the urbanization process in China since the 1980s. Finally, even more needs to be done to incorporate China's urbanization into the relevant theories and where necessary, to modify those theories accordingly. It seems that there is still a long way to go in contributing some insights into the urbanization problems posed above by studying China's experience.

1.3 RESEARCH OBJECTIVES

On the basis of the above proposed research questions and reviewed research backgrounds, the main objectives of this study are defined as follows.

1.3.1 TO REVEAL THE CHARACTERISTICS OF THE NEW URBANIZATION PATTERNS IN CHINA, ESPECIALLY FUJIAN PROVINCE

This will involve:

(1) Revealing the temporal characteristics of the new urbanization patterns. In this part the urbanization process since 1949 will be reviewed. Major efforts will be made to reveal the new tracks of urbanization since 1978, which are not properly covered by the official definitions and statistics, and their increasing importance in the urbanization process.

(2) Revealing the spatial features of the new urbanization patterns. This will be achieved by reviewing the evolution of the urban system and the residential hierarchy, by examining the proximate causes of urbanization, especially the increasing importance of reclassification and more dispersed patterns of migration.

1.3.2 To Analyze the Underlying Causes of the New Urbanization Patterns

This will involve:

(1) Examining the need for urbanization as the outlet for rural surplus labor;

(2) Reviewing government policies toward rural-urban migration and urbanization and their effects on urbanization patterns;

(3) Analyzing the mechanism of structural changes in the economy and their implications for urbanization under the new patterns, focusing on the roles of township and village enterprises and foreign investment, and the relevant government policies;

(4) Articulating other factors which contribute to the characteristics of the new urbanization patterns but have not been paid enough attention in previous studies. These factors include the new demographic context, the improvement of transport and communication, the links with Chinese overseas[4], Hong Kongers and Taiwanese, and some cultural and institutional factors.

1.3.3 To Examine the New Urbanization Patterns from an International and Historical Perspective

This will involve:

(1) Revealing in more detail why the new urbanization patterns have taken their current forms, by looking at them from an international and historical context;

(2) Assessing the desirability and applicability of the new urbanization patterns from an international and historical perspective.

1.3.4 To Draw Some Theoretical and Policy Implications from the Study

This will involve:

---

[4] Following Wang (1993:926-7), in this book "Chinese overseas" refers to everyone of Chinese descent living outside Mainland China, Taiwan, Hong Kong and Macau. The more commonly used term "overseas Chinese" is a direct translation of the Chinese term *Huaqiao* which implies Chinese citizenship. Wang considers that this is misleading when applied to the ethnic Chinese living in other countries, many of whom are citizens of those countries.

(1) Proposing conceptual revision of urbanization studies according to the changing conditions in developing countries;

(2) Discussing the inadequacy and the elaboration of existing theories regarding urbanization and regional development by taking into account the new realities emerging from the study such as the flexibility of the relationship between the structural changes and spatial clustering, the non-polarized spatial patterns of development and foreign investments;

(3) Discussing the policy implications of the new urbanization patterns, focusing on their implications for China's urban and regional development policies and China's urban planning theories and practice. The implications for other developing countries will also be discussed.

1.4 GENERAL RESEARCH DESIGN AND DATA SOURCES

1.4.1 THE DEFINITION OF URBANIZATION AND THE SCOPE OF THIS STUDY

No consensus has yet been reached on the definition of "urban" and "urbanization" in the literature (Lin 1994:2). In this study urbanization is regarded as a multi-dimensional phenomenon (Goldstein and Sly 1975:14; Lin 1994:5) and continuing process (Yu and Ning 1983:20). From this perspective, the demographic definition of urbanization, that is, the rise in the proportion of persons living in urban areas (IUSSP 1982:44; Jones 1991:5), is too narrow for the needs of this study. According to the United Nations, urbanization consists of at least four components: first, the definition of urban areas; secondly, the growth of population in these urban areas which is generally caused by rural-urban migration, natural increase and reclassification; thirdly, an increase in the numbers of people engaged in non-agricultural activities; finally, the distinctive environment and organization of cities which enable urban ways of life (United Nations 1993:2-1). This definition does not make a clear distinction between urban growth and urbanization, but covers the main aspects of the urbanization process, and will be the basis of the following discussions. Thus in the following my study will not be restricted to the demographic dimensions of urbanization such as population size and density; rather it will be related to all components of and processes leading to urbanization, especially the rural industrialization in my fieldwork sites.

1.4.2 GENERAL RESEARCH STRATEGY

As mentioned above, case study research will be the predominant research activity in this study. Yin gives the definition of case study and describes its use as follows.

A case study is an empirical inquiry that investigates a contemporary phenomenon within its real-life context, when the boundaries between phenomenon and context are not clearly evident; and in which multiple sources of evidence are used (Yin 1984:23).

The most important use of case study is to "explain the causal links in real-life interventions that are too complex for the survey or experimental strategy" (Yin 1984: 25).

Urbanization is certainly a phenomenon which interweaves with various socio-economic processes. If it is to be examined deeply, complex and large amounts of information are needed. Therefore the case study strategy can best accommodate the nature of this study.

1.4.3 DATA SOURCES

An important characteristic and a major strength of case study research is that it uses multiple sources of evidence. In this study data are collected from the following different sources.

(1) Census and survey data. These mainly include the data from the 1982 and 1990 censuses, and the data from the one percent sample survey conducted in October 1995. They are mainly used for the analysis of the temporal and spatial characteristics of urbanization.

(2) Annual statistical reports and relevant publications. Data of this kind serve two purposes: first to provide a basis for the analysis of the temporal and spatial characteristics of urbanization, secondly to provide socio-economic information needed for exploring the causes of urbanization.

(3) Government documents and archival records. These include government regulations regarding rural-urban migration and urban planning; urban and regional planning documents of the fieldwork sites; and some more detailed socio-economic information which is not published in the statistical reports.

(4) Interviews and direct observation. Government officials and scholars engaged in the study and planning of urban and regional development, and even the ordinary residents in the fieldwork sites are asked for more information.

These interviews are of an open-ended nature. In some situations respondents are even asked to propose their own insights into certain occurrences, and such propositions are used as the basis for further inquiry. Direct personal observations are made to gain the first perceptual knowledge, to identify problems for further investigation, and to get more information.

The most important advantage of the data sources is their wide coverage of the political, social, and economic changes in the study areas. The access to government documents, archival records, and officials is particularly important, because they often provide me with some very useful information. Such data sources allow me to explore a wide range of factors relating to the urbanization process in a broad context, and to get insights into some important issues through in-depth personal discussions and personal observation. The shortcoming of the data sources is that there is no systematic data set for me to conduct more detailed analysis at the micro-level. This could have been avoided by conducting my own survey. But given the constraints of time and resources, this can only be left to research in the future.

1.4.4 RESEARCH PROCEDURES AND ANALYTICAL METHODS

In general this study is conducted at three levels. First the theoretical and international backgrounds are established, and the study is put in this context. Secondly, the characteristics of the urbanization patterns in Fujian Province are examined at the provincial level. Some general characteristics of urbanization and factors influencing urbanization patterns in China as a whole are also reflected at this level. Thirdly, in-depth investigations are conducted at the municipality level to explore the causes of the new urbanization patterns. Three case study sites are chosen to serve different purposes (see also Figure 2.1 in Chapter 2): (1) Fuzhou is chosen as the fieldwork site to explore the roles of the government's direct policy intervention and the urbanization of its suburban areas in the formation of the new urbanization patterns; (2) Fuqing is chosen as the fieldwork site to explore the roles of foreign investment in the formation of the new urbanization patterns; (3) Jinjiang is chosen as the fieldwork site to explore the role of township and village enterprises in the formation of the new urbanization patterns.

Three methods are used in the data analysis. (1) Quantitative analysis is primarily used to analyze the characteristics of the new urbanization patterns. This involves estimating the urbanization trend in Fujian Province since the 1980s and examining the spatial features of the urbanization patterns. (2) Qualitative analy-

sis is the major method in the analysis of the underlying causes of the new urbanization patterns, the assessment of the new urbanization patterns, and the generalization of the theoretical and policy implications. This is partly because of the
fact that urbanization patterns in China are very much related to policy, which is
difficult to quantify, and partly because systematic data are not easily available.
Besides it is intended in this research to examine in depth the roles of some contributing factors (for example township and village enterprises) to the new urbanization patterns, rather than to touch all the relevant factors without focal
points. It seems that the qualitative method is more suitable for this purpose. (3)
In some cases cartographic methods are used to illustrate the spatial patterns of
urban and regional development more clearly.

1.5 CHAPTER OUTLINE

Chapter 2 gives a brief introduction to some regional situations and their
historical development in Fujian Province. It serves as an account of the broad
context within which the new urbanization patterns have been developing.

Chapter 3 examines the temporal characteristics of urbanization patterns in
China. It briefly reviews urbanization processes in both China as a whole and
Fujian Province in particular since 1949, but places the emphasis on revealing the
new tracks of "urbanization from below" caused by profound socio-economic
changes since 1978, and estimating the urbanization trend by integrating these
new urbanization processes.

Chapter 4 explores the spatial features of Fujian's urbanization patterns. It
examines the evolution of Fujian's urban system, especially the influences of the
new rural-urban transformation processes on the evolution of the urban system. It
also analyzes the proximate causes of Fujian's urbanization to identify the importance of reclassification and short-distance migration in the new urbanization
processes.

Chapter 5 uses the cases of three municipalities as examples to investigate
the government policies towards rural-urban migration and urbanization, the
emergence and development of township and village enterprises and foreign investment and the relevant government policy changes; and to explore the roles of
the State, TVEs and foreign investment in influencing the new urbanization patterns.

Chapter 6 assesses the new urbanization processes both in the light of past
urbanization processes in developed countries and in the context of developing

countries' conditions. It also explores the effects of some enabling factors to the new urbanization patterns, such as high population density, improved transport and communication conditions, the connections of Chinese overseas, Hong Kongers and Taiwanese to their ancestral regions, and the Chinese culture.

Chapter 7 discusses the theoretical and policy implications of the study. It analyzes the inadequacy of existing urbanization and regional development theories in relation to the realities revealed in this study, and proposes some possible directions in improving relevant studies. The discussion on the policy implication of the study focuses on urban and regional development policies and new urban planning issues.

Chapter 8 summarizes the major findings of the study and draws some conclusions from a comprehensive perspective based on these findings.

CHAPTER 2

REGIONAL AND HISTORICAL CONTEXT OF URBANIZATION

Before the urbanization process in Fujian Province of China is examined, a brief introduction to some regional situations and their historical development is necessary. This not only provides general information about Fujian Province, but also describes the broad context within which the new urbanization patterns mentioned in Chapter 1 have been developing.

2.1 GEOGRAPHICAL AND HISTORICAL BACKGROUNDS

Fujian Province lies along the southeast coast of China, bordering Zhejiang, Jiangxi, and Guangdong provinces in its northeast, northwest and southwest parts respectively in the inland area, and facing Taiwan across the narrow Strait in its southeast (Figure 2.1). It comprises six prefecture-level municipalities and three prefectures, and is further divided into 50 counties, 14 county-level municipalities, and 17 districts of prefecture-level municipalities[5]. Its total area is 121,400 square kilometers, with mountains and hills covering 90 percent of its territory. Its total population is 31.65 million (Statistical Bureau of Fujian Province 1996:47), with a population density of 261 persons per square kilometer. Physically Fujian is an independent geographical unit in landscape, river system, and climate (Chen and Huang 1991:7). Its landscape structure is the most important factor influencing regional development. Two major mountain systems, the Minxi mountain system and Mindong mountain system, occupy most areas of the

---

[5] For more information on China's administrative hierarchy see Appendix 1 and Chan 1994:248-51.

Figure 2.1 A sketch map of Fujian Province

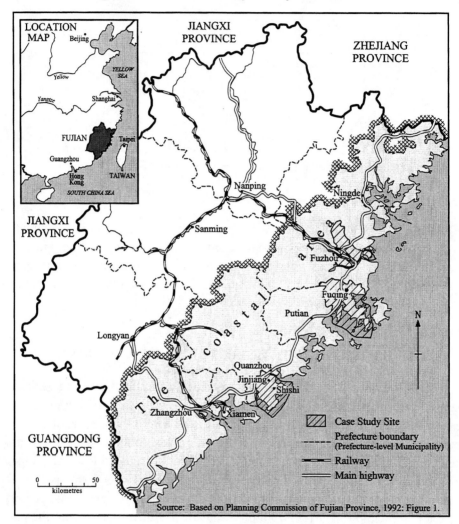

Source: calculated according to China, State Statistical Bureau 1994:60, 329.

province, with a narrow valley between them. Rivers cut through mountains and hills, forming valleys and small basins alternating with each other. On the lower reaches of the major rivers there are some relatively large plains, which lie along the coast. As the inland area of the province is occupied by the mountains, communications between Fujian and other provinces in China through land transport are relatively difficult. This has resulted in Fujian being one of the most isolated provinces in China in respect to the connections between provinces.

The relatively remote geographical location of central China where the Chinese nation originated, and the mountainous landscape, also led to Fujian's later development than other provinces in China. In fact Fujian was not conquered by the Han until the Qin dynasty (211-206 B.C.), which set up Minzhong county with its capital at the present site of Fuzhou city (Chen and Huang 1991:54; Chu and Zheng 1992:201). Until the Han dynasty (206 B.C.-A.D. 220) the influences of the central government and Han culture were still limited in Fujian, which remained largely settled by the indigenous population known as Min Viet. Only after the fall of the Han dynasty did waves of Han migration start moving into the area, largely because of the war in northern China, turning it into a settlement frontier. The settlement of Han migrants developed gradually from north to south, from the inland mountains to the coastal areas. In the Tang (A.D. 618-907) and Song (A.D. 960-1279) dynasties Fujian experienced three large waves of Han migration, which led to rapid population growth, economic development, and settlement and exploitation of most of its areas, especially its coastal areas. The large-scale immigration basically ended after this period (Chen and Huang 1991:59-60).

The mountainous landscape is related to the shortage of arable land in Fujian. Land suitable for farming is mostly located in the coastal plains and river valley basins, which are very limited in area. There is some arable land in the mountain valleys, but with low productivity because of the low temperature. In fact the area of arable land constitutes only 10-11 percent of the total land area in Fujian. In comparison with other provinces Fujian's per capita land area is only 0.57 *Mu* (0.038 ha.), ranking among the lowest in China (Figure 2.2).

**Figure 2.2 Per capita cultivated land by provinces, China
1993**

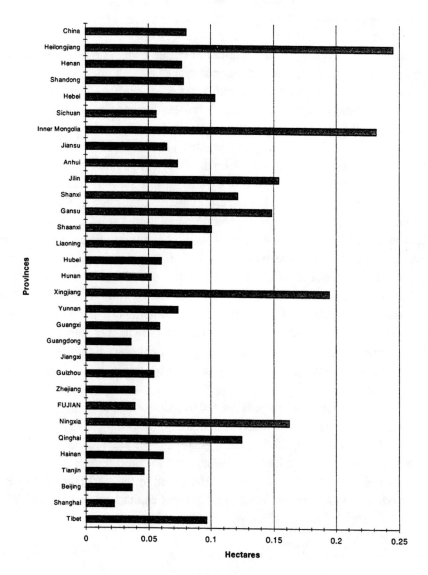

Source: based on the data in China, State Statistical Bureau 1986:53;
Statistical Bureau of Fujian Province 1989:25.

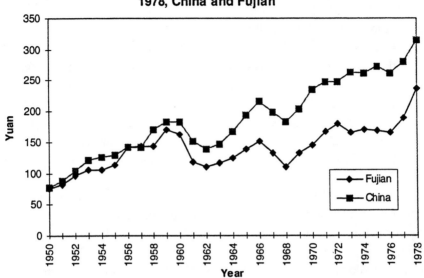

Figure 2.3 Per capita national income of production 1950-1978, China and Fujian

Sources: based on the data in China, State Statistical Bureau 1991:31, 1994:32; Statistical Bureau of Fujian Province 1996:27.

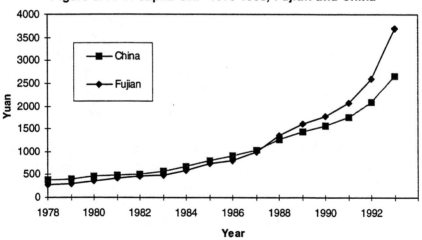

Figure 2.4 Per capita GNP 1978-1993, Fujian and China

Sources: based on the data in China, State Statistical Bureau 1991:31, 1994:32; Statistical Bureau of Fujian Province 1996:27.

This kind of geographical background has some important implications for regional development in Fujian.

First, while inland communication with other provinces was not convenient, long ago the sea route became the major way of connecting Fujian to the outside world. As the saying goes, Fujian opens its door on the sea. There are many sea bays with good conditions along the 3300-kilometers-long coastline in Fujian, which facilitates not only the fishing industry, but more importantly, Fujian's trade with other parts of the world. As early as 2000 years ago people in Fujian had begun to trade with other countries by sea. By the time of the West Han dynasty some people from the coastal areas of Fujian had already travelled to Sumatra, Burma, India, Sikkim, and Japan. In the Tang and Song dynasties foreign trade in Fujian reached its climax, with Quanzhou becoming the biggest port in China, and one of the three largest trading ports in the world. Foreign trade in Fujian was further stimulated by the looming population pressure. During the Ming dynasty, foreign trade began to serve the purpose of using trade surplus to buy food to make up for food shortages (Chen and Huang 1991:29). The development of trade was further connected to the diversification of agricultural production by using Fujian's favorable geographical conditions. For example forestry, tea production, and the production of forestry by-products such as mushrooms and dried bamboo shoots were promoted to make use of the land on mountains and hills; fishing, seawater agriculture, and even marine industries were promoted to make use of marine resources; the production of sugarcane, lychee, and longan was promoted to make use of the subtropical climate. Many of the products from the diversified economy were used for trading with other regions (Chen and Huang 1991:78), and therefore agricultural diversification and trade promoted each other. So people in Fujian, especially in its coastal area, have a long tradition and expertise in adjusting economic structure and trading with other countries and regions. The entrepreneurship displayed recently in Fujian can be traced back to this development.

Secondly, although Fujian as virgin land took in many migrants during its early development, as trade with other regions developed, more and more people from Fujian migrated to other countries and regions and some of them stayed there. The emigration was further stimulated by increasing acute population pressure, especially in the coastal area, and migration was not only the result of trade with the outside world, but also the outlet for overpopulation. According to incomplete statistics, in Southeast Asia overseas Chinese from Fujian already numbered 500,000 by the seventeenth century (Wu et al. 1994:2). The Ming Dynasty (A.D. 1368-1644) was the turning point in the balance between immigration and emigration in Fujian, according to Chen and Huang (1991:35-6). The problems of too many people with too little land and not being self-sufficient in food supply appeared in this period, and migration overseas increased correspondingly (Chen and Huang 1991:29). At the end of the Qing Dynasty (A.D. 1644-1911) a large number of Fujian people in the coastal areas migrated to Southeast Asia, doing business or opening waste lands.

Taiwan was also a major destination of emigration from Fujian. As early as the Sui (A.D. 89-618) and Tang (A.D. 618-907) dynasties people from the coastal area of Fujian Province began to trade in Taiwan. In the late Tang Dynasty people from Fujian began to settle and open up waste land in the western plain of Taiwan. In the Ming and Qing dynasties the number of migrants to Taiwan greatly increased, with the development areas expanded from the western plain area to the southern and northern areas (Fu and Chen 1990:36-7). One of the purposes of migrating to Taiwan was to produce food and transport it to Fujian to make up for the food shortage there (Chen and Huang 1991:35-6). Because of the emigration from Fujian to Taiwan the connections between Fujian and Taiwan are particularly close. People on both sides of the Taiwan strait have the same ancestors and close ties of blood. They speak the same dialect and share the same social customs and religious beliefs (Wu et al. 1994:3-4).

As a result of those emigrations Fujian become one of the major places of origin of Chinese overseas and the ancestral home of 80 percent of Taiwanese. More than 8 million Chinese overseas are from Fujian or of Fujian origin (Table 2.1). This constitutes one-third of the total number of Chinese overseas, ranking second among the provinces (next to Guangdong) in China. According to available statistics, of the 50 richest persons of Chinese origin in the world half are of Fujian origin (Wu et al. 1994:3). In addition, there are 800,000 Hong Kong people with their origin in Fujian. All this has had many implications for the social and economic development of Fujian since the 1980s.

Thirdly, owing to the geographical conditions and historical development mentioned above, the population of Fujian and its urban areas is mainly distributed along the narrow strip of its coastal area. There are clear distinctions between the inland, mountainous area and the coastal, plain area, with the latter more advanced in social and economic development and leading the changes in all fields. The coastal area includes 44 counties, county-level municipalities and districts of prefecture level municipalities. These administrative units are under the jurisdiction of five prefecture-level municipalities and one prefecture. The coastal land area is 48,600 square kilometers, only 39.2 percent of Fujian's total area. But at the end of 1990 the population in this area was 21 million, 70.1 percent of the province's total. In the same year 68.7 percent of Fujian's GNP was also produced here (Planning Commission of Fujian Province 1992:1-2). So most of the socio-economic changes in Fujian since 1978 started, and have continued here. Consequently the coastal area is the main focus of this study.

Table 2.1 Distribution of Chinese overseas with Fujian origin

Countries and regions	Total number of Chinese overseas (000s)	Chinese overseas with Fujian origin	
		Number (000s)	% of total
Indonesia	6,000.0	3,600.0	60.0
Malaysia	4,530.0	1,767.0	39.0
Philippines	1,000.0	900.0	90.0
Singapore	1,922.6	865.0	45.0
Thailand	4,800.0	384.0	8.0
Burma	700.0	280.0	40.0
Vietnam	700.0	140.0	20.0
Brunei	64.0	19.2	30.0
Cambodia	50.0	10.0	20.0
Laos	10.0	2.0	20.0
East Timor	8.3	1.7	20.0
USA	1,200.0	120.0	10.0
Japan	67.9	16.3	24.0
Total	21,052.8	8,105.2	38.5

Source: Tang 1991:10.

2.2 OPENING-UP TO THE OUTSIDE WORLD SINCE 1978

As mentioned above Fujian has a long tradition of opening to the outside world. But there were two major disruptions to this development. One happened in the Ming and Qing dynasties, when a maritime prohibition was issued in 1523, lasting almost until 1743. This turned the coastal area of Fujian into an inwardly-oriented and downward transitional periphery. In 1644, the Qing government even ordered an evacuation of all households along the coast to facilitate its campaign against the remainder of the Ming regime, turning it into a no-man's-land (Chu and Zheng 1992:203). This led to the stagnation and recession of marine trade and diversified economy, making population pressure in the coastal area even more serious. Fujian's emigration at that period was very much related to this historical event (Chen and Huang 1991:78). The other disruption was in 1949-1978. For well-known reasons, China was isolated from the outside world, and Fujian was even more closed because of its geographical position directly facing Taiwan. Fujian's economic development was negatively influenced not only by the setback to diversified economy and trade, but also by the lack of State investment, which was important for regional development in China before 1978 (Planning Commission of Fujian Province 1992:5-6). The lesson from Fujian's history is that the regional economy will develop smoothly when Fujian opens its door to the outside world, and be set back when the door is closed (Planning Commission of Fujian Province 1992:6).

Since the Third Plenary Session of the Eleventh Central Committee of the Chinese Communist Party (CCP) in late 1978, Fujian has resumed its long tradition of opening to the outside world. In this process more and more areas have been covered by the comprehensive open-door and reform policies, which make Fujian Province the leading province of China in this respect.

In September 1979 the State Council approved the adoption by Fujian and Guangdong provinces of "special policies and flexible measures" in foreign economic activities, so that the two provinces might take advantage of their close ties with Hong Kong, Macau, and Taiwan, speed up their economic development, and go one step ahead of other provinces in economic reform.

In July 1979 the central government decided to set up four special economic zones (SEZ), of which one is located in Xiamen city of Fujian Province. The special economic zone in Xiamen was initially known as an export manufacturing zone, which was located in Huli, the northeast part of Xiamen island with an area of 2.5 square kilometers. In March 1984, the central government made the decision to expand the Xiamen SEZ to the whole of Xiamen island, with an area of 131 square kilometers, and allowed Xiamen to adopt some free-port policies. Later Xiamen was further endowed with a series of preferential policies and measures.

In May 1985 the central committee of the CCP and the State Council decided to open up 14 coastal port cities and establish economic-technological development zones (ETDZ) in these cities. Fuzhou, the capital of Fujian Province, is one of those cities. A series of preferential policies and measurements were introduced to encourage foreign investment and economic reform. Fuzhou ETDZ, located on the outskirts of Fuzhou with an area of 4.4 square kilometers, was established at that time.

In February 1985 the central committee of the CCP and the State Council decided to set up the Yangtze River Delta, Pearl River Delta, and Xiamen-Zhangzhou-Quanzhou triangle area in Fujian as the coastal economic open areas. Later the coastal economic open area in Fujian was expanded several times, and currently it covers 70 percent of Fujian's total population. These areas are supposed to promote foreign trade and production based on foreign trade, adjust agricultural structure, introduce new technology, enhance the economic ties with the inland area, and drive the economic development in the inland area.

In 1988 the central government set Fujian as a national trial region for comprehensive reform and opening-up, and approved 11 measures proposed by the Fujian provincial government concerning deepening reform, expanding opening-up, and accelerating foreign-oriented economic development.

In 1989 the State Council approved the setting up of Taiwan investment zones in Xiamen and Fuzhou ETDZ, which are the only two in China.

From the above description it is evident that Fujian has almost all kinds of open areas at all levels, which makes it one of the most open provinces in China, along with Guangdong and Hainan provinces (Tang 1991:18-22; Planning Commission of Fujian Province 1992:6). It has also introduced more market-oriented economic reforms than most of the provinces, taking the lead in China. The opening-up process is closely related to the market-oriented reform, since the planned economy does not fit in with international economic practice. These reforms and opening-up processes have paved the way for economic renaissance in Fujian since the 1980s.

2.3 ECONOMIC TAKE-OFF FROM A RELATIVELY LOW LEVEL

Fujian was a relatively backward province in the coastal area of China before 1978 (Chen and Huang 1991:51; Planning Commission of Fujian Province 1992:6). In 1950 Fujian's economic development started almost at the level of China's average, but by the end of 1978, when China first adopted reform and open-door policies, Fujian's level of economic development was far behind the nation's average in terms of per capita national income of production[6]. Figure 2.3 shows clearly that the gap between China and Fujian increased in the period 1950-1978. In 1978 Fujian's per capita GNP was also only 273 *Yuan*, far below China's average (375 *Yuan*), ranking 22nd among 29 provinces, autonomous regions and municipalities directly under the jurisdiction of the central government in mainland China (Planning Commission of Fujian Province 1992:6). This is not the place to explore comprehensively why Fujian's economic performance was worse than that of China as a whole, but it certainly had much to do with China's closed-door policies and the lack of State investment here.

Since the late 1970s the situation has totally changed: Fujian has been one of the provinces with the fastest economic development in China. Figure 2.4 shows that Fujian's per capita GNP caught up with and surpassed China's average in the 1980s; this totally reversed the trend before the 1980s. As a result Fujian became one of the relatively developed provinces in China. Figure 2.5 shows that Fujian's per capita GDP ranked ninth among the provinces in mainland China, in sharp contrast to the situation in 1978. Given the close relationship between economic development and urbanization, it is not surprising that there were dramatic changes in the process of urbanization as well.

2.4 DEMOGRAPHIC CHANGES AND URBAN DEVELOPMENT

2.4.1 POPULATION GROWTH AND DISTRIBUTION

Although it is a mountainous province, Fujian's population density is twice the national average (248 and 121 persons per km^2 respectively in 1990). While its total area is only 1.26 percent of the national total, its population is 2.66 percent of China's total population. The high population density can be partly attributed to its fast population growth since 1949: for most of the years since then Fujian's population growth rate has been higher than the national average (Fu

---

[6] GNP was not calculated in China at that time. According to the State Statistical Bureau (China, State Statistical Bureau 1988:919; 1994:52-3), the national income of production refers to the newly created value in a given period by workers engaged in material production sectors; it is the sum of the net output value of agriculture, industry, construction, transport, postal services, and commerce, obtained by deducting the value of input material consumption of those sectors from the total product of society. The total product of society is the sum total of gross output in value terms produced by the above sectors.

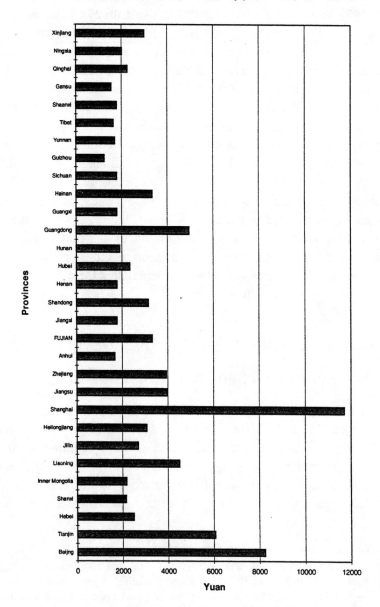

Figure 2.5 Per capita GDP by provinces, China 1993

Source: based on the data in China, State Statistical Bureau 1994:36-7

and Chen 1990:51-3). Its total population was only 11.86 million in 1949, but had reached 31.65 million in 1995, with an average annual growth rate of 2.2 percent.

For Fujian Province as a whole, population growth is largely caused by natural increase (Wu et al. 1994:10). As can be seen in Figure 2.6, the natural increase rate of Fujian's population was between 2.4 and 3.0 percent for most of the years until 1973. In 1963 and 1965 it was as high as 3.6 percent and 3.3 percent. This trend of fast population growth was only interrupted by the so-called "three years economic difficulties" from 1959 to 1961, but Fujian still distinguished itself from most other provinces and China as a whole in that it still had positive population increase while others experienced negative population growth. Since 1974, as in China as a whole, Fujian's population growth has been effectively controlled by the family planning program, and the population growth has slowed down tremendously. But further reduction of population growth has been much less since the 1980s, because implementation of the family planning program has been more difficult since the economic reform and since the large cohorts born in the 1960s have entered the reproductive age. Furthermore, as the population volume had grown bigger, the volume of population growth was even larger in the 1980s than in the 1970s. Although these are common phenomena in China as a whole, the situation in Fujian was regarded as particularly serious, because its average annual population growth rate between the 1982 and the 1990 censuses was 1.89 percent, 0.39 percentage points higher than the national average (Wu et al. 1994:12-3). Obviously, population pressure will remain high in Fujian in future.

One of the most important consequences of the long-lasting rapid population growth has been rapid increase in the labor resource[7]. Between the 1964 and 1990 population censuses the number of Fujian's labor resource increased at an average annual growth rate of 2.9 percent, reaching 17.1 million persons in 1990, 56.9 percent of the total population. It is predicted that between 1990 and 2000, the net annual increase in Fujian's labor force will be 400,000 persons (Wu et al. 1994:256-7). This is the most important reason why the employment problem has occupied, and will still occupy pride of place in Fujian's rural-urban transformation, as will be discussed in the later chapters.

---

[7] In China labour resource includes females aged 16-54 and males aged 16-59.

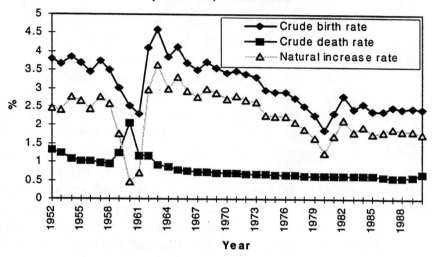

Figure 2.6 Natural increase of Fujian's Population, 1952-1990

Source: based on the data in Wu et al. 1994:8-9.

The distribution of Fujian's population further intensifies its effects on Fujian's socio-economic development. As mentioned earlier, most of Fujian's population is distributed along the narrow strip of its coastal area. Therefore, the actual population density of the areas where most people reside is much higher than the provincial average. In fact, the population density of the coastal area was 432 person per km^2 in 1990, compared to the provincial average of 248. The population density of Jinjiang, one of the field sites of this study, was as high as 1,245 persons per km^2 in the same year. In the inland mountain area, population density is also very high in some small river valley basins, but their population scale is insignificant compared to that in the coastal area. Thus, the population and employment pressure is much more acute than is suggested by analysis based on the provincial average data.

2.4.2 URBAN DEVELOPMENT

Cities and towns emerged in Fujian as early as in the Qin and Han dynasties more than 2000 years ago. At the early stage their historical development corresponded very much to the migration history and regional exploitation process, with the peak of the numbers of cities and towns and their populations being reached in the Tang and Song dynasties. The development of towns and cities was negatively influenced by the maritime prohibition and the slow economic growth afterwards. As a result Fujian started from a low urbanization level when the communists took power in 1949. At that time there were only two cities, Fuzhou and Xiamen, and some market towns in Fujian. The total urban population was 1.713 million, accounting for 14.4 percent of the total population. Corresponding to the population distribution, cities and towns and their populations in Fujian were mostly distributed in the coastal area (Zhu 1994b).

Since 1949 the difference in urban development between coastal and inland areas has narrowed. This can be mainly attributed to the construction of a railway (see Figure 2.1), which promoted the industrialization of the areas along it. The emergence of Shaowu, Nanping, Sanming, Yongan, and Longyan was a result of this development (Figure 2.7). Nevertheless, there is an indication that this difference is widening again owing to the fast development of township and village enterprises and small towns in the coastal area. In addition, as can be seen in Figure 2.7, the coastal area is dominant in the number of cities and towns, and has the largest and second largest cities of the province.

It is important to note that Fujian's cities are quite small by Chinese standards. Fuzhou, the largest and capital city of Fujian Province, had a non-agricultural population of only 889,920 according to the 1990 census. Xiamen, the second largest city and one of China's special economic zones, had a non-agricultural population of only 390,947 according to the same census. Half of the remaining 12 cities have non-agricultural populations of less than 200,000, and

Figure 2.7 Cities and towns in Fujian Province, 1990 Census

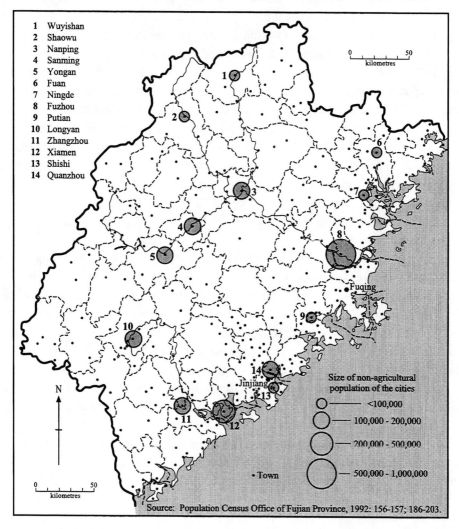

1 Wuyishan
2 Shaowu
3 Nanping
4 Sanming
5 Yongan
6 Fuan
7 Ningde
8 Fuzhou
9 Putian
10 Longyan
11 Zhangzhou
12 Xiamen
13 Shishi
14 Quanzhou

Size of non-agricultural
population of the cities

<100,000
100,000 - 200,000
200,000 - 500,000
500,000 - 1,000,000

• Town

Source: Population Census Office of Fujian Province, 1992: 156-157; 186-203.

the rest have non-agricultural populations of less than 100,000[8] (Figure 2.7). In fact, among the coastal provinces of China, Fujian is one of a few provinces without a million-plus city in terms of the non-agricultural population of cities and towns. This could be partly attributed to its long-lasting low level of economic development, but also to the limited area of hinterland, which is the result of the mountain barrier. Similarly the influence of other cities in China is also weak in Fujian. This is different from other coastal provinces, especially Zhejiang and Jiangsu, whose developments are very much affected by Shanghai; and Guangdong, whose development is very much affected by Hong Kong.

2.5 SUMMARY AND CONCLUSIONS

Before proceeding to the next chapter some points need to be made or reiterated here.

1. Conditioned by its geographical and demographic features there have been strong "push factors" in Fujian Province. Before industrialization was possible as a solution, emigration had been a major response to the push power. If the experience of many developing countries were applicable here, there would be great potential for urban growth and rural-urban migration in Fujian during its process of industrialization, which is examined later.

2. Promoting a foreign-oriented and diversified economy is another way of responding to the geographic conditions in Fujian. Although this happened in a basically agricultural society a long time ago, it still has much bearing on Fujian's recent development. Entrepreneurship, connections to the outside world, and the ability to adjust to the changing environment and economic structure, are some of the legacies from this development. Their significance for Fujian's urbanization process is shown in the following chapters.

3. Fujian's status as one of the trial cases for China's open-door and reform policies has much to do with the aforementioned historical development. Fujian has benefited considerably from this status, which made many socio-economic

---

[8] As can be seen later (Chapter 3; Appendix 1; Appendix 2), the total population of a city is not a good index for city size in China, especially in the case of county-level cities where too much village population is included. Therefore the total populations of the cities in Fujian are not listed here. Nevertheless, this is less a problem in the cases of Fuzhou and Xiamen, where the proportions of their suburban populations in the total populations are not very high. The total population of Fuzhou was 1,402,584 according to the 1990 Census; that of Xiamen is 662,270. These two figures can be taken as reference. There is more analysis on the sizes of cities in Fujian in later chapters.

changes possible, including those in urbanization. The coastal area of Fujian has most of both its population and its cities and towns, and is the focus of such changes. Nevertheless, the isolated geographical condition and the weak urban system makes it difficult for Fujian to benefit from the spread-effect of large cities.

4. The radical change in Fujian's economic growth in the 1980s makes it interesting and important for students of urbanization to study it closely. Its good economic performance and high population pressure makes it a particularly good case for examining the relationship between urbanization and economic development in the context of developing countries. To some extent Fujian represents a trend in regional development patterns, since it is one of the trial cases of the government policies in China, and the results of those trials have been quite satisfactory in terms of economic development. Compared with areas around Hong Kong and Shanghai its experiences are more applicable to other parts of China because its development relies more on itself than on some very big cities, which are not common everywhere. Students of urbanization will be interested to ask such questions as: has the rapid growth of the economy led to the high concentration of population and mega-city problems, as often seen in many developing countries? Under what patterns of urbanization was that development achieved? What are the underlying forces behind those developments? Answers to these questions will be illuminating to many developing regions.

CHAPTER 3

TEMPORAL ASPECTS OF URBANIZATION PATTERNS

Identifying the real urbanization trend in China is a necessary step towards understanding China's urbanization more deeply. China's changing political, social, and economic developments and urban definitions make it a difficult task, especially since 1978. In this chapter an attempt will be made to tackle this problem by using the case of Fujian. Special efforts will be made to relate Fujian's urbanization trend to the profound socio-economic changes since 1978 so that the real trend of urbanization and its temporal characteristics can be revealed.

3.1 URBANIZATION BEFORE 1978: A SINGLE TRACK OF "STATE-SPONSORED URBANIZATION"

A brief review of Fujian's urbanization before the reform era will help the later analysis. However, one must first appreciate the dichotomy between "agricultural" population and "non-agricultural" population in China's household registration system. This system assigns all people a registration status as either "agricultural" or "non-agricultural" (Zhou 1989:2). This classification reflects not only people's occupation, but more importantly, their household registration (*Hukou*) status. Before the reform era those persons officially registered as non-agricultural enjoyed many privileges provided by the State, which supplied heavily subsidized food and housing, free education, medical care, old-age pensions and other subsidized services. After schooling they were assigned jobs by the local government (Zhou 1989:2; Ebanks and Cheng 1990:38; Laquian

1991:261; Mallee 1995:2-7). Since 1978 many of these benefits have been reduced, but they still exist to some extent.

Not surprisingly, most of the non-agricultural population (NAP) has been living in the urban areas in China. In Fujian, the non-agricultural population of cities and towns (NAPCT) accounted for more than 80 percent of the NAP for most of the time (Table 3.1). Cities and towns are in fact the places where most of the recipients of the aforementioned non-agricultural benefits live. In this sense urbanization implies increasing responsibilities which the State bears for this part of the population, so that the increase of the non-agricultural population, especially the NAPCT, has been strictly controlled by the State (Fu and Chen 1990:132). As these people have been officially recognized, regularly counted, and sponsored by the government, they are here called the "State-sponsored urban population", and the process of their increasing proportion of the total population "State-sponsored urbanization".

Table 3.1 NAP and NAPCT, Fujian 1961-1978

Year	NAP (000s) (1)	NAPCT (000s) (2)	(2)/(1) (%)
1961	3,189.3	2,435.1	76.4
1962	2,869.9	2,351.8	81.9
1963	2,837.1	2,264.1	79.8
1964	2,796.1	2,290.5	81.9
1965	2,873.4	2,344.6	81.6
1966	2,953.6	2,387.7	80.8
1967	3,005.2	2,433.7	81.0
1968	3,114.0	2,478.2	79.6
1969	2,973.6	2,415.3	81.2
1970	2,853.9	2,425.7	85.0
1971	2,962.8	2,357.9	79.6
1972	2,989.4	2,409.9	80.6
1973	3,086.2	2,478.2	80.3
1974	3,133.3	2,544.3	81.2
1975	3,173.0	2,573.3	81.1
1976	3,240.6	2,629.4	81.1
1977	3,276.5	2,671.5	81.5
1978	3,361.1	2,755.2	82.0

Source: Statistical Bureau of Fujian Province 1996:49.

It needs stressing that the NAPCT represents only the *de jure* urban residents eligible for the aforementioned benefits. There are still some *de facto* urban residents classified as "agricultural" by household registration, who are actually engaged in non-agricultural activities, or cater to nearby urban markets, and use the urban infrastructure intensively in the urban administrative area (Hu and Zhang 1984:269; Kirkby 1985:89-93; Tian 1989:5; Linge and Forbes 1990:193). Another commonly-used urban statistical criterion in China, the total population of cities and towns (TPCT), covers both the agricultural and non-agricultural population inside the urban administrative areas, and was regarded by many scholars as a reasonable representation of the size of the urban population until 1982 and internationally comparable[9] (United Nations 1974:9; Linge and Forbes 1990:194; Chan 1994:252).

With the above knowledge about the data of China's urban population and their relationship to the agricultural and non-agricultural dichotomy, we can now look at the data in Table 3.2 and Figure 3.1. Two important points about the nature of urbanization before 1978 arise from the figure.

First, Figure 3.1 shows that the non-agricultural population of cities and towns always constituted the larger part (59 to 75 percent) of the total population of cities and towns. Its proportion of the TPCT exhibited a decreasing trend, but changed only slightly before 1978 (calculated according to Statistical Bureau of Fujian Province 1996:47-9). The urbanization trends measured by the TPCT and the NAPCT were very similar. This suggests that urban growth in Fujian before 1978 was mainly a "State-sponsored" process, that is, an increase in the NAPCT. The increase in the *de facto* urban population was an accompanying subsidiary process, resulting from the inclusion of suburban areas in the designated cities and towns.

Secondly, the trend in urban growth and urbanization in Fujian before 1978 very much resembled that of China as a whole. It followed the same checkered path, with a net result of limited increase in the proportion of the TPCT and decrease in the proportion of the NAPCT[10]. This indicates that the State was the major driving force of urbanization at that time. The stagnation of urbanization is

---

[9] Detailed information about the sources and definitions of the data on urbanization in China is given in Appendix 2. See also Ma and Cui (1987) and Zhou (1988).

[10] For more discussion about the urbanization process between 1949 and 1978 in China, see Kirkby 1985:103-33; Chan 1988; Gu 1991:107-9; for that in Fujian see Fu and Chen 1990:170-92; Zhu 1994b:192-6.

Table 3.2 TPCT and NAPCT: numbers and their proportions of total population, Fujian 1949-1978

Year	Total population (000s)	Total population of cities and towns		Non-agricultural population of cities and towns	
		Number (000s)	% of total population	Number (000s)	% of total population
1949	11,879.0	1,713.0	14.4	n.a.	n.a
1954	13,385.1	2,519.2	18.8	n.a.	n.a.
1955	13,666.2	2,067.4	15.1	n.a.	n.a.
1956	14,004.4	2,273.8	16.2	1,707.5	12.2
1957	14,525.1	2,369.8	16.3	1,750.4	12.1
1958	14,933.8	3,020.6	20.2	n.a.	n.a
1959	15,430.5	3,455.0	22.4	n.a.	n.a.
1960	15,726.2	3,735.2	23.8	n.a.	n.a.
1961	15,978.1	3,629.9	22.7	2,435.1	15.2
1962	16,396.5	3,535.1	21.6	2,351.8	14.3
1963	16,783.7	3,390.4	20.2	2,264.1	13.5
1964	17,034.9	3,478.0	20.4	2,290.5	13.4
1965	17,597.6	3,567.0	20.3	2,344.6	13.3
1966	18,136.8	3,634.2	20.0	2,387.7	13.2
1967	18,608.1	3,797.5	20.4	2,433.7	13.1
1968	19,176.4	3,882.7	20.2	2,478.2	12.9
1969	19,744.9	3,834.1	19.4	2,415.3	12.2
1970	20,287.5	3,895.6	19.2	2,425.7	12.0
1971	20,896.9	4,003.6	19.2	2,357.9	11.3
1972	21,506.8	4,026.2	18.7	2,409.9	11.2
1973	22,104.1	4,130.6	18.7	2,478.2	11.2
1974	22,579.2	4,243.4	18.8	2,544.3	11.3
1975	23,102.7	4,391.8	19.0	2,573.3	11.1
1976	23,619.1	4,483.2	19.0	2,629.4	11.1
1977	24,111.9	4,570.8	19.0	2,671.5	11.1
1978	24,527.7	4,679.5	19.1	2,755.2	11.2

Source: Statistical Bureau of Fujian Province 1996:47-9.

Figure 3.1 TPCT[a] and NAPCT[b] as proportions of the total population before 1978, Fujian and China

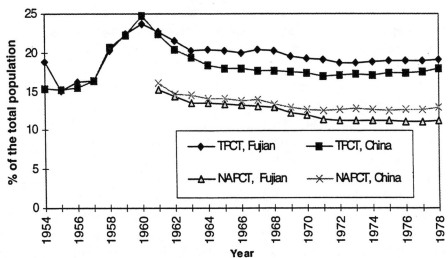

[a] TPCT: total population of cities and towns.
[b] NAPCT: non-agricultural population of cities and towns.
Sources: based on Statistical Bureau of Fujian Province 1996:47-9; China, State Statistical Bureau, Population and Employment Section 1996:365.

not surprising, given that the State took full responsibility for looking after all the "State-sponsored urban population" and firmly controlled rural-urban migration after the 1950s, and that economic development was limited before 1978. The peak in 1960 was a result of the "Great Leap Forward" and was only an exception. As there was only one track of government-sponsored urbanization, this process was fairly easy to record statistically by using the two urban criteria, TPCT and NAPCT, which generally reflected the real situation at that time.

3.2 THE URBANIZATION PROCESS SINCE 1978: TWO DIFFERENT TRACKS

Since China adopted reform and open-door policies in 1978, the urbanization process in Fujian has been much more complicated. One problem is that the

1980s saw many changes in urban definitions and administration systems. As a result it is becoming more difficult to analyze the urbanization trend in China by using the TPCT and NAPCT data, because of the problem of data comparability. Another problem is that even if the old definitions were still useful, they could not cover many "spontaneous urbanization" processes properly. The *in situ* transformation of formerly agricultural populations into quasi-urban ones, which has largely been driven by the development of township and village enterprises and facilitated by the creation of many small urban centers, and the increase of temporary residents, are the major forms of "spontaneous urbanization". They are neither sponsored by the State nor officially recognized by the official definition and statistics, and thus contrast with "State-sponsored urbanization". Although there are still cases where government statistics based on different definitions are uncritically used (World Bank 1994:264-5), the first problem has been increasingly realized by students of urbanization in China (Ebanks and Cheng 1990; Goldstein 1990; Jones 1991; Chan 1994). Nevertheless the second problem attracted far less attention than the first one. People happily treat the urbanization data for China as a "statistical artifact" (Goldstein 1990:697), without appreciating the profound socio-economic implications behind those data. In fact, what has not been fully recognized about China's urbanization since 1978 is that it has been proceeding along two different tracks: one is the conventional, "State-sponsored" urbanization; the other is the "spontaneous" process, which is mainly the result of rural industrialization. As previously mentioned, a *de facto* urban population already existed before 1978 in the form of agricultural population in the urban administrative areas. This can be regarded as the initial form of "spontaneous urban population". But because of its limited scope, it did not attract attention and was not the focus of urbanization studies. This has no longer been the case since the 1980s. As will be seen later, "spontaneous urbanization" has been more important than the State-sponsored process. It is the major purpose of the following section to examine urbanization in Fujian by integrating the "spontaneous" process. But it begins by examining the conventional data: the annual statistics on TPCT and NAPCT, and the census information.

3.2.1 URBANIZATION TRENDS SINCE 1978 REFLECTED IN TPCT, NAPCT AND CENSUS DATA

Like data on urbanization in China as a whole, official data on Fujian's urban growth and urbanization seem extremely confusing (Table 3.3). Compared with the same data series before 1978 there are two important differences. First, as already mentioned, the urbanization trends measured by two different criteria, i.e. the total population of cities and towns and the non-agricultural population of cities and towns, were very similar before 1978. But they started to differ in 1983, and have differed greatly since 1984, as is evident in Figure 3.2.

Secondly both the TPCT and NAPCT have exhibited a steady upward trend, with the former increasing much more quickly. Clearly urban growth and urbanization have entered a new era of accelerating development in Fujian, but given the large gap between the TPCT and NAPCT, it is no longer easy to assess Fujian's urbanization level according to these data series.

Despite this it is still worthwhile to analyze the changing trend of total population of cities and towns and non-agricultural population of cities and towns and their proportions of the total population. Some stages of development can be identified. As the result of reform and open-door policies, urbanization began to gain its upward momentum in Fujian between 1978 and 1983. The TPCT and NAPCT increased by 27.8 percent and 19.9 percent respectively in five years, with annual growth rates of 5.0 percent and 3.7 percent. These are far faster than the average annual growth rate of the TPCT between 1949 and 1978 (3.5 percent), and that of the NAPCT between 1956 and 1978 (2.2 percent). The proportion of the TPCT increased from 19.1 percent in 1978 to 22.7 percent in 1983, whereas the proportion of the NAPCT increased from 11.2 percent to 12.5 percent during the same period.

Table 3.3 TPCT and NAPCT: numbers and their proportions of total population, Fujian 1978-1995

Year	Total population (000s)	Total population of cities and towns		Non-agricultural population of cities and towns	
		Number (000s)	% of total population	Number (000s)	% of total population
1978	24,527.7	4,679.5	19.1	2,755.2	11.2
1979	24,879.3	4,841.6	19.5	2,905.0	11.7
1980	25,177.8	4,980.0	19.8	3,004.5	11.9
1981	25,569.0	5,358.7	21.0	3,115.9	12.2
1982	26,040.2	5,481.8	21.1	3,197.9	12.3
1983	26,398.0	5,980.0	22.7	3,304.3	12.5
1984	26,768.3	9,979.0	37.3	3,599.7	13.4
1985	27,131.0	11,622.9	42.8	3,850.2	14.2
1986	27,493.0	12,024.7	43.7	3,957.2	14.4
1987	28,005.2	12,749.2	45.5	4,072.3	14.5
1988	28,452.5	14,245.7	50.1	4,241.2	14.9
1989	28,890.5	15,284.3	52.9	4,410.4	15.3
1990	29,998.2	16,983.2	56.6	4,549.4	15.2
1991	30,390.9	18,014.2	59.3	4,656.9	15.3
1992	30,668.5	23,644.2	77.1	5,020.7	16.4
1993	30,991.7	25,183.9	81.3	5,414.4	17.5
1994	31,268.7	25,818.3	82.6	5,610.6	17.9
1995	31,646.3	26,556.7	83.9	5,734.4	18.1

Source: Statistical Bureau of Fujian Province 1996:47-9.

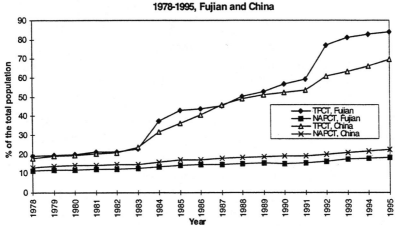

Figure 3.2 TPCT[a] and NAPCT[b] as proportions of the total population, 1978-1995, Fujian and China

[a] TPCT: total population of cities and towns.
[b] NAPCT: non-agricultural population of cities and towns.
Sources: based on Statistical Bureau of Fujian Province 1996:47-9; China, State Statistical Bureau, Population and Employment Section 1996:365.

After 1983 the trend of growth in the NAPCT remained very much the same. The average annual growth rate of the NAPCT was 4.7 percent between 1983 and 1995, and its proportion of the total population increased from 12.5 percent to 18.1 percent. In general the NAPCT has increased at a stable rate from the beginning of reform until now, faster than the world average urban population growth rate (4.5 percent, Laquian 1991:238).

But the growth trend of the TPCT has differed widely from that of the NAPCT since 1984. Between 1983 and 1995 it increased sharply, with an average annual growth rate of 13.2 percent. Its proportion of the total population increased incredibly from 22.7 percent to 83.9 percent. If Fujian's urbanization level were judged by this criterion, Fujian would be one of the most advanced regions in the world. Broadly, these points can also be made about the urbanization trend in China, as can be seen in Figure 3.2.

Examined in statistical terms, there were two major causes of the growth in the TPCT, which corresponded to two major stages of the growth. As stated in detail in Appendix 2, the State Council lowered the criteria for the designation of official town status (China, State Council, 1984a), and promoted the policies of "abolishing townships and establishing towns" (*chexiang jianzhen*) and "town administering village" (*zhengguancun*) whereby townships were abolished and their territories and population were placed under the jurisdiction of towns (China, State Council 1984a; Ma and Cui 1987:384-5; Lee 1989). This resulted immediately in the conversion of many townships into designated towns and the inclusion of a large number of agricultural population into town population statistics, and the TPCT jumped from 5,980,000 to 9,979,000 in the same year in Fujian Province. Later, in 1986 the State Council also lowered the criteria for the designation of city status, with a smaller impact on Fujian's urban growth than the former one[11]. The second major increase in the TPCT happened in 1992, when Fujian's provincial committee of the CCP and the provincial government sought to convert all coastal area townships into towns, and in 1993, when the provincial government further suggested reclassifying all townships in the inland area into towns (personal communication, Fujian Provincial Civil Affairs Department, August 1996). The Civil Affairs Department, which is responsible for the designation of cities and towns, suggested the addition of the words "if the requirements are met", but this idea was ignored by the provincial government. The encouragement by the provincial government of the designation of small towns brought about another wave of rapid growth in the TPCT. In 1992 the TPCT and its proportion of the total population jumped again from 18.0 million (59.3 percent) to 23.6 million (77.1 percent). This unusual growth continued in 1993. In this process many townships, which did not even meet the new 1984 criteria to be designated as towns, gained official town status[12]. Given these circumstances, the TPCT no longer represents the real urban population.

---

[11] In 1993 there was another city definition change, but it had little effect on the total number of urban population, because it only converted some town populations, which had already been included in the TPCT and NAPCT, into city populations.

[12] The provincial and local governments have been eager to designate cities and towns because urban status is closely related to the local economic benefits (Zhou and Shi 1995:290; Khakee 1996:114). In Fujian Province these benefits are mainly as follows: (a) An official urban place is better-known. This will help attract investment and get more attention from the superior government; (b) More autonomy will be given to urban places in decision making, such as approving foreign investment projects; (c) It will be more legitimate for the governments of urban places to promote non-agricultural sectors in the local economy and pay less attention to agricultural development; (d) There are some financial benefits such as being entitled to collect more "urban maintenance and construction tax" and getting more funding for urban infrastructure construction (personal communication, Fujian Provincial Civil Affairs Department, August 1996).

Census data on Fujian's urbanization have not been exempt from the influence of the urban definition changes. Since the early 1980s two population censuses have been conducted in China: the third census in 1982 and the fourth census in 1990. In both censuses a criterion similar to TPCT was used, and the results in Fujian (21.2 percent and 54.1 percent respectively of TPCT as a proportion of the total population) are also very similar to those in the annual statistics. Recognizing the exaggerating effect of the TPCT on the real level of urbanization, a new criterion, commonly called the "second criterion" was introduced in the fourth census in 1990. However, the application of this criterion in Fujian produced even more confusion, because it showed the urbanization level to be 21.4 percent, only marginally increased since the 1982 census. This is by no means the real urbanization level in Fujian, given its fast economic growth since 1978. Officials in the Census Bureau of Fujian Province have explained that the town population based on the second criterion was enumerated by residents' committees. But as these had not yet been formed in many newly established towns, much of the town population was missed (personal communication, Census Bureau of Fujian Province, August 1996).

It seems that there is no statistical criterion which can reasonably, let alone precisely, represent the real urbanization situation in Fujian. The total population of cities and towns includes too many of the agricultural population on the outskirts of cities and towns. The definition of non-agricultural population of cities and towns is too narrow to cover all urban residents, especially those who are classified as agricultural population but working in the non-agricultural sectors in the urban areas or the newly emergent rural urban centers. The "second criterion" used since the fourth census in 1990 is widely regarded as adequately reflecting the urbanization levels and changes during the 1980s in China as a whole (Zhou 1993), but this is obviously not true of Fujian, because the result was so unreasonable. In fact this also casts doubt on the representativeness of the "second criterion" for the whole of China, because it is hard to imagine that a criterion supposed to be representative for the whole country is totally invalid for some of its provinces[13]. The question thus remains how the urbanization trend in Fujian

---

[13] In fact, a similar problem exists for other provinces like Jiangsu in using the "second criterion" (Zhou 1993:127). On the other hand, urbanization level is exaggerated by using this criterion in Guangdong (Zhong 1995). Zhou (1993:122-8) pointed out further that the "second criterion" takes different criteria for city population and town population, making the urban population data incomparable among cities and towns and different regions. Thus the acceptability of the "second criterion" for measuring the urbanization level in China as a whole is more out of coincidence than out

since the 1980s can be determined, as it would be inadequate simply to analyze official urban statistical data. One needs to look beyond the urbanization data to learn more about it.

3.2.2 DIFFERENT TRACKS OF URBANIZATION: THE REALITIES BEHIND THE DATA

The dilemma in urban definitions reflects in fact deep socio-economic changes in China since 1978. Instead of being merely a "statistical artifact" or "administrative fiat" (Goldstein 1990:697), it is to a great extent caused by the fact that new processes of "urbanization from below" have emerged in China, especially in a province like Fujian which leads in the reform and open-door policies. As those forms of urbanization are spontaneous and informal, they cannot be properly reflected in the official data, which therefore should be re-examined in connection with some important socio-economic changes in order to gain a better understanding of Fujian's urbanization process.

3.2.2.1 Relaxation of Urban Definitions and the Creation of New Urban Centers

As will be examined more intensively in the later chapters, the rapid rural industrialization has been the most remarkable change in rural China since the 1980s. The change in criteria for the designation of official town status was one of the major government measures to facilitate this development (Laquian 1991:250-4; Ma and Lin 1993:587-9). As a result the number of towns increased sharply. In 1982 there were only 119 officially designated towns in Fujian, but within three years in 1985 the number had reached 209 and it was 258 by 1990. There was another wave of newly designated towns, bringing the number to 581 in 1995[14]. Similarly there was also a big increase in the number of cities, but with a much lower growth rate and effect on the size of the TPCT.

Reviewing Figure 3.2 one can see that while the increase in the number of cities and towns coincided with the increase in the total population of cities and towns, it had little effect on the increase in the non-agricultural population of

---

of reasonableness. For more criticism on the "second criterion" see also Gu 1991; Guo and Deng 1995; Kojima 1995; and Yu 1995.

[14] Towns under the municipal administration are included in all these cases.

cities and towns. This is a clear indication that relaxing the criteria for designating cities and towns was not intended to promote the State-sponsored urbanization, which dominated the urbanization process before the reform era, but rather to promote the establishment of new urban centers without much new government investment. This can be confirmed by the fact that almost at the same time as the criteria were lowered, the State Council released another document (China, State Council 1984b), allowing peasants and their dependants to move to designated towns (excluding county seats) for permanent settlement, provided they had permanent residences in the towns, were able to run a business or had a permanent job in township enterprises, and could meet their own needs for food grain and cooking oil through purchase at prices higher than those paid by regular town dwellers. Thus the implementation of new criteria actually marked a major step in "urbanization from below".

Although the subsequent sharp increase in the TPCT is statistically exaggerated, it should not be regarded totally as a statistical artifact. First, one reason for adopting this measure was that small town development had been restricted during the 1960s and the 1970s by the strict criteria for official town status, which led to many towns being demoted to commune status, both nominally and functionally. In Fujian Province the number of towns was cut from 225 in 1956 to 127 in 1963, and further to only 98 in 1966 (Li, Chen and Yu 1988:746). Those towns existing before the 1960s and abolished afterwards were mostly the market towns forming naturally in the process of regional development and had long served as regional centers. For the most part the newly established towns were simply those that had been abolished in the 1960s. Very few were artificially created. The new criteria merely enabled those towns to recover their function as regional centers.

Secondly, for those towns the regional center function became very different from what it had previously been: they became increasingly involved in rapid rural industrialization, especially the development of township and village enterprises, which certainly promoted the urbanization process in Fujian. Thirdly, although the 1984 criterion for the designation of towns was lowered, the requirement for the number of non-agricultural population residing in the township seat was still very close to the urban definitions adopted by such countries as Germany, Netherlands, Angola, Argentina, Kenya (see United Nations 1995:33-43), and therefore still reasonable. It can be inferred from the criterion that, for most cases, only those townships with more than 2,000 non-agricultural residents in the township seat can be designated as towns[15]. If the *de facto* non-agricultural population, which was quite substantial in many rural centers, had been added, the total non-agricultural population in those township seats would have been even larger. Generally speaking, the designation of towns in 1984 was made strictly according to the official criteria; therefore much of the increase in those urban centers was real urban growth.

The second wave of the designation of towns was to a greater extent an "administrative fiat". Its direct cause was that some top leaders of Fujian Province visited Guangdong Province, found that the designation of more towns could help promote the local economy, and wanted Fujian Province to emulate Guangdong (personal communication, Fujian Provincial Civil Affairs Department, August 1996). The increasing gap between the proportion of the TPCT in Fujian and that in China was a result of the designation of towns at that time. Although this administrative change resulted in the inclusion of a large amount of rural population in the urban statistics, it still had the effect of promoting rural industrialization[16], thus accelerating the transformation of agricultural areas into quasi-urban areas.

In summary, the designation of new cities and towns in the 1980s was an important aspect of a large-scale "urbanization from below". Failure to recognize this would miss a significant explanation for Fujian's urban development. Unfortunately, there is no statistical criterion which can properly cover the real number of population involved in this kind of urbanization, and this problem will be tackled later.

3.2.2.2 Township and Village Enterprises and the Structural Change in Employment

Considerable changes have taken place in the employment structure of the population in Fujian since the 1980s (Table 3.4). In 1982 agricultural activities were still dominant in the employment structure in Fujian Province, but in 1995 almost half the work force was in the non-agricultural sectors. Judging from the relationship between structural change of the economy and spatial clustering, it is hard to believe that Fujian's urbanization rate was only 22.7 percent, as the 1995 one percent population sample survey indicated, or even only 18.1 percent, as the

---

[15] For detailed information see China, State Council 1984a and Ma and Cui 1987:377-8.
[16] For details see note 12.

NAPCT shows. In Java, the most populous island of Indonesia, when half of the employed population were working in the non-agricultural sectors, the urbanization level was about 35 percent (G. W. Jones, personal communication, April 1996). How should the big gap between Fujian's official urbanization level and the employment structure be explained?

Table 3.4 Employment structure in Fujian Province, selected years (%)

	1982[a]	1990	1995
Primary sector	69.7	58.4	50.3
Secondary sector	18.0	20.6	23.7
Tertiary sector	12.3	21.1	26.1

[a] 1982 census data.
Sources: Population Census Office 1984:122-7; Statistical Bureau of Fujian Province 1996:59.

A simple answer to this question could be that Fujian's urbanization has lagged behind the structural change in the economy, thus leading to the low urbanization rate (Gu 1991; Liao 1992). From the perspective of State-sponsored urbanization this is indeed the case. However, this unusually low level of urbanization can be examined from the perspective of "invisible urbanization" or "latent urbanization", a new concept that has emerged in the Chinese literature on urbanization (Li 1993; Wang and Zhou 1993; Zhong 1997) to embrace the idea that a new urbanization process has been taking place in China but has not been officially recognized. This "invisible urbanization" serves a substitute for the conventionally understood urbanization, and the transformation of the employment structure has been its main result.

The major form of "invisible urbanization" is the development of township and village enterprises. Table 3.5 shows that there have been large increases in the numbers of both TVEs and their employees in Fujian Province since 1978. These enterprises are located in the seats of towns and townships, and even in the villages. It is those enterprises that provide the main substitute for the conventionally understood urbanization, which is still sponsored by the government.

Table 3.5 Number of TVEs and their employees, Fujian 1978-1995

Year	Enterprises	Employees
1978	34,247	870,824
1979	40,685	1,093,381
1980	43,129	1,214,350
1981	44,066	1,260,378
1982	45,775	1,303,866
1983	70,518	1,453,890
1984	149,464	1,746,286
1985	257,931	2,036,363
1986	203,941	2,125,455
1987	404,303	2,581,024
1988	446,694	2,746,816
1989	462,936	2,767,318
1990	471,993	2,791,569
1991	495,870	2,952,087
1992	534,885	3,371,644
1993	671,962	4,063,322
1994	774,055	4,673,724
1995	667,385	4,709,956

Source: Statistical Bureau of Fujian Province 1996:186.

Given the dispersed nature of TVEs one would be reluctant to regard their development as a part of the urbanization process. But in regions like Fujian with high population densities, spatial concentration is not as important a component of urbanization as suggested by the conventional theories, which are based on the past experiences of developed countries. A comparison can be made to illustrate this point: the average population density of Jinjiang Municipality, one of the most famous places for fast development of TVEs in Fujian, was 1,245 persons per km^2 in 1990, much higher than that of the urbanized areas in USA in 1990 (1,001 persons per km^2)[17] (U. S. Bureau of the Census 1990, cited in Zhou and Shi 1995:295). In a way urbanization has already been achieved in terms of population concentration; functional urbanization (de Vries 1990:48-9), and to a

---

[17] This point will be further discussed in Chapters 6 and 7.

lesser extent changes in lifestyles, both of which can be achieved through TVE development, are more important for these areas to achieve urbanization. This is why the development of TVEs should be considered as part of urbanization[18]. In fact the people involved in this development are in a very similar situation to that of the agricultural population in the suburban area, which was considered to be the *de facto* urban population (Linge and Forbes 1990:194), before the reform began.

If we regard urbanization as a multi-dimensional phenomenon (Goldstein and Sly 1975: 4) and continuum process (Yu and Ning 1983:20), this point will be clearer. First, as stated in Chapter 1, urbanization includes four components: the definition of urban area; the growth of population in these urban areas; the increase of non-agricultural activities, and the distinctive urban way of life (United Nations 1993:2-1). This suggests that any progress in one of the four components will help promote the urbanization process. The function of the development of TVEs as part of an urbanization process in Fujian is very evident in this sense. As mentioned, it has been the major driving force for the transformation of the employment structure in Fujian. During the period 1985-1995 the number of people engaged in non-agricultural activities increased by 3.36 million in Fujian Province, while the employees in the TVEs increased by 2.67 million. This suggests that almost 80 percent of the increase in non-agricultural employment in this period may be attributed to the development of TVEs, which also greatly promoted rural economic growth and spread the urban way of life.

Secondly, even if the changes brought about by the development of TVEs are insufficient to qualify a place as urban, they can be seen as a stage in the urbanization process. As TVEs develop and industrialization proceeds, more and more urban features will accumulate in the rural areas, and one day the criteria for a real urban area will be met and the spontaneous urbanization will be officially recognized. Many Western countries experienced such a development stage[19] (Li 1993:141), and many newly designated cities and towns in Fujian have gone, or are going, through this process too. In other words, the development of TVEs

---

[18] On the contrary, in today's developing countries rural-urban migration is not necessarily a more complete urbanization process than what has happened in Jinjiang in terms of functional urbanization and the changes of lifestyles. As pointed out by Young (1994:94-7), if opportunities are limited, rural dwellers moving to the city "may continue to produce foodstuffs and other products, but sell them informally in the urban market economy". "Their lifestyles may change only slightly, both culturally and socially, from those of the villages which they left".

[19] This will be discussed in more detail in Chapter 6.

will first lead to the *in situ* transformations of formerly agricultural areas into quasi-urban ones, which will eventually become fully urbanized. This process should not be neglected, because it represents a new way of achieving urbanization in China.

3.2.2.3 Temporary Residents: Another Kind of Spontaneous Urban Population

Another aspect of spontaneous urbanization consists of "temporary residents", sometimes also referred to as "floating population", although the latter also includes those who are migrating for a short period of time for the purposes of tourism, shopping, visiting relatives and friends, and business trips, and hence is different from the former. In fact "temporary residents" is not necessarily a precise term because "temporary residents" can live in an area (including cities and towns) for as long as they like, so long as they can find a job and residence, although there are major differences between them and the normal residents in what job they do, where they live, and to what extent they can enjoy the social welfare provided for the normal urban residents.

Since the 1980s a major change in the policies regarding migration in China has been that it is becoming progressively easier for a person to live and work in any place, including cities and towns, as a "temporary resident", although it is still difficult for a farmer to be officially registered as a permanent resident in an urban area. Table 3.6 shows the proportion of the population of Fujian and of certain areas which consisted of people who had left the places of their household registration for a certain period of time. It indicates that the proportion of temporary residents has increased drastically since the 1982 population census in Fujian Province, especially in urban places and those areas where township and village enterprises have been developing quickly. The volume of temporary residents is impressive. In the 1982 census there were only 232,856 temporary residents in Fujian Province, but in the 1990 census this number increased to 795,136, with an average annual growth rate of 16.6 percent. In Xiamen city there were only 7,658 temporary residents in the 1982 census, but this number increased to 49,799 in the 1990 census, with an average annual growth rate of 26.4 percent. These figures refer only to those temporary residents who had crossed the county-level border and left their places of household registration for more than one year: if all registered temporary residents, including those crossing township-level borders and staying for only a few days[20], are counted in, the total will of course be much higher. There were 335,352 temporary residents in Xiamen city at the end of 1994, equivalent to 51.2 percent of the number of permanent residents. In Jinjiang, which is famous for its TVEs and was designated as a city only in 1992, the total number of temporary residents reached 186,217 at the end of 1994, or 19.3 percent of the number of permanent residents (local government statistics collected during fieldwork, October 1996).

Table 3.6 Proportions of temporary residents[a] in Fujian and its selected areas (% of the total population)

	Fujian	Districts[b] of Fuzhou	Districts of Xiamen	Districts of Putian	District of Quanzhou	Jinjiang Municipality	Shishi Municipality	District of Zhangzhou
1982 census	0.9	1.9	1.5	0.6	1.4	0.2	0.02	1.3
1990 census	2.6	8.2	9.5	5.4	4.3	3.3	5.1	3.6
1995 sample survey	4.4	19.3	14.6	11.8	n.a.	12.0	n.a.	4.2

[a] "Temporary residents" are those who had left the county-level places where they had their household registration for one year or more in the case of the 1982 and 1990 censuses; or those who had left the township-level places where they had their household registration for half a year or more in the case of the 1995 sample survey.
[b] Districts in this table are "city-administered districts" (*shixiaqu*) of the relevant cities. They include suburban districts.
Sources: calculated according to the data in Population Census Office 1990:14-6; and 1995 one percent sample survey data provided by the Population Census Office of Fujian Province.

Several important characteristics of temporary residents should be mentioned. First, temporary residents obviously cannot have their official household registration at the place where they work and live, nor can they enjoy all the

---

[20] But most registered temporary residents had lived there for more than one month. This is because only those temporary residents who intend to stay for longer than one month need to apply for a temporary residence permit. Those who intend to stay for less than one month are required theoretically to be registered by the local public security bureau, but this is often ignored. See also Table 3.9 and Chapter 5.

privileges and benefits provided for the normal urban residents, although these privileges are gradually losing their meaning as the reform progresses. For example, they are ineligible for low-priced food grain, housing and job security guaranteed by the State. When their child goes to school they have to pay more than the normal residents. Secondly, most temporary residents are engaged in industry. According to the government statistics of Jinjiang Municipality, this accounted for 86.8 percent of the purposes of temporary residence (Table 3.7). They usually work in non-State owned enterprises, especially in foreign-funded enterprises or TVEs in the case of Fujian. In Jinjiang, for example, foreign-funded enterprises and TVEs absorbed as many as 250,000 temporary residents in 1991 (Zhu 1994a:18). Thirdly, the accommodation of temporary residents is very much of a temporary nature. Unlike most normal urban residents who are provided with a housing unit by their working units or local housing office, temporary residents usually rent a small living space from local residents or, if lucky, they will be provided with a dormitory in their working units, because most of them are single and young. However, a considerable proportion simply live in huts at their working sites. Table 3.8 shows the housing arrangements of temporary residents in Jinjiang, and this probably gives a fairly representative picture. Fourthly, as the term implies, temporary residents change their places of living and working frequently. As can be seen from Table 3.9, most temporary residents in Jinjiang at the end of 1994 had lived there for less than one year. Their numbers fluctuated in line with the local labor demand. Whereas there were as many as 250,000 temporary residents in Jinjiang in 1991, this decreased to 186,217 in 1994, and to 151,222 in 1995. These temporary residents keep coming and going to and from a certain area, as well as changing places inside an area.

Table 3.7 Purpose of temporary residence in Jinjiang Municipalities, 1994

	Working in the factory	Working as a farmer	Trad-ing	Servicing business	Business trip	Education and training	Medical treatment and recu-peration	House keeper	Living together with relatives	Visiting friend	Tourist	Others	Total
Number of persons	161,633	4,893	3,256	6,919	641	925	54	392	746	413	47	6,298	186,217
%	86.80	2.60	1.80	3.70	0.30	0.50	0.03	0.20	0.40	0.20	0.03	3.40	100.00

Sources: local government statistics collected during fieldwork.

Table 3.8 Living places of the temporary residents in Jinjiang Municipality, 1994

	Hotel	Home of local resident	Inside the working unit	Working site	Rented housing	Others	Total
Number of persons	416	26,812	61,894	27,413	64,465	5,217	186,217
%	0.22	14.40	33.24	14.72	34.62	2.80	100.00

Source: as for Table 3.7.

Table 3.9 Temporary residents by the period of residence, Jinjiang, 1994

	Less than one month	One month to one year	More than one year	Total
Number of persons	9,682	155,147	21,388	186,217
%	5.19	83.32	11.49	100.00

Source: as for Table 3.7.

These characteristics clearly show that temporary residents cannot be included in the State-sponsored urbanization. They are allowed or even encouraged because government does not need to take much responsibility, especially in financial terms, and temporary residents are easily controlled because their residential status in the city is still reversible—at least in theory. Yet there is no doubt that the reality of their presence in urban areas has increased the urbanization levels in Fujian.

3.3 THE ESTIMATION OF THE URBANIZATION TREND: A SUMMARY AND AN ILLUSTRATION

In the preceding analysis Fujian's urbanization has been divided into two major different tracks: State-sponsored urbanization, which can be roughly represented by the non-agricultural population of cities and towns, and spontaneous urbanization, which cannot be properly measured by any existing statistical criterion. It is time now to make a summary of the preceding analysis, and, as an illustration, to estimate roughly the urbanization trends on the basis of the aforementioned analytical framework, so that the implications of the new urbanization trends, especially that of spontaneous urbanization, can be easily appreciated.

As already noted, the trend of State-sponsored urbanization has been quite stable and is well covered by the official statistics, i.e. the NAPCT. This is largely due to the fact that the State is still responsible for many aspects of the life of this part of the population. Since 1978 this kind of population has been growing because of the economic boom, but it cannot grow at a faster rate than the State can cope with financially. This is the basic explanation for the trend of the NAPCT. In fact the Construction Commission, which is the government department responsible for urban planning, still tends to use the NAPCT for its planning purposes; literature written by urban planners reflects this situation (e.g. Xing et al. 1990; Zhang 1995. Also personal communication, officials at the Construction Commission of Fujian Province). This is another example of the close link between the NAPCT and the State roles in urbanization.

However, spontaneous urbanization has a totally different trend from that of State-sponsored urbanization since the 1980s. The driving forces behind it are also very different, and so are the consequences of its development, which will be examined in later chapters. Two forms of spontaneous urbanization were identified: the *in situ* rural-urban transformation driven by TVE development and facilitated by the creation of new urban centers (especially towns), and the increase in temporary residents.

An attempt can be made to examine the urbanization trend in Fujian Province on a more realistic basis by estimating the trends of State-sponsored and spontaneous urbanization separately. Since the State-sponsored urban population is represented by the NAPCT, the key problem is to estimate the spontaneous urban population. As mentioned before, prior to 1983 the agricultural population in suburban areas was the initial form of spontaneous urbanization; because the TPCT before 1983 is generally considered to be a reasonable representation of the size of the total urban population in China[21] and internationally comparable (Linge and Forbes 1990:194; Chan 1994:252), it can be disaggregated into the State-sponsored component, which is the NAPCT, and the spontaneous component, which is the difference between the TPCT and the NAPCT. After 1983 the spontaneous urban population can no longer be represented by this difference because of the problems with the TPCT previously mentioned. In Fujian Province rural industrialization mostly started on the outskirts of cities and towns. We may assume then that the spontaneous urban population after 1983 was increasing on the basis of the spontaneous component of the TPCT in 1982. So if we can estimate the growth rate of the spontaneous urban population, then we can get the number of spontaneous urban population after 1983 by applying this rate to the spontaneous urban population in 1982. The preceding analysis has shown that spontaneous urbanization in Fujian has been closely related to the development

---

[21] In the last few years I had a chance to discuss urban statistics with many relevant professional persons from both academic circles and government departments in Fujian Province, and most of them also regarded the urban statistics in the 1982 census, which was based on the TPCT, as reasonable for Fujian Province.

of TVEs since 1983. It is reasonable to assume therefore that the spontaneous urban population has been growing at a similar rate to that of TVE employees; and to use this rate to estimate the spontaneous urban population. In addition to the local State-sponsored and spontaneous urban population, temporary residents should also be estimated[22]. The proportion of temporary residents to local State-sponsored and spontaneous urban populations can be estimated from the 1982 and 1990 census data for the current 23 municipalities[23]. Hence we can use the following formulae to estimate Fujian's urbanization trend since 1983:

Uss_i = number of non-agricultural population of cities and towns in i year
$Ulsp_i = Ulsp_{i-1}*(1+R_i)$
$Utr_i = (Ussi_i+Ulsp_i)*TR_i$
$Usp_i = Ulsp_i+Utr_i$
where i is year;

Ulsp$_{i-1}$ is the number of local spontaneous urban population in i-1 year;
$Ulsp_i$ is the number of local spontaneous urban population in i year;
R_i is the growth rate of the number of employees in TVEs in i year;
TR_i is the proportion of the number of temporary residents living for more than one year to the number of local State-sponsored plus spontaneous urban population in i year;
Utr_i is the number of temporary residents in i year;
Usp_i is the total number of spontaneous urban population in i year.

---

[22] Statistics on the TVEs in Fujian do not include the employees with temporary resident status. Therefore estimation for the spontaneous urban population based on the growth rate of TVEs does not cover the temporary residents.

[23] Because it is difficult to obtain detailed information about temporary residents in both China as a whole (Guo and Deng 1995:37) and in Fujian as well, a proxy has to be used for the estimation. As the above 23 municipalities cover most urban areas and the areas with well-developed TVEs in Fujian Province, the proportion of temporary residents to the local population in these areas is the best proxy available for the proportion of temporary residents to local State-sponsored and sponta-neous urban populations. These municipalities do not cover some towns in the counties, and this may cause over-representation of cities and overestimation of the proportion of temporary resi-dents. However, these municipalities include some townships, and this can cancel some of the ef-fect of overestimation of temporary residents, as the proportion of temporary residents in townships is usually lower than in urban areas. In fact, the bias for the whole estimate caused by the exclusion of some towns would not be serious, as the long-term temporary residents in Fujian are not very much concentrated in the cities, as will be shown in Chapter 4, and in any case they account for less than 2.6 percent of the total population, as shown in the result of the estimate presented in Table 3.10.

Table 3.10 shows the processes and results of this estimation. An important characteristic of Fujian's urbanization trend since 1983 stands out according to this estimation, which can be further illustrated by Figure 3.3: while the proportion of the non-agricultural population of cities and towns increased steadily during the 1983-1995 period, it was greatly overshadowed by the increase in the proportion of spontaneous urban population. In 1987 the spontaneous urban population began to surpass the State-sponsored urban population as a proportion of the total population, and since 1990 this difference has increased noticeably each year. This increase was mainly caused by the local spontaneous urbanization, which was driven by the development of TVEs. The number of temporary residents as a proportion of the total population did not seem to be high, but its growth was quite noticeable. This result suggests a major change in Fujian's urbanization patterns: the State-sponsored *de jure* urbanization has become less important in the urbanization process, while the spontaneous quasi-urbanization driven by the local economic development and market forces has been playing an increasingly important role. Given the large proportion of population involved, and the fast rate of this spontaneous quasi-urbanization, as can be seen in Table 3.10 and Figure 3.3, it represents to a great extent the likely future direction of Fujian's urbanization; and the analysis of urbanization without this component would only provide an incomplete and superficial picture of Fujian's urbanization[24].

---

[24] The proportion of spontaneous urban population in Fujian is probably higher than that of China as a whole and those of most other provinces, as Fujian is one of a few provinces with the most developed TVEs.

Table 3.10 Estimation of Fujian's urbanization trend, 1983-1995

Year	Total population[a] (000s) (1)	NAPCT (000s) (2)	Employees in TVEs: growth rate (3) (%)	Local spontaneous urban population (000s) (4)	Temporary residents: proportion of local population (5) (%)	Temporary residents (000s) (6)	Estimate of total spontaneous urban population (000s) (7)	State-sponsored+ spontaneous urban population (000s) (8)	Proportion of State-sponsored urban population in total population (9) (%)	Proportion of local spontaneous population in total population (10) (%)	Proportion of temporary residents in total population (11) (%)	Proportion of total spontaneous urban population in total population (12) (%)	Proportion of State-sponsored+ spontaneous urban population in total population (13) (%)
1982	26,040.2	3,197.9		2,283.9	1.3	71.3							
1983	26,398.0	3,304.3	11.5	2,546.5	1.7	99.5	2,646.0	5,950.3	12.5	9.6	0.4	10.0	22.5
1984	26,768.3	3,599.7	20.1	3,058.4	2.0	133.2	3,191.6	6,791.3	13.4	11.4	0.5	11.9	25.4
1985	27,131.0	3,850.2	16.6	3,566.1	2.4	178.0	3,744.1	7,594.3	14.2	13.1	0.7	13.8	28.0
1986	27,493.0	3,957.2	4.4	3,723.0	2.7	207.4	3,930.4	7,887.6	14.4	13.5	0.8	14.3	28.7
1987	28,005.2	4,072.3	21.4	4,519.7	3.1	266.4	4,786.1	8,858.4	14.5	16.1	1.0	17.1	31.6
1988	28,452.5	4,241.2	6.4	4,809.0	3.4	307.7	5,116.7	9,357.9	14.9	16.9	1.1	18.0	32.9
1989	28,890.5	4,410.4	0.8	4,847.5	3.8	351.8	5,199.3	9,609.7	15.3	16.8	1.2	18.0	33.3
1990	29,998.2	4,549.4	0.9	4,891.1	4.2	396.5	5,287.6	9,837.0	15.2	16.3	1.3	17.6	32.8
1991	30,390.9	4,656.9	5.8	5,174.8	4.5	442.4	5,617.2	10,274.1	15.3	17.0	1.5	18.5	33.8
1992	30,668.5	5,020.7	14.2	5,909.6	4.9	535.6	6,445.2	11,465.9	16.4	19.3	1.7	21.0	37.4
1993	30,991.7	5,414.4	20.5	7,121.1	5.2	651.8	7,772.9	13,187.3	17.5	23.0	2.1	25.1	42.6
1994	31,268.7	5,610.6	15.0	8,189.2	5.6	772.8	8,962.0	14,572.6	17.9	26.2	2.5	28.7	46.6
1995	31,646.3	5,734.4	0.8	8,254.7	5.9	825.4	9,080.1	14,814.5	18.1	26.1	2.6	28.7	46.8

Notes: (1) Source: Statistical Bureau of Fujian Province 1996:47. (2) Statistical Bureau of Fujian Province 1996:49. (3) calculated according to the data in Statistical Bureau of Fujian Province 1996:186. $(4)_n = (4)_{n-1} * (1+(3))$. $(4)_{1982}$ is calculated according to the data in Statistical Bureau of Fujian Province 1996:48-9. (5) based on the proportion of temporary residents to the permanent residents in 23 municipalities in 1982 and 1990 census provided in Population Census Office 1990:14-6. Figures between 1982 and 1990 and after 1990 are interpolated or extrapolated respectively. $(6)=((2)+(4))*(5)$. $(7)=(4)+(6)$. $(8)=(7)+(2)$. $(9)=(2)/(1)$. $(10)=(4)/(1)$. $(11)=(6)/(1)$. $(12)=(7)/(1)$. $(13)=(8)/(1)$. [a] Total population is not adjusted for including temporary residents from outside Fujian. According to the 1990 census those temporary residents accounted for less than 0.8 percent of the total population (Zhu 1994a:19).

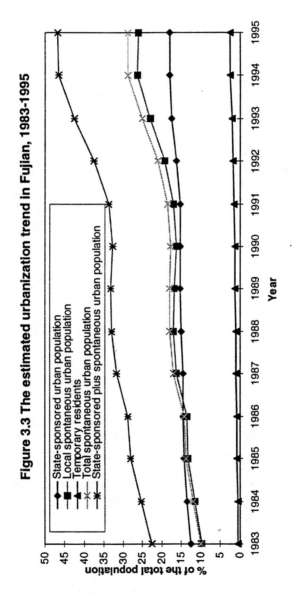

Figure 3.3 The estimated urbanization trend in Fujian, 1983-1995

% of the total population

State-sponsored urban population
Local spontaneous urban population
Temporary residents
Total spontaneous urban population
State-sponsored plus spontaneous urban population

Year

Source: Table 3.10.

Two points should be reiterated here. First, the above estimation, including the calculation of the "State-sponsored plus spontaneous urban population" as a proportion of the total population, is not meant to give a precise statistical account of the urban population and urbanization experience in Fujian. Rather, it serves as an illustration of how our understanding of Fujian's urbanization process, and to a great extent China's too, will be changed, if account is taken of those neglected factors. It strongly suggests that the confines of China's official data on urbanization prevent a full appreciation of the essence of the urbanization process since 1978. Secondly, spontaneous urbanization has largely been treated here as functional urbanization. By other criteria spontaneous urbanization may not be quite up to the standard of full urbanization. What this estimation of Fujian's spontaneous urban population provides is a measure of how many people entered the urbanization process as potential urban population in an spontaneous way rather than how many completed it as conventionally understood[25]. But sooner or later those spontaneous urban populations will complete this process in life style and residential status, which is an irreversible process. As urbanization is regarded as a multidimensional phenomenon and continuing process in this study, they can be regarded as part of the urbanization process. As will be seen in the following chapters, this part of the urbanization process has far-reaching theoretical and policy implications and needs to be examined further.

---

[25] Those spontaneous urban populations, such as TVE employees and temporary residents in the built-up areas of cities and towns and their dependants, can be considered to have completed this process. Nevertheless, the distinction between them and other members of the spontaneous urban population is not clear-cut, if we regard spontaneous urbanization as a continuing process and note that many villages with well-developed TVEs are densely populated and incorporated in Fujian, as mentioned in this chapter and as will be discussed further in the following chapters.

CHAPTER 4

SPATIAL ASPECTS OF URBANIZATION PATTERNS

Exploring the spatial features of the new urbanization patterns in China is one of the most important aspects of this study. This is not only because it has great theoretical and practical significance in general, but also because it is indispensable for fully appreciating the implications of the newly emergent spontaneous urbanization examined in Chapter 3. This chapter examines Fujian's urban system and residential hierarchy, especially those after 1978, by using different methods and from different perspectives, so that some insights into this issue can be obtained.

4.1 THE CLASSIFICATION OF CITIES AND TOWNS ACCORDING TO THEIR POPULATION SIZES

Before Fujian's urban system is analyzed, another definitional problem needs to be approached. Besides the distinction between cities and towns, cities in China are further classified into different categories according to the size of their non-agricultural population. The criteria for this kind of classification are partly stipulated in the Urban Planning Act of the PRC (China, Standing Committee of NPC 1990:176-7). Cities with a non-agricultural population of more than 500,000 are classified as "large cities"; those with a non-agricultural population between 200,000 and 500,000 are "medium-sized cities", and those with a non-agricultural population of less than 200,000 are small cities. In practice, cities with a non-agricultural population of over one million are called "very large cities" (Liu, Wu and Li 1986:367; Laquian 1991:238-9).

Two problems need to be sorted out here. First, as pointed out in Chapter 3, urban population would be underestimated by using the non-agricultural population of cities and towns (NAPCT). In analysis of the proportion of population in the cities of different sizes, this is less a problem because the effects of underestimation on the cities of different sizes will cancel each other out, as implied by Kojima (1995:140). Nevertheless this is not necessarily the case since the 1980s. Cities of different sizes can have different proportions of spontaneous urban population, which is quite obvious when one notes that Fujian's urbanization process has been characterized by the development of township and village enterprises. So this chapter first looks at Fujian's urban system based on the NAPCT, and then examines the effects of the development of township and village enterprises and temporary residents on Fujian's residential system. Data based on the total population of cities and towns are used only for reference, because they not only exaggerate the urban population, but also do so disproportionately for the cities and towns of different sizes[26]. Secondly the official classification of the population sizes of cities should be regrouped for analytical purposes. As towns and their status in the urban system are very different from cities, and their development is currently strongly promoted by the government, they are separated from small cities. Because the population size of 100,000 is an important criterion for designating a city in China, and is regarded by some scholars as the lower limit of the population size of secondary cities (Rondinelli 1983:48), cities larger or smaller than 100,000 are also separated. The final categories are set out in Table 1. The following analysis is conducted in the light of the above criteria and classification.

Table 4.1 Categories of cities and towns

Category	Town	Small city (1)	Small city (2)	Medium-sized city	Large city	Very large city
Number of NAP	<100,000	<100,000	100,000-200,000	200,000-500,000	500,000-1,000,000	>1,000,000

---

[26] Because different criteria are used for defining city and town populations (see Chapter 3, footnote 13), the "second criterion" of the 1990 census will not be used in the analysis of this chapter either.

4.2 URBAN SYSTEM IN TERMS OF STATE-SPONSORED URBANIZATION

Although the analysis based on the NAPCT cannot fully represent the real situation of Fujian's urban system, for a number of reasons it is necessary to do such analysis. First, there are far more data on State-sponsored urbanization than on spontaneous urbanization, and therefore it is easier to carry out such analysis. Unlike temporal changes of urbanization, spatial patterns of urbanization are less influenced by urban definition problems. The analysis of spatial patterns of urbanization based on the non-agricultural population of cities and towns is relatively useful and can be taken as reference for the understanding of the real urban system. In addition, the analysis based on the NAPCT serves as a reference frame for the analysis based on the spontaneous urban population. Secondly, the classification of population size of cities and towns in the "Urban Planning Act of the PRC" is based on the non-agricultural population of cities and towns. The urban development strategy stipulated in the same Act, that is "strictly control the size of large cities, reasonably develop the medium-sized and small cities", is also based on the NAPCT. Clearly the government is more concerned with the spatial distribution of the NAPCT, and therefore it is necessary to deal with it separately. In a way the following examination of Fujian's urban system in terms of the non-agricultural population of cities and towns is a test of the effectiveness of government urban development policies in Fujian province.

4.2.1 PERCENTAGE DISTRIBUTION OF NAPCT IN CITIES AND TOWNS OF DIFFERENT SIZES

This section examines the percentage distribution of the non-agricultural population of cities and towns in the cities and towns of different sizes. First the evolution of the urban system before the reform era is briefly reviewed. Fujian's urban system was long characterized by the small size of cities and the large proportion of town population at that time. Table 4.2 shows that in terms of the non-agricultural population of cities and towns, small urban places dominated Fujian's urban system before 1978. About half of the NAPCT were distributed in urban places with a non-agricultural population of less than 100,000. If the government definition of small cities with 200,000 is taken as the upper limit of population size, then as much as 60-70 percent of the urban population lived in the small cities and towns. A corollary of this is that medium-sized cities and large cities were relatively underdeveloped in Fujian. In fact there was not a single large city in the province until the provincial capital Fuzhou developed into a large city in 1959. If Fujian's urban system is analyzed in terms of the total population of cities and towns the situation will be quite similar, since the proportions of the agricultural population in the total population of cities and towns (TPCT) were limited and stable at that time. There were higher proportions of the agricultural population in the total population of cities than in towns, and therefore the proportions of the TPCT distributed in the big urban places were higher than those of the NAPCT. Nevertheless this would not change the dominating role of small urban places in the urban system. For example in 1978, 41.7 percent of the TPCT were distributed in the towns, while only 23.1 percent of the TPCT were distributed in the capital city, Fuzhou.

Compared with the urban system of China as a whole Fujian is quite exceptional in this respect, because it is widely recognized that China's urban system has been characterized by the overdevelopment of large cities and underdevelopment of small cities and towns (Wei 1990; Gu 1991:111-3; Laquian 1991). If related to Fujian's political and economic situation before 1978, this may be partly explained by Fujian's frontier status with regard to Taiwan, slower economic development, and limited government investment (Zhu 1994b:192). But an interesting question is: has Fujian's urban system changed much, as the experience of many developing countries and the conventional theories suggest, since Fujian opened up to the outside world and its economic development took off in the late 1970s?

The distribution of the non-agricultural population of cities and towns in the cities and towns of different sizes since 1978 is presented in Table 4.3. Comparing Table 4.3 and Table 4.2 shows that there have been some changes in Fujian's urban system since 1978. But these changes have not altered the fundamental characteristics of Fujian's urban system. First the proportion of town population declined, but this was accompanied by a corresponding increase in the proportion of population in the cities smaller than 100,000. When these two are combined, small urban places with a non-agricultural population of less than 100,000 still dominate Fujian's urban system, although the percentage of their population slightly declined.

Table 4.2 NAPCT in cities and towns of different sizes, Fujian 1955-1978

Year	Total		Towns		Cities with NAP of less than 100,000		Cities with NAP of 100,000-200,000		Cities with NAP of 200,000-500,000		Cities with NAP of 500,000 or more	
	Number (000s)	% of total	Number (000s)	% of total	Number (000s)	% of total	Number (000s)	% of total	Number (000s)	% of total	Number (000s)	% of total
1955	n.a.	n.a.	n.a.	n.a.	81.9	n.a.	307.2	n.a.	430.5	n.a.	0.0	n.a.
1956	1,707.5	100.0	848.3	49.7	220.6	12.9	185.2	10.8	453.4	26.6	0.0	0.0
1957	1,750.4	100.0	872.4	49.8	232.8	13.3	190.9	10.9	454.3	26.0	0.0	0.0
1958	n.a.	n.a.	n.a.	n.a.	280.9	n.a.	0.0	n.a.	733.0	n.a.	0.0	n.a.
1959	n.a.	n.a.	n.a.	n.a.	56.8	n.a.	324.3	n.a.	255.3	n.a.	536.5	n.a.
1960	n.a.	n.a.	n.a.	n.a.	n.a.	n.a.	488.7	n.a.	266.2	n.a.	602.7	n.a.
1961	2,435.1	100.0	1,165.0	47.8	97.2	4.0	330.7	13.6	253.2	10.4	589.0	24.2
1962	2,351.8	100.0	1,145.3	48.7	52.8	2.2	334.4	14.2	237.0	10.1	582.3	24.8
1963	2,264.1	100.0	1,072.1	47.4	57.9	2.6	325.9	14.4	233.6	10.3	574.6	25.4
1964	2,290.5	100.0	1,084.0	47.3	58.7	2.6	329.5	14.4	237.2	10.4	581.1	25.4
1965	2,344.6	100.0	1,119.4	47.7	63.5	2.7	334.2	14.3	241.5	10.3	586.0	25.0
1966	2,387.7	100.0	1,130.8	47.4	71.9	3.0	346.1	14.5	246.7	10.3	592.2	24.8
1967	2,433.7	100.0	1,143.7	47.0	77.4	3.2	359.1	14.8	252.0	10.4	601.5	24.7
1968	2,478.2	100.0	1,161.8	46.9	80.5	3.2	373.6	15.1	253.9	10.2	608.4	24.6
1969	2,415.3	100.0	1,190.6	49.3	82.9	3.4	352.8	14.6	230.0	9.5	559.0	23.1
1970	2,425.7	100.0	1,216.0	50.1	90.4	3.7	339.9	14.0	221.8	9.1	557.6	23.0
1971	2,357.9	100.0	1,141.1	48.4	97.4	4.1	353.2	15.0	230.2	9.8	536.0	22.7
1972	2,409.9	100.0	1,165.6	48.4	0.0	0.0	457.3	19.0	237.9	9.9	549.1	22.8
1973	2,478.2	100.0	1,202.5	48.5	0.0	0.0	465.6	18.8	247.6	10.0	562.5	22.7
1974	2,544.3	100.0	1,253.1	49.3	0.0	0.0	471.5	18.5	249.7	9.8	570.0	22.4
1975	2,573.3	100.0	1,279.1	49.7	0.0	0.0	469.7	18.3	255.0	9.9	569.5	22.1
1976	2,629.4	100.0	1,309.2	49.8	0.0	0.0	476.9	18.1	260.9	9.9	582.4	22.1
1977	2,671.5	100.0	1,333.5	49.9	0.0	0.0	482.9	18.1	266.3	10.0	588.8	22.0
1978	2,755.2	100.0	1,365.8	49.6	0.0	0.0	499.6	18.1	274.9	10.0	614.9	22.3

Source: calculated according to Statistical Bureau of Fujian Province and Public Security Bureau of Fujian Province 1989:80-103.

Table 4.3 NAPCT in cities and towns of different sizes, Fujian 1978-1995

Year	Total		Towns		Cities with NAP of less than 100,000		Cities with NAP of 100,000-200,000		Cities with NAP of 200,000-500,000		Cities with NAP of 500,000 or more	
	Number (000s)	% of total	Number (000s)	% of total	Number (000s)	% of total	Number (000s)	% of total	Number (000s)	% of total	Number (000s)	% of total
1978	2,755.2	100.0	1,365.8	49.6	0.0	0.0	499.6	18.1	274.9	10.0	614.9	22.3
1979	2,905.0	100.0	1,453.0	50.0	0.0	0.0	522.9	18.0	286.3	9.9	642.8	22.1
1980	3,004.5	100.0	1,508.5	50.2	0.0	0.0	538.7	17.9	292.5	9.7	664.8	22.1
1981	3,115.9	100.0	1,479.4	47.5	90.0	2.9	555.5	17.8	301.2	9.7	689.8	22.1
1982	3,197.9	100.0	1,517.5	47.5	94.4	3.0	570.3	17.8	306.4	9.6	709.3	22.2
1983	3,304.3	100.0	1,456.0	44.1	223.7	6.8	583.1	17.6	314.5	9.5	727.0	22.0
1984	3,599.7	100.0	1,584.4	44.0	230.5	6.4	702.2	19.5	328.1	9.1	754.5	21.0
1985	3,850.2	100.0	1,738.2	45.1	146.0	3.8	838.1	21.8	343.7	8.9	784.2	20.4
1986	3,957.2	100.0	1,788.6	45.2	152.8	3.9	859.2	21.7	351.1	8.9	805.5	20.4
1987	4,072.3	100.0	1,838.9	45.2	159.9	3.9	881.4	21.6	360.2	8.8	831.9	20.4
1988	4,241.2	100.0	1,827.8	43.1	293.4	6.9	903.7	21.3	370.1	8.7	846.2	20.0
1989	4,410.4	100.0	1,816.3	41.2	418.1	9.5	939.6	21.3	373.2	8.5	863.2	19.6
1990	4,549.4	100.0	1,810.8	39.8	502.1	11.0	974.9	21.4	386.8	8.5	874.8	19.2
1991	4,656.9	100.0	1,811.6	38.9	567.4	12.2	988.6	21.2	398.1	8.5	891.2	19.1
1992	5,020.7	100.0	1,915.9	38.2	765.0	15.2	818.2	16.3	612.5	12.2	909.1	18.1
1993	5,414.4	100.0	1,904.9	35.2	883.9	16.3	596.8	11.0	1,102.1	20.4	926.7	17.1
1994	5,610.6	100.0	1,826.5	32.6	689.0	12.3	1,046.8	18.7	1,096.0	19.5	952.3	17.0
1995	5,737.4	100.0	1,764.8	30.8	773.3	13.5	884.2	15.4	1,332.2	23.2	982.9	17.1

Sources: Statistical Bureau of Fujian Province and Public Security Bureau of Fujian Province 1989:104-13; Statistical Bureau of Fujian Province 1990-1996.

In fact some non-agricultural population in the cities with a population of less than 100,000 still live in the towns which are under the administration of a city[27]. If this fact is taken into account, the position of towns in the urban system is more important than is indicated in Table 4.3. Secondly, the position of small cities with a non-agricultural population between 100,000 and 200,000 in the urban system fluctuated. The proportion of their population in the urban system increased through most of the 1980s, but decreased again in the 1990s, which was obviously the result of upgrading of some cities into medium-sized cities due to their population growth. This can be confirmed by the fact that the decrease in the proportion of population in the small cities was accompanied by an increase in the proportion of population in the medium-sized cities. Thirdly, the proportion of population in the big city decreased noticeably. This is a clear indication that the spatial patterns of Fujian's urbanization in terms of the NAPCT since the 1978 has not conformed with the experience of many developing countries and much of the conventional theory. The above analysis is further illustrated in Figure 4.1.

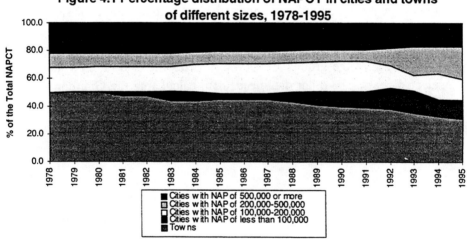

Figure 4.1 Percentage distribution of NAPCT in cities and towns of different sizes, 1978-1995

Source: Table 4.3.

<hr>

[27] In China cities are also divided into two categories: cities with districts and cities without districts. Usually cities with a population of less than 100,000 are those without districts. They are composed of one big town, which is usually the seat of the municipal government, and several other towns and townships. See also Appendix 1.

4.2.2 CHANGES IN URBAN POPULATION CONCENTRATION MEASURED BY THE GINI CONCENTRATION RATIO

Another way to examine the evolution of Fujian's urban system with regard to the non-agricultural population of cities and towns is to compute and analyze the Gini concentration ratio, which has been widely used for the measurement of concentration (Arriaga 1975:66-71). In this case the index is used to measure how uniformly the urban non-agricultural population is distributed in relation to the numbers of different sized cities and towns. Calculating the Gini concentration ratio of the urban non-agricultural population in relation to the land area is another option, but it is too difficult to get such data. Besides it is not the urban population distribution in relation to the land area, rather the urban population distribution in relation to the city size that is of interest here. The formula used in the calculation is as follows:

$$CR = (\sum_{k=2}^{m} PP_k * N_{k-1} - \sum_{k=2}^{m} PP_{k-1} * N_k) / 10,000$$

where PP_K and N_K are the percentage of population and city numbers accumulated for each subgroup of city sizes and m is the total number of subgroups of city size in the calculation. Before calculation of the cumulative percentages of the subgroups, they are ranked from the smallest to the largest according to the population sizes of the groups. Table 4.4 presents the data on city numbers for the selected years. The other data needed for calculating the Gini concentration ratio can be found in Table 4.2 and Table 4.3, and are not listed here to avoid repetition. The calculation result is shown in the last column of Table 4.4 and further illustrated in Figure 4.2.

Table 4.4 Number of cities[a] and towns in Fujian and Gini concentration ratio, selected years

Year	Town[b]	Cities with NAP of less than 100,000	Cities with NAP of 100,000-200,000	Cities with NAP of 200,000-500,000	Cities with NAP of 500,000 or more	Gini concentration ratio
1956	225[c]	3	1	1	0	0.485940
1964	120[d]	1	3	1	1	0.489468
1975	114[d]	0	4	1	1	0.461558
1982	119[d]	1	4	1	1	0.480718
1985	188[c]	2	6	1	1	0.508865
1990	218[e]	8	6	1	1	0.552384
1995	364[f]	10	7	5	1	0.649378

[a] City numbers are from Statistical Bureau of Fujian Province and Fujian Public Security Bureau 1989:81, 89, 100, 107, 110; and Statistical Bureau of Fujian Province 1991:461-2; 1996:420-1.

[b] Towns under municipal administration are not included. Sources of their numbers:

[c] Li et al. 1988:746-7;

[d] Fu and Chen 1990:178, 184;

[e] Population Census Office of Fujian Province 1992:186-203;

[f] Statistical Bureau of Fujian Province 1995:1922; and data provided by Fujian Provincial Civil Affairs Department.

Figure 4.2 Gini concentration ratio for NAPCT in Fujian, selected years

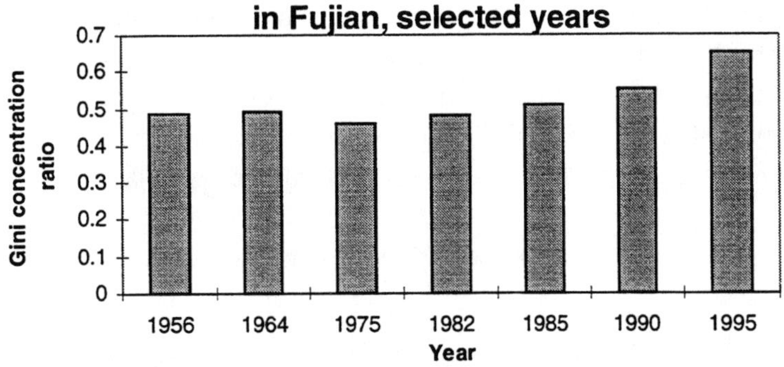

Source: Table 4.4.

The result shows that the concentration degree of Fujian's urban system did not change much before the 1980s, but has increased noticeably since then. This conclusion seems to contradict the dispersed urbanization trend identified in Chapter 3, but if comprehended correctly it is not surprising. Reviewing the analysis in section 4.2.1 this can be seen as mainly a result of increasing concentration of the NAPCT in the small and medium-sized cities, rather than the large city, in relation to the numbers of different sized cities and towns. Furthermore, the spontaneous urban population, which is the major cause of dispersed urbanization, has not yet been included in the analysis. The concentrating trend revealed here represents only the spatial pattern of the non-agricultural population of cities and towns, although this should not be neglected because it is another reflection of the differences between State-sponsored urbanization and spontaneous urbanization.

4.2.3 CHANGES IN DEGREE OF URBAN POPULATION CONCENTRATION MEASURED BY THE TWO-CITY AND FOUR-CITY PRIMACY INDICES

The third way of exploring the evolution of the urban system is calculating the urban primacy index. It has been noted that although there was a trend of concentration in Fujian's urban system, the proportion of the non-agricultural population of cities and towns distributed in the large city was decreasing. This is an indication that the concentration did not lead to urban primacy. The urban primacy indices can be used to test this proposition.

Two urban primacy indices, the two-city primacy index and the four-city primacy index, are used here[28]. The two-city primacy index is the division of the population of the largest city by that of the second largest city. The four-city index is the population of the largest city divided by the sum of the population of the second-, third-, and fourth-ranked cities (Arriaga 1975:63-4). The indices measure the concentration of population in the largest city in relation to the second-ranked city, or the second-, third-, and fourth-ranked three cities. The greater the index value, the greater the degree of concentration of population in the largest city.

In symbols the two indices can be expressed respectively as follows:

$$PI_2 = C1/C2$$

---

[28] In some cases it might be preferable to compute an eleven-city index. But in the case of Fujian there were fewer than eleven cities until 1988, so it is not meaningful to calculate this index.

$$PL_4 = C1/\sum_{K=2}^{4} C_K$$

where PI_2 is the two-city primacy index;

　PL_4 is the four-city primacy index;

　C_1 is the population of the largest city;

　C_2 is the population of the second largest city;

　C_K for K = 2, 3, 4 represents the population of the second, third, and fourth ranked cities respectively.

Data needed for the calculation of the two indices and the corresponding results are presented in Table 4.5. The results are further illustrated in Figure 4.3.

Figure 4.3 Two-city and four-city primacy indices in Fujian, 1955-1995

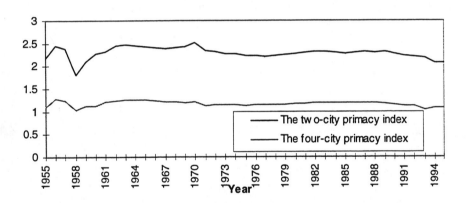

Source: Table 4.5

More insights into the spatial patterns of Fujian's urbanization can be gained from the above results. Figure 4.4 shows clearly that both the two-city and four-city primacy indices exhibited stable and slightly downward trends, except for the period around 1960 when there were some big fluctuations, which were the results of faster growth of the second- and third-ranked cities than the largest city in the "Great Leap Forward" and the adjustment afterwards. It is particularly important to note that the general trends of both indices after the 1980s were downward, indicating that there was no spatial concentration in the provincial capital, even after the economic development took off. This further confirms the previous analysis that the general trend of concentration identified in section 4.2.2 was not the result of growth of the largest city, rather the result of relatively fast growth of small and medium-sized cities in relation to the growth of towns.

Table 4.5 Two-city and four-city primacy indices in Fujian, 1955-1995

Year	Non-agricultural population of largest city: Fuzhou (000s)	Non-agricultural population of second-ranked city: Xiamen (000s)	Non-agricultural population of third-ranked city (000s)	Non-agricultural population of fourth-ranked city (000s)	Two-city primacy index	Four-city primacy index
1955	430.5	197.3	109.9	81.9	2.18	1.11
1956	453.4	185.2	87.5	82.1	2.45	1.28
1957	454.3	190.9	90.3	86.3	2.38	1.24
1958	471.8	261.2	95.4	94.0	1.81	1.05
1959	536.5	255.3	114.8	107.6	2.10	1.12
1960	602.7	266.2	153.9	113.7	2.26	1.13
1961	589.0	253.2	116.9	112.9	2.33	1.22
1962	582.3	237.0	126.1	105.9	2.46	1.24
1963	574.6	233.6	111.9	107.7	2.46	1.27
1964	581.1	237.2	112.3	108.9	2.45	1.27
1965	586.0	241.5	115.7	111.3	2.43	1.25
1966	592.2	246.7	117.9	115.0	2.40	1.23
1967	601.5	252.0	122.0	119.4	2.39	1.22
1968	608.4	253.9	126.3	124.5	2.40	1.21
1969	559.0	230.0	121.8	117.3	2.43	1.19
1970	557.6	221.8	124.3	110.5	2.51	1.22
1971	536.0	230.2	129.7	114.7	2.33	1.13
1972	549.1	237.9	128.3	115.0	2.31	1.14
1973	562.5	247.6	128.8	117.4	2.27	1.14
1974	570.0	249.7	130.1	118.1	2.28	1.14
1975	569.5	255.0	127.1	119.7	2.23	1.13
1976	582.4	260.9	127.4	120.7	2.23	1.14
1977	588.8	266.3	128.0	121.5	2.21	1.14
1978	614.9	274.9	132.6	125.1	2.24	1.15
1979	642.8	286.3	137.4	133.8	2.25	1.15
1980	664.8	292.5	141.8	139.5	2.27	1.16
1981	689.8	301.2	145.4	143.0	2.29	1.17
1982	709.3	306.4	148.5	144.2	2.31	1.18
1983	727.0	314.5	150.7	148.2	2.31	1.19

1984	754.5	328.1	155.3	153.0	2.30	1.19
1985	784.2	343.7	159.4	157.1	2.28	1.19
1986	805.5	351.1	165.3	161.4	2.29	1.19
1987	831.9	360.2	169.4	167.4	2.31	1.19
1988	846.2	370.1	174.0	172.2	2.29	1.18
1989	863.2	373.2	191.1	177.9	2.31	1.16
1990	874.8	386.8	195.1	185.2	2.26	1.14
1991	891.2	398.1	198.3	190.3	2.24	1.13
1992	909.1	410.8	201.7	196.4	2.21	1.12
1993	926.7	426.3	256.8	213.7	2.17	1.03
1994	952.3	458.6	217.9	211.7	2.08	1.07
1995	982.9	472.3	221.6	217.9	2.08	1.08

Sources: data for the period 1955-1988 are from Statistical Bureau of Fujian Province and Public Security Bureau of Fujian Province 1989:81-113; data for the period after 1989 are from Statistical Bureau of Fujian Province 1990-1996.

4.2.4 SUMMARY

Combining the findings from the three preceding sections gives a clearer and more comprehensive picture of the evolution of Fujian's urban system in terms of the NAPCT. Unlike many developing regions which inherited the historical legacy of urban concentration and urban primacy, Fujian started its urban evolution from a basis dominated by small urban places. The economic development since the 1980s brought about a change in the urban system in the direction of more concentration, but this change did not alter the basic characteristics of the urban system, and was mainly caused by the increasing importance of small and medium-sized cities. The economic development did not lead to an increase in urban primacy; this is best demonstrated by both the two-city primacy index and the four-city primacy index, which exhibited almost the same trend over time. In short, it is safe to conclude that up to now no major spatial concentration has occurred in Fujian in terms of the NAPCT, and there has been no sign of polarization.

4.3 SPATIAL EFFECTS OF SPONTANEOUS URBANIZATION

Up to now the analysis in this chapter has been confined to the non-agricultural population of cities and towns, but a complete understanding of the spatial patterns of Fujian's urbanization can only be achieved when the spatial effects of spontaneous urbanization are incorporated into the analysis.

In this section, efforts will be made to reveal these effects. The basic idea is to take the distribution of the non-agricultural population by the residential hierarchy as the reference frame, and compare it with the distribution of TVE employees and temporary residents to identify the general direction of such effects. It should be noted that the residential hierarchy rather than the urban system, and the non-agricultural population rather than the non-agricultural population of cities and towns, are used for the analysis. The difference between the residential hierarchy and the urban system is that while the urban system consists of large, medium-sized, and small cities and towns, the residential hierarchy includes one more residential level at the bottom: the rural townships. There are three reasons to choose the residential hierarchy rather than the urban system as the reference frame for the following analysis. First, the number of township and village enterprise employees and temporary residents in the towns cannot be separated from those in the townships with the available data, so that the following analysis can only be conducted on the basis of the residential hierarchy, rather than of the urban system. Secondly, as many TVEs are in places which have not been designated as urban places, it is necessary to use the residential hierarchy rather than the urban system so that those TVEs can be included in the analysis. Thirdly, the difference between the distribution of the NAP by residential hierarchy and the NAPCT by urban system is small. It is caused by the inclusion of the NAP living in the rural area, whose number was only 165,900, 2.9 percent of the NAPCT in 1995. In fact the non-agricultural population is even used as a proxy for urban population by many Chinese scholars (Yu 1995:40). Therefore the conclusions in the following analysis for the residential hierarchy can be largely used to infer the situation in the urban system.

4.3.1 SPATIAL EFFECTS OF THE DEVELOPMENT OF TOWNSHIP
AND VILLAGE ENTERPRISES

Table 4.6 shows the distribution of township and village enterprise employees by residential hierarchy in Fujian in 1995. It is further compared with the distribution of the non-agricultural population in Figure 4.4. While it is not surprising that a dispersed spatial pattern of TVEs can be clearly identified from this table, it should be noted that once these TVE employees and their dependants are incorporated, there will be significant changes in Fujian's urban system, which would not be revealed by merely analyzing the distribution of the non-agricultural population of cities and towns.

In general the incorporation of TVE employees and their dependants will further decentralize Fujian's urban system. As Figure 4.4 clearly shows, compared with the non-agricultural population, a much higher proportion (nearly 90 percent) of township and village enterprise employees were distributed in small places, that is townships and towns under county administration, and cities with a non-agricultural population of less than 200,000. Correspondingly, the proportions of township and village enterprise employees distributed in the medium-sized and large cities were much lower, compared with the distribution of the NAP. Only 4 percent of the TVE employees were distributed in the largest cities in Fujian Province, compared to 16.7 percent of the NAP. This comparison suggests that as spontaneous urbanization progresses further, the lower level of the urban system will be greatly strengthened and the higher level relatively weakened.

This change in the urban system will largely be realized by a significant increase in the number of towns and town population. This is because TVE employees in the towns or townships under county administration accounted for more than half of the total number of TVE employees. While the development of TVEs in existing towns will promote the growth of town population, the development of TVEs in townships will facilitate the emergence of new towns, leading to a strengthened lower level of the urban system. In addition, the effect of the development of township and village enterprises on the residential hierarchy and the urban system should also be appreciated in the sense that if those employees had not been absorbed in local non-agricultural activities, they would have migrated to the primate city, leading to a higher degree of urban population concentration.

Table 4.6 Number and percentage distribution of TVE employees by residential hierarchy, Fujian 1995

	Total		Towns or townships[a]		Cities with NAP of less than 100,000		Cities with NAP of 100,000- 200,000		Cities with NAP of 200,000-500,000		Cities with NAP of 500,000 or more	
	Number	% of total	Number	% of total	Number	% of total	Number	% of total	Number	% of total	Number	% of total
	4,709,954	100	2,436,796	51.74	824,053	17.50	914,497	19.42	336,985	7.15	197,623	4.20

[a] Towns and townships only refer to those under county administration.

Source: calculated according to Statistical Bureau of Fujian Province 1996:442-3.

Figure 4.4 Comparison of the distribution of TVE employees with that of NAP in Fujian, 1995

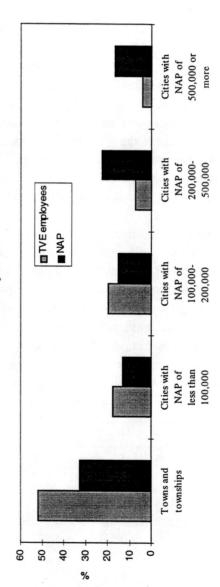

Sources: based on Table 4.6 and Statistical Bureau of Fujian Province 1996:49.

The spatial effect of the development of TVEs can be examined from another perspective. As can be seen from Table 4.7, the rank of places according to the number of township and village enterprise employees is totally different from that of the non-agricultural population (and non-agricultural population of cities and towns). The place with the largest number of township and village enterprise employees is Jinjiang, which was just designated as a city in 1992 and had a non-agricultural population of only 107,700 in 1995. But it had as many as 393,600 township and village enterprise employees in the same year, compared to 197,600 in the largest city, Fuzhou. The place with the second-largest number of township and village enterprise employees is Nanan, which was designated as a city even later than Jinjiang. It is noteworthy that in Table 4.7, only one place, the provincial capital Fuzhou, appears in both lists of ten top cities with the largest non-agricultural populations and ten top places with the largest numbers of TVE employees. In fact most places with the largest numbers of township and village enterprise employees are newly designated cities or even still counties. On the other hand most of the cities among the top ten with the largest NAPs are administrative centers, being either the provincial capitals, or the government seats of prefectures, or prefecture-level municipalities. The correlation coefficient between the number of TVE employees and the number of the NAP, calculated according to the data for 69 cities and counties in Fujian, is only 0.3338 (P=0.005), which can be mostly attributed to the overlapping distribution of TVE employees with the non-agricultural population in the towns. This suggests that the development of township and village enterprises will lead to the creation of many new economic growth centers, rather than enhance the old administrative centers, at least in terms of employment. One result of the emergence of those new growth centers is to enhance the lower part of the urban system, as just mentioned; the other result is that the distribution of urban centers will be geographically more dispersed, leading to a more regionally-based, rather than city-based urbanization process.

**Table 4.7 Ten top cities with the largest NAPs and ten top places with
the largest numbers of TVE employees, 1995**

NAP (000s)		TVE employees (000s)	
Name	Number	Name	Number
Fuzhou	982.9	Jinjiang	393.6
Xiamen	472.3	Nanan	280.2
Longyan	221.6	Putian (county)	263.0
Quanzhou	217.9	Fuzhou	197.6
Nanping	217.7	Fuqing	179.0
Zhangzhou	202.7	Huian	178.9
Sanming	184.2	Xianyou	168.1
Fuding	137.3	Longhai	156.2
Yongan	122.6	Shishi	137.3
Putian (city)	120.6	Minhou	120.9

Source: Statistical Bureau of Fujian Province 1996:420-1;
442-3.

In addition to the direct spatial effects of TVE development, the development of TVEs has an indirect effect on the position of small cities in the urban system. Since 1986 the designation of cities in China has been related to the economic performance of localities. According to 1984 city definitions, the designation of a city was related to the annual gross product. In 1993, criteria on the economic structure were introduced in the definition to stress the importance of the development of secondary and tertiary sectors, and the criterion concerning gross domestic product was further increased (see Appendix 2 for more detail). As a result of those changes, township and village enterprises are important not only for town development, but also for the development of small cities, because TVE is the major source of economic development in many places of Fujian Province. The designation of many small cities in the coastal area with a non-agricultural population of up to 100,000 can largely be attributed to this reason. Cities designated after the late 1980s, such as Fuqing, Jinjiang, Longhai, Changle, Nanan, and Shishi are mostly places with rapid growth of township and village enterprises. The case of Jinjiang can best illustrate this situation. When it was designated as a city in 1992, the number of the official non-agricultural population was only 95,500, actually below the official criterion. But its gross domestic product was 3,498,000,000 *Yuan*, 8.7 times that of the official economic criterion for the designation of a city. This high level of economic development was largely a result of township and village enterprises development, because 74.3 percent of Jinjiang's total product was produced by township and village enterprises in that year[29]. The problem of not being up to the official standard in terms of its non-agricultural population (120,000) was sorted out by including temporary residents who were engaged in non-agricultural activities in the official non-agricultural population (personal communication, local officials in the Civil Affairs Department, September 1996). This is reasonable for places like Jinjiang because many temporary residents are *de facto* urban population, as analyzed in Chapter 3.

So in this way the development of township and village enterprises not only influences the spatial pattern of Fujian's urbanization in a broader sense, but also influences the urban system in terms of the non-agricultural population of cities and towns. The designation of new cities does not have much effect on the urbanization level, because most newly designated cities are largely composed of towns, with only a small proportion of places still being townships. But it changes the relative position of small cities in the urban system. In fact the increasing proportion of small city population shown in Figure 4.1 was to a great extent a result of this development. Besides, at the micro-level the urban population in these cities is very much distributed in many towns, which is different from the traditional patterns of internal population distribution in small cities. This will have a considerable effect on the urban planning strategy in these areas.

Unfortunately, because there are no regionally disaggregated data on the distribution of township and village enterprise employees among towns and townships, it is not possible to estimate the spontaneous urban population for each city and town as proposed for Fujian Province as a whole in Chapter 3. Therefore it is not possible to calculate the proportion of urban population distributed in the cities of different sizes, towns and townships, Gini concentration ratio, and urban primacy indices, when spontaneous urbanization is incorporated into the analysis. Nevertheless, from the above analysis it is reasonable to argue that the develop-

---

[29] Unfortunately no gross domestic product is calculated for TVEs in China. But it should be reasonable to use the proportion of TVE product to the total product of society to indicate the contribution of TVEs in the economic development.

ment of township and village enterprises would lead to a more decentralized spatial pattern of urbanization, in the residential hierarchy, urban system and geographical distribution.

4.3.2 SPATIAL EFFECTS OF TEMPORARY RESIDENTS

Another spontaneous urbanization process influencing the spatial pattern of Fujian's urbanization is the emergence and increased importance of temporary residents. Assessment of the effects of this kind of population on the spatial pattern of Fujian's urbanization is also difficult, because data in this aspect are either limited or only for internal use in the government departments. Nevertheless a similar approach to that used in the preceding section can also be taken to explore the general trend.

One useful piece of information about the spatial distribution of temporary residents can be obtained from the 1990 population census data. As was done for the township and village enterprise employees, the distribution of those temporary residents, who had lived in a county-level place other than where they had their household registration for one year or more, can be calculated by residential hierarchy (Table 4.8). As can be seen in Figure 4.5 it very much resembles the distribution of the non-agricultural population in the same year. This can be confirmed by the fact that the correlation coefficient between the number of temporary residents in the 1990 census and the number of the non-agricultural population calculated according to the data for all 69 cities and counties in Fujian in the same year is as high as 0.9310 (P=0.0001). Comparison of Table 4.8 and Table 4.6 shows less similarity between the spatial distribution of temporary residents by residential hierarchy and that of township and village enterprise employees. The correlation coefficient between the number of TVE employees and the number of temporary residents, calculated in the same way, is only 0.3519 (P=0.003), and the partial correlation coefficient (R=0.1187, P=0.335) is not significant, when the number of the NAP is controlled.

Table 4.8 Number and percentage distribution of temporary residents[a] by residential hierarchy, Fujian 1990 census

	Total		Towns or townships[b]		Cities with NAP of less than 100,000		Cities with NAP of 100,000-200,000		Cities with NAP of 200,000-500,000		Cities with NAP of 500,000 or more	
	Number	% of total	Number	% of total	Number	% of total	Number	% of total	Number	% of total	Number	% of total
	734,912	100	340,315	46.31	81,632	11.11	144,544	19.67	58,753	7.99	109,668	14.92

[a]Temporary residents here are those who had lived in a county-level place other than where they had their household registration for one year or more.

[b] Towns and townships only refer to those under county administration.

Source: calculated according to Population Census Office of Fujian Province 1992:8-11

Figure 4.5 Comparison of the distribution of temporary residents with that of NAP in Fujian, 1990

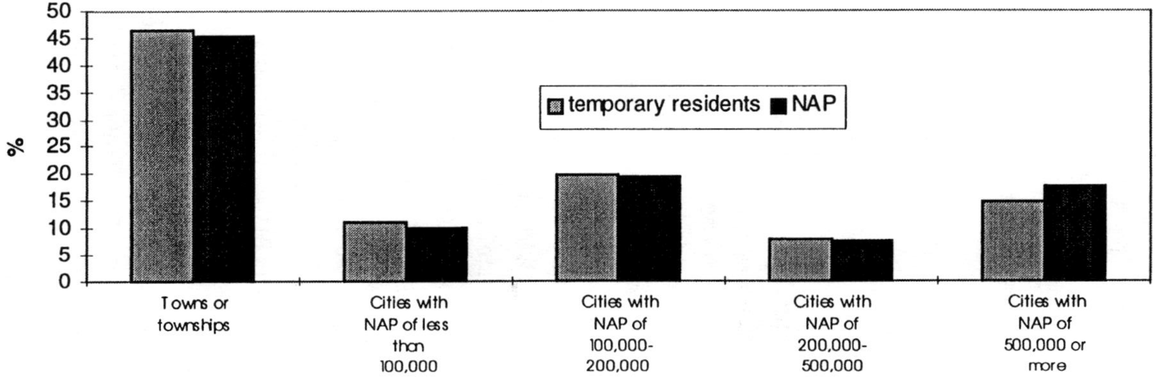

Sources: based on Table 4.8 and Statistical Bureau of Fujian Province 1991:43, 461-2.

The above analysis suggests in general that the distribution of temporary residents mainly follows the distribution of the non-agricultural population. Given the fact that most of the NAP (more than 90 percent) are distributed in cities and towns, and the dispersed distribution of the NAPCT already analyzed, it is clear that the temporary residents will not cause a highly concentrated urban population distribution. The fact that 46.3 percent of the temporary residents lived in towns or townships and only 14.9 percent of them lived in the largest city is already a good indication of this. In fact it suggests that as with the distribution of the NAPCT, most long-term temporary residents tend to stay in small residential places.

The above analysis has to be further extended for two purposes. First, the number of temporary residents has increased rapidly since 1990, so it is necessary to examine the new situation since then. Secondly, as pointed out in Chapter 3, most temporary residents live in a place for less than one year. They should also be included in the analysis. It is difficult to conduct both these kinds of analysis because of the problem of data availability, but some information, although not ideal, can be used for the purposes.

Table 4.9 provides some information about the distribution of temporary residents by residential hierarchy obtained from the 1995 one percent population sample survey. The temporary residents here are those who had lived in a township-level place other than where they had their household registration for half a year or more by October 1995. Although not absolutely reliable, it should represent to a great extent the real distribution of temporary residents, because urban-rural distribution was one of the main criteria for selecting the sample population in that survey (personal communication, Provincial Population Census Bureau, October 1996). Comparing Table 4.9 to Table 4.8 one can find two noticeable differences between them. As can be expected, the number of temporary residents in Table 4.9 is much higher, which is mainly a result of both the increase of temporary residents over time and the inclusion of shorter-staying temporary residents. Inferred from Table 4.9 the total number of temporary residents under the corresponding definition will be 1,568,400, almost double that in Table 4.8. Another difference is that a much smaller proportion of temporary residents were distributed in the towns or townships, while a much higher proportion of temporary residents were distributed in the medium-sized and large cities, especially the former[30]. It is noteworthy that Xiamen, one of China's special economic zones, accounted for a significant proportion (43.9 percent) of temporary residents in medium-sized cities. But on the whole the distribution of temporary residents under the new definition still does not exhibit much of a trend towards concentration, and does not lead to urban primacy, as the proportion of this kind of temporary residents located in the largest city is very similar to that of the non-agricultural population.

Table 4.10 provides further information about the distribution of temporary residents. The area covered by this table is economically the most developed in Fujian Province, and many cities, including the largest and second-largest cities in Fujian Province, are located here. Theoretically the temporary residents in this table are all temporary residents regardless of how long they had lived there, but as analyzed in Chapter 3, most of them had lived in their provisional living places for more than one month. If the proportion of temporary residents in this area to the total temporary residents in Fujian Province is the same as the proportion of this area's population to Fujian's total population (64 percent), it can be inferred from this table that the temporary residents who had lived in a township-level place other than where they had their household registration for more than one month could be as many as 1,993,100 in Fujian Province in 1994. Interestingly, as more short-staying temporary residents are included, the proportion of temporary residents in towns and townships decreases again, with increasing

---

[30] The inclusion of inter-township (town) migrants plays only a minor role in leading to the above two differences, because most temporary residents in Fujian are inter-county (municipality) migrants. This is confirmed by a survey in Fuzhou, Quanzhou, Fuqing, and Jinjiang, which shows that 95 percent of the temporary residents are from outside the above municipalities, mostly the rural areas of inland provinces and economically-backward counties of Fujian Province (data provided by the Institute of Geography, Fujian Normal University, November 1996; Liu 1993). These temporary residents were already covered by the 1990 census data if they had stayed in their provisional places for a year or more.

Table 4.9 Number and percentage distribution of temporary residents[a] by residential hierarchy, Fujian 1995 1% population sample survey

Total		Towns or townships[b]		Cities with NAP of less than 100,000		Cities with NAP of 100,000-200,000		Cities with NAP of 200,000-500,000		Cities with NAP of 500,000 or more	
Number	% of total	Number	% of total	Number	% of total	Number	% of total	Number	% of total	Number	% of total
15,684	100	4,660	29.71	1,931	12.31	3,043	19.40	3,257	20.77	2,793	17.81

[a] Temporary residents here are those who had lived in a township-level place other than where they had their household registration for half a year or more.

[b] Towns and townships are those under county administration.

Source: calculated according to the data provided by Population Census Bureau of Fujian Province.

Table 4.10 Number and percentage distribution of temporary residents[a] by residential hierarchy, selected areas[b] in Fujian, 1994

Total		Towns or townships[c]		Cities with NAP of less than 100,000		Cities with NAP of 100,000-200,000		Cities with NAP of 200,000-500,000		Cities with NAP of 500,000 or more	
Number	% of total	Number	% of total	Number	% of total	Number	% of total	Number	% of total	Number	% of total
1,275,412	100	201,311	15.78	144,490	11.33	309,469	24.26	407,051	31.92	181,145	14.20

[a] Temporary residents here are those who had lived in a township-level place other than where they had their household registration for one month or more.

[b] Including counties and city districts under the administration of Fuzhou, Putian, Quanzhou, Zhangzhou, and Xiamen.

[c] Towns and townships are only those under county administration.

Source: provided by Public Security Bureau of Fujian Province.

proportions of temporary residents in cities with a NAP of 100,000-200,000 and cities with a NAP of 200,000-500,000, especially the latter. Again Xiamen, the special economic zone, played a big role, absorbing 82.4 percent of temporary residents living in medium-sized cities. The proportion of temporary residents living in the largest city still did not increase, on the contrary it decreased. If this is not coincidence, it seems to indicate that towns and townships are less likely to be the destination for short-term temporary residents than for the longer-term ones, and medium-sized cities, especially the special economic zone, are most likely to be their provisional living places. This is illustrated in Figure 4.6.

Figure 4.6 Distribution of temporary residents by residential hierarchy

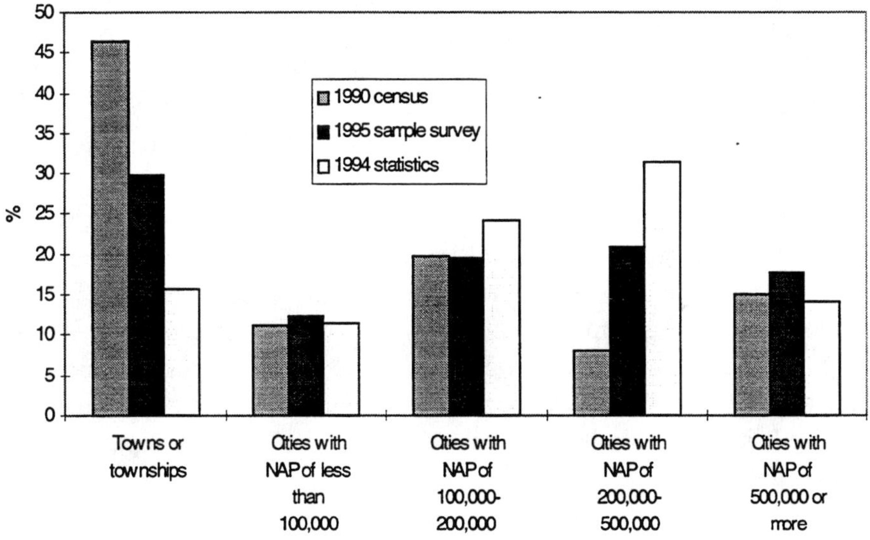

Sources Tables 4.8; 4.9; 4.10.

4.3.3 SUMMARY AND SOME ADDITIONAL NOTES

Section 4.3 focused on the spatial effects of spontaneous urbanization. Because of the limitation of available data I mainly analyzed the influence of spontaneous urbanization on the urban system by taking as a reference frame the distribution of the non-agricultural population by the residential hierarchy, which is very similar to the distribution of the non-agricultural population of cities and towns by urban system. The major conclusions can be summarized as follows:

1. The development of township and village enterprises will lead to a much more decentralized urban system than is suggested by the analysis based on the NAPCT. The creation of new towns and small cities on a widespread geographical basis, and the growth of existing small urban centers, are the most important effects of TVE development.

2. The increase in temporary residents is less a decentralizing factor than the development of TVEs. In fact the distribution of long-term, long-distance temporary residents tends to correspond to that of the NAP. Because there has been a trend for the NAPCT to be more concentrated in small and medium-sized cities, temporary residents may enhance this trend. It is a noteworthy trend that the less time temporary residents stay in their provisional places, the more likely it is that they are staying in medium-sized cities. In this sense, short-term temporary residents tend to increase the concentration of the residential hierarchy and the urban system. Nevertheless, no evidence has been identified that temporary residents, whether short-term or long-term, will increase the urban primacy, as their proportion in the largest city is very similar to that of the non-agricultural population.

3. The effects of township and village enterprise development on the evolution of the residential hierarchy and the urban system are much stronger than those of the temporary residents. This is because the number of the TVE employees amounted to 4.7 million in 1995, while the number of estimated short-term temporary residents was less than 2 million. Therefore, temporary residents will reduce the effects of TVE development on the urban system at the level of medium-sized cities, but the decentralizing effects of the TVE development will still predominate.

At the end of this section, it is necessary to add one comment on the internal distribution of the population in Fuzhou. As can be seen from Table 4.11, a much higher proportion of spontaneous urban population than of State-sponsored urban population is distributed in the suburbs of Fuzhou. This suggests that compared with State-sponsored urbanization, the distribution of spontaneous urbanization inside the large city is also more balanced. It seems that spontaneous urbanization helps to avoid not only the problem of over-concentration in the urban system, but also population congestion inside the large city.

Table 4.11 Distribution of various populations in Fuzhou (%)

	NAP of 1990 census[a]	TVE employees[b]	Temporary residents of 1990 census[c]	Temporary residents of 1994 statistics[d]
City proper	87.6	0	62.4	69.7
Suburbs	12.4	100	37.6	30.3

Sources: [a] calculated according to Population Census Office of Fujian Province 1992:16-9; [b] as literally meant; [c] calculated according to Population Census Office of Fujian Province 1992:8-11; [d] provided by Public Security Bureau of Fujian Province.

4.4 SPATIAL FEATURES OF URBANIZATION PATTERNS REFLECTED IN THE PROXIMATE CAUSES OF URBANIZATION

Before completing Chapter 4 it is worthwhile to look at the proximate causes of Fujian's urbanization, because they reflect the spatial features of Fujian's urbanization from another angle. "There are three components of urban population growth: natural increase of the urban population, rural-urban migration, and the reclassification of areas previously defined as rural" (Jones 1991:9). In urbanization studies the relative importance of natural increase and migration has been intensively examined, but the role of reclassification in the process of urban growth and urbanization is often neglected (Arriaga 1975:76; United Nations 1993:2-21). The distance of migration is also an under-researched topic. These two aspects make Fujian's urbanization unusual, and need further examination.

From the estimation of Fujian's urbanization trend in Chapter 3 a broad understanding of this aspect can be obtained. According to Table 3.10, the number of local spontaneous urban population, which is largely generated by the development of township and village enterprises, has exceeded the non-agricultural population of cities and towns since 1987. In 1995, among the "total State-sponsored plus spontaneous urban population", 55.7 percent were local spontaneous urban population, 38.7 percent were NAPCT, and 5.6 percent were temporary residents. As can be inferred from the analysis in Chapter 3, the local spontaneous urban population, which was more than half of the "total State-sponsored plus spontaneous urban population", were non-migrants or came from nearby villages (within the same county or even the same town or township). Analyzing the proximate causes of urban growth can illustrate from another angle to what extent this kind of "urbanization on the spot" contributes to the whole urbanization process in Fujian.

To do this we can try to decompose the components of natural increase and migration across county (city) borders for the period 1986-1990, for which minimum necessary data are available. The method used here is the "residual method" (United Nations 1974), which was successfully used by Chan (1988, 1994) for reconstructing China's urbanization trend. The procedure can be divided into three stages.

4.4.1 ESTIMATION OF STATE-SPONSORED AND SPONTANEOUS URBAN POPULATION GROWTH THROUGH NATURAL INCREASE

Several problems need to be solved in the estimation of natural increase of State-sponsored and spontaneous urban population. First, as in the situation Chan met when he estimated the natural increase rate for cities and towns in China, no complete time-series data are available for Fujian Province in this aspect. Proxies have to be used or calculated by collecting data from different sources and making some reasonable estimation. In this case the principle proposed by Chan (1988:56-9, 82) is adopted to estimate the natural increase rate of the non-agricultural population of cities and towns. Detailed data sources and method of calculation are given in Table 4.12.

Secondly, according to the analysis of spontaneous urban population, it can be reasonably assumed that the natural increase rate of spontaneous urban population is close to that of town population. Therefore we distinguish between the natural increase rate of the NAPCT and that of spontaneous urban population, assuming that spontaneous urban population has the same natural increase rate as the town population. On the basis of the above assumptions the natural increase in the NAPCT and that of spontaneous urban population are calculated separately. The results can be found in columns (9) and (11).

Table 4.12 Estimation of State-sponsored and spontaneous urban population growth through natural increase, Fujian 1986-1990

Year	Natural increase rate (%)			Urban population weight		Natural increase rate of NAPCT (%) (6)	Natural Increase rate of spontaneous urban population (%) (7)	Mid-year NAPCT (000s) (8)	Natural increase of NAPCT (9)	Midyear spontaneous urban population (000s) (10)	Natural increase of spontaneous urban population (11)
	Cities (1)	Counties (2)	Towns(3)	Cities (4)	Towns (5)						
1986	0.951	1.218	1.085	0.548	0.452	1.011568	1.085	3,903.7	39,489	3,839.4	41,657
1987	1.36	1.636	1.498	0.548	0.452	1.422376	1.498	4,014.75	57,105	4,360.8	65,325
1988	0.994	1.211	1.103	0.569	0.431	1.040979	1.103	4,256.75	44,312	4,955.5	54,659
1989	1.477	1.98	1.729	0.573	0.427	1.584604	1.729	4,325.8	68,547	5,161.5	89,242
1990	1.477	1.98	1.729	0.593	0.407	1.579564	1.729	4,479.9	70,763	5,240.7	90,612
Sum									280,215		341,495

Sources: (1) and (2): data for 1986-1988 are from Statistical Bureau of Fujian Province and Public Security Bureau of Fujian Province 1989:125-6; data for 1989 are the arithmetic average of the data for individual cities and counties in 1990 census; data for 1990 are assumed to be the same as for 1989 because the natural increase rate for the whole province was almost the same as that of 1989.

(3)=((1)+(2))/2;
(4) and (5) are from Statistical Bureau of Fujian Province 1995:49;
(6)=(1)*(4)+(3)*(5);
(7): it is assumed that the natural increase rate of spontaneous urban population is the same as that in towns (3);
(8): calculated from Table 3.10;
(9)=(6)*(8);
(10): calculated from Table 3.10;
(11)=(7)*(10).

4.4.2 ESTIMATION OF STATE-SPONSORED AND SPONTANEOUS URBAN POPULATION GROWTH THROUGH MIGRATION ACROSS COUNTY (CITY) BORDERS

No direct information is available about Fujian's rural-urban migration in the period 1986-1990. But the 1990 population census data, which reflect the migration across county (city) borders during the period from 1 July 1985 to 30 June 1990 (Population Census Office of Fujian Province 1992:1507), can be used to make some reasonable estimation, on the assumption that the net rural-urban migration during the period 1 January 1986 to 30 December 1990 was close to that during the period 1 July 1985 to 30 June 1990.

Table 4.13 provides some information about rural-urban migration in Fujian from this census. It can be used to infer the broad scope of State-sponsored and spontaneous urban population growth through migration across county-level borders, although some reservations need to be made at the same time. First, it can be calculated from Table 4.13 that 506,938 migrants moved from townships to cities and towns across the county (city) border. This figure is on the high side of the real in-migrant number to the real urbanized areas because it covers the whole administrative areas of cities and towns. Secondly, the total number of out-migrants from cities and towns is estimated as 142,718 persons. This figure also includes some out-migrants from not-really urbanized areas inside the administrative areas of cities and towns, but the number of such out-migrants should be smaller than that of the in-migrants who should not have been included in the above in-migrant number, given the general trend that there are more in-migrants to cities and towns than out-migrants from them.

In addition, this figure is on the low side of the real number of out-migrants from the administrative areas of cities and towns, because migrants from the suburbs of cities are not included. On the basis of the two figures and corresponding

Table 4.13 Estimation of rural-urban net migration in Fujian, 1/7/1985-30/6/1990

In-migration to cities and towns					Out-migration from city streets and towns				Estimation of net migration to cities and towns (10)
Inter-Fujian migration		Migrants from outside Fujian		Total number of in-migrants to cities and towns (5)	Inter-Fujian migration		Number of migrants from city streets and towns to outside Fujian (8)	Total number of out-migrants from city streets and towns (9)	
Number of township-city migrants (1)	Number of township-town migrants (2)	Number of migrants from outside Fujian (3)	% of (3) who migrated to cities and towns (4)		Number of migrants from city streets to county townships (6)	Number of migrants from towns to county townships (7)			
254,642	81,561	251,044	68.01	506,938	17,590	21,925	103,203	142,718	364,220

Sources and notes:

(1), (2), (3): from Population Census Office of Fujian Province 1992:146-51.

(4): according to Wu et al. 1994: 207.

(5)=(1)+(2)+(3)*(4).

(6), (7), (8): from Population Census Office of Fujian Province 1992:146-51.

(9)=(6)+(7)+(8).

(10)=(5)-(9).

analysis, the estimated number of net migration to cities and towns, 364,220, should represent the upper limit of urban population growth through migration across county (city) borders.

4.4.3 THE ROLE OF RECLASSIFICATION AND SHORT-DISTANCE MIGRATION IN FUJIAN'S URBANIZATION

In the preceding two sections the natural increase of population and the net rural-urban migration across county (city) borders were decomposed from the total increase of State-sponsored and spontaneous urban population growth in Fujian during the period 1 January 1986 to 31 December 1990. According to Table 3.10, the total State-sponsored and spontaneous urban population increased by 2,236,524 during this period, so the natural increase in population (621,710) accounted for only 27.8 percent of the total increase in State-sponsored and spontaneous urban population, and the net increase of rural-urban migration across county (city) borders (364,220) accounted for only 16.3 percent of the total increase in State-sponsored and spontaneous urban population. It is clear now that reclassification[31] and short-distance migration played a key role in Fujian's urbanization process: they accounted for 55.9 percent of the total growth of State-sponsored and spontaneous urban population. This kind of "urbanization on the spot" is another important characteristic of Fujian's urbanization patterns. In this way massive rural-urban migration has been avoided. The implication of this finding for urbanization studies on China is that when examining the proximate causes of urbanization, it is not enough just to distinguish between natural increase and migration, which is not distinguished from reclassification. Simply attributing much of China's urban growth to "rural-urban migration" without making distinctions between long-distance migration, short-distance migration, and reclassification, would be misleading, because it does not reflect the fact that urbanization in Fujian has been largely a process of transforming local rural

---

[31] Because spontaneous urbanization is included in the analysis, the reclassification here should be mainly understood as *de facto* upgrading of rural settlements to urban or quasi-urban ones as a result of rural industrialization. The scope of such reclassification is smaller than that of official reclassification since the 1980s, which exaggerated the real urban growth, as discussed in Chapter 3.

communities into more urbanized ones. It would be ideal to further examine the relative importance of reclassification and short-distance migration. As no information is available on this aspect, this will be a task for future studies.

CHAPTER 5

MAJOR POLICY CHANGES AND URBANIZATION PATTERNS: CASE STUDIES IN THREE MUNICIPALITIES

Chapters 3 and 4 have described a new trend in China's urbanization process by examining Fujian's urbanization patterns: the State-sponsored and strictly controlled urbanization has been transformed into a very dynamic development mainly promoted by local economic activities. In this process Fujian's urban system has enhanced its decentralized characteristics, and the importance of the largest city in Fujian, Fuzhou, has been even further reduced. As this is at odds with both the experience of many developing countries and conventional theories, it may be asked how this transformation has been achieved and why it is possible. The following two chapters try to answer these questions. Chapter 5 reviews major relevant government policies in China and traces their changes, especially those since 1978, the effects of which on Fujian's urbanization have partly been demonstrated in the preceding chapters. In this chapter they are further scrutinized by using three municipalities, where I conducted fieldwork, as examples. Chapter 6 examines the new urbanization process from international and historical perspectives. One of its major purposes is to reveal the enabling factors for the implementation of the new policies. But first government policies regarding rural-urban migration and urbanization will be briefly reviewed.

5.1 THE CHANGING ROLES OF THE HOUSEHOLD REGISTRATION SYSTEM IN CHINA'S URBANIZATION

5.1.1 HOUSEHOLD REGISTRATION SYSTEM BEFORE 1978

Until the onset of the reform in 1978, the central mechanism controlling rural-urban migration and urbanization in China was the household registration (*hukou*) system (Mallee 1995:1-2). Its emergence was directly related to the need to curb the "blind flow" of farmers into cities. According to Sun et al. (1996:85), at the beginning of the establishment of the People's Republic of China, State control over population migration was loose. There was no restriction on residents moving between urban and rural areas to find jobs or live with relatives or friends. But from 1953, the large-scale economic construction caused by the implementation of the first five-year plan attracted a large number of farmers to cities, leading to heavy pressures on employment, the supply of daily necessities, housing, communication, and infrastructure in cities. As a result the State Council released a directive on preventing the rural "blind flow" from moving into cities in 1956 (China, State Council 1986c). In 1957 the central committee of the CCP and the State Council released another directive, instructing governments at various levels to use administrative measures, mainly the household registration system, to intervene in rural-urban migration. All this finally led to the promulgation of the "PRC regulation on household registration" in 1958, which stipulated the following regulations on rural-urban migration in the form of law:

When moving from the countryside to a city, a citizen has to provide proof of employment from the urban Labor Bureau, or proof of enrolment in an urban educational institution, or proof that in-migration has been granted by the urban registration authorities, in order to be able to complete the out-migration formalities by the household registration office of his residential area (China, Standing Committee of the NPC 1986:84).

The household registration system not only precluded unauthorized migration from rural to urban areas, but also prevented people from moving from a place lower in the residential hierarchy to one higher in the residential hierarchy. This was reflected in a notice released by the State Council, which stipulated the need for control over transfers of household registration from town to city, from small city to large city, from normal-sized city to one of the three centrally administered cities of Shanghai, Beijing, or Tianjin, and even from rural regions to the city outskirts, or to the outskirts of a town located in a rural region, or near

State farms, vegetable production teams, or economic crop regions. On the other hand, the transfers of household registration from cities and towns to rural areas, and from large cities to small cities, should be approved; the transfer of household registration between cities and towns of the same size, and rural areas, should also be approved (China, State Council 1991).

The household registration system alone did not guarantee effective controlling of rural-urban and urban-urban migration. Its success depended strongly on State control over employment, commodity supply, and housing (Mallee 1995:4). As pointed out in Chapter 3, this system assigns all people a registration status as either "agricultural" or "non-agricultural"[32], and it was extremely difficult for an average peasant to have his or her agricultural *hukou* transferred into a non-agricultural one. The only ways of obtaining non-agricultural status included assignment after military service, enrolment in an institution of higher education, and promotion to commune-level jobs (Zhao 1992:181-2; Mallee 1995:4). Even a rural resident married to an urban one could not change his or her agricultural registration status, unless the urban resident met two of the following conditions: he or she had to be older than 45 years, to have worked for 25 years, and to have been married for 15 years (Policy Research Institute 1991:8-9). While those persons having officially registered as non-agricultural could enjoy many benefits provided by the State, those without non-agricultural status had virtually no access to urban employment, subsidized State supply of daily commodities, especially staple foods, and urban housing (State Commission on Economic Reform 1996). This means that transferring household registration status for rural-urban migration was not only a matter of going through a strict formality, but also vitally necessary for a migrant to survive in a city. This was particularly the case when there were shortages in the supply of daily necessities, housing, and employment, which was not uncommon before the reform era. On the other hand, the increase in the urban population implied a greater burden on the State budget,

---

[32] Some scholars often confuse "non-agricultural status" with "urban status". Strictly speaking there are some differences. As can be expected by commonsense, urban residents are mostly non-agricultural by household status. But there are some rural residents, for example rural cadres, who are also non-agricultural by household registration status, but enjoy the benefits provided by the State for urban non-agricultural residents. Therefore, strictly speaking, what the Chinese government controls is the transfer of household status from agricultural to non-agricultural, one of the main purposes of which is to avoid the burden on the State budget. But as the non-agricultural population is mainly urban, it can effectively restrict migration from rural to urban areas. In this sense controlling agricultural to non-agricultural transfer of household registration is almost identical to controlling rural-urban migration.

which made it more necessary for the government to control rural-urban migration. Thus before the reform era, the Chinese government had to, and could, effectively use household registration as the major means to regulate its urbanization.

The above analysis about the household registration system in China had little regional variation before 1978. It largely applies to the situation in Fujian. This is reflected in the findings in Chapter 3 that there was only very limited increase in Fujian's urbanization level before 1978, and that its trend at that time was very similar to that in China as a whole. In short, before 1978 the household registration system was crucial and effective in controlling China's urbanization patterns.

5.1.2 HOUSEHOLD REGISTRATION SYSTEM SINCE 1978

Since 1978, it has not been as simple as it used to be to control rural-urban migration and migration up the urban hierarchy in China by applying only administrative measures. It has become relatively easy for household registration to be changed from agricultural to non-agricultural, or for a person to live or work in cities and towns without official household registration status. There are several aspects which constitute the relaxation of State control over household registration status.

First, since 1978 several groups of people have been granted non-agricultural status. The most famous occurrence in this regard was that at the beginning of the 1980s all those who had been sent to the rural areas during the "up to the mountains and down to the villages" campaign, and their dependants, were allowed to go back to the urban areas and granted non-agricultural status. Later, family members of certain other groups, like those who were mistreated in the "Great Cultural Revolution"; middle-and high-level technicians, cadres, and teachers; miners, forest workers, and returned overseas-Chinese were also accorded non-agricultural status (personal communication, Public Security Bureau of Fujian Province, October 1996).

Secondly, some "informal" types of non-agricultural household status have been created. A major step in this regard was the introduction of "urban registration with self-supplied grain", which, as mentioned in Chapter 3, was one of the government measures to promote small town development. In the late 1980s, many localities even started experimenting with "blue seal" household registration status[33] (Mallee 1995:15; personal communication, Public Security Bureaus in the fieldwork sites, August to October 1996). Rural people can get urban non-agricultural household registration status by paying a certain amount of money, or buying an apartment from the real estate market. In Fujian this was done experimentally in many county seats, and even in Xiamen city. This kind of household registration is superior to "urban registration with self-supplied grain" because its holder can obtain permanent residence in urban places at or above the county-seat level, and have access to urban privileges in the places of issue, neither of which is the case for "urban registration with self-supplied grain". But this registration status is only valid at the local place (personal communication, Public Security Bureau of Fujian Province, October 1996).

Thirdly, perhaps the biggest change in the household registration system since 1978 has been the emergence of a grey area: temporary residents. As mentioned in Chapters 3 and 4, temporary residents have been playing increasingly important roles in Fujian's urbanization. The Chinese government has realized that population mobility, especially the mobility of rural surplus labor, is inevitable at the current stage of development, and temporary residents have positively contributed to economic development (General Office of the Central Committee of CCP 1995; Wang 1996). Nevertheless, the emergence and increasing number of temporary residents have also led to a wide range of social-economic problems, the most serious being heavy burdens on the urban public facilities, increasing crime rates, and deteriorating public security. The formal change of household registration status into urban for temporary residents is still not possible, as this will create further strains on the State budget. Therefore, neither official nor illegal household registration status for temporary residents has come into existence. Because of their slightly ambiguous status, temporary residents can be controlled when necessary. In city planning, temporary residents have begun to be taken into account in some aspects, but they are still not included in the official statistics of urban population size (personal communication, Planning Department, Construction Commission of Fujian Province, August 1996). All this reflects the government's ambivalent attitude towards temporary residents.

Fourthly, economic development and reform have undermined the supporting mechanism for a rigid household registration system. In rural areas, the implementation of the household land-contract production responsibility system re-

---

[33] This household registration status is named after the blue color of the seal on the registration booklet; normally seals were red.

vealed and intensified the once invisible problem of surplus rural labor. According to Taylor and Banister (1991:90-1), at the beginning of reform in 1979, there were 64.8 million surplus rural workers, accounting for 22.7 percent of the total agricultural workers. During the next three years the number of surplus rural laborers further increased to 132.3 million, accounting for 42.5 percent of the total agricultural workers. A similar situation existed in Fujian. This was a serious problem for policy-makers, and softening the control over the migration of rural workers to urban areas was almost unavoidable for the government. More importantly, as a result of economic reform, rural migrants have got more and more access to urban employment opportunities, supply of daily commodities, and urban housing since the 1980s, mostly through non-State sectors. In Fujian Province, subject to the approval of certain authorities, and on certain conditions, companies and enterprises can recruit migrants from rural areas or outside Fujian (Labor Bureau of Fujian Province 1996; personal communication, Labor Bureaus in the fieldwork sites, August to October 1998). Migrants can rent housing from local residents, so long as they comply with certain regulations (General Office of Fuzhou Municipal Committee of CCP 1996). As the availability of daily commodities, especially staple foods, increased substantially, rationing was virtually abolished in the 1980s, and migrants can now easily get their daily necessities from the free market (Chen H. 1996). All these factors make it possible for temporary residents to live and work in any places, including urban areas, without official household registration status.

The relaxation of the control over non-agricultural household registration status has had some influence on both temporal and spatial changes of the State-sponsored urban population. This was reflected in the analysis in Chapters 3 and 4, especially in the faster increase of the non-agricultural population of cities and towns since 1978. But it has to be realized that official non-agricultural urban status is still under government control, and relatively difficult to obtain. Furthermore, as also can be seen in Chapter 3, the increase in the non-agricultural population of cities and towns has been playing a diminishing role in the new urbanization process. Thus the official transfer of household registration status is not very significant in shaping the new urbanization patterns. As temporary residents are now allowed to live and work in the urban areas, they pose a much greater challenge for the government. Theoretically it is now possible for any rural resident to move into urban areas, and potentially this could cause a large-scale rural-urban migration, especially migration into major cities, given the large number of rural people who are waiting to be absorbed in non-agricultural sectors. The central mechanism controlling urbanization since 1978 has no longer been the transfer from rural to urban household registration status. As rural residents gain the freedom to migrate, those factors which can influence the farmer's movements are at the center of urbanization policies. Chapter 3 showed that potential migrants released from the agricultural sector have two different choices: they can either stay in the rural areas to participate in non-agricultural activities, and create new urban centers on the spot; or they can migrate to the existing cities to earn their living. Therefore the new patterns of urbanization depend on the urban and regional development policies at both ends of the residential hierarchy: on the one hand, urban planning and urban management policies will affect migrants' job prospects and their distribution in the existing cities; on the other hand, regional development policies and investment patterns will affect farmers' likelihood of finding non-agricultural employment in rural areas, and their decision on whether to move. The former can be demonstrated by the case of Fuzhou, while the latter can be demonstrated by the cases of Jinjiang and Fuqing, in the following sections.

5.2 URBAN MANAGEMENT AND DEVELOPMENT: THE CASE OF FUZHOU[34]

The focus of discussion in this section will be some urban planning and management policies regarding the expansion of existing cities, and their role in transforming rural into urban population since 1978. Fuzhou, the capital city of Fujian Province, is chosen as the case for discussion.

Fuzhou is a city with 2,100 years of history. It has been Fujian's political and cultural center since A.D. 733 (Tang Dynasty), and the capital city of Fujian Province since the establishment of the People's Republic in 1949. Most provincial government institutions are located here. It is also the largest center for commercial activities, education, science and technology, and the most important hub of communication in Fujian Province. Perhaps the most noticeable feature of Fuzhou is its fast industrial development and foreign investment since 1978. It is one of the 14 coastal open cities in China, and various development zones, investment zones, industrial zones etc. have been set up here, attracting a large

---

[34] In this section "Fuzhou" only refers to the scope of its city districts (including the suburban district), excluding counties under its administration.

amount of foreign investment[35]. The average annual growth rate of industrial output value between 1978-1990 was as high as 21.6 percent, which was twice as fast as the industrial growth rate between 1950 and 1978 (Department of Land and Ocean Science 1992). Given the important status of Fuzhou as described above, what roles has it played in Fujian's urbanization and how has it achieved this?

To answer this question some basic information about Fuzhou is needed. Table 5.1 provides figures about Fuzhou's total population, non-agricultural population, total area, and built-up area (*Jian Cheng Qu*) in selected years. Temporary residents are not included in the population figures. As mentioned in Chapter 4 there were 21,456 and 109,668 temporary residents who had lived in Fuzhou for more than one year according to the 1982 and 1990 censuses respectively (Table 4.7).

Table 5.1 Population and area of Fuzhou, selected years

	Total population (000s)	Non-agricultural population (000s)	Suburban population (000s)	Total area (km^2)	Built-up area (km^2)
1949	577.0	341.0	n.a.	206.0	11.0
1978	1,027.6	615.6	466.8	1,043.3	34.3
1990	1,292.0	874.8	455.9	1,043.3	49.8
1995	1,375.2	982.9	447.9	1,043.3	68.0

Sources: Population Census Office of Fujian Province 1992:8; Liu 1993:26; Statistical Bureau of Fujian Province 1996:387.

With the above knowledge of Fuzhou's demographic, social and economic situation, it is now possible to analyze some major factors which influence Fuzhou's role in Fujian's urbanization.

5.2.1 THE ROLE OF NATIONAL URBAN DEVELOPMENT STRATEGY

China's urban development strategy has had much influence on Fuzhou's development. Sponsored by the State Construction Commission and approved by the State Council, an important conference regarding urban planning was held in

---

[35] See Section 5.4.1 for more information about foreign investment in Fuzhou.

Beijing in 1980. The main task of this conference was to discuss and formulate the draft of the *"Urban Planning Act of PRC"*, and work out strategies, policies and measures of urban planning. It was concluded that before 1978 China's urban planning had ceased to be binding for a long time, and that this had caused serious consequences such as unchecked development of large cities and under-development of small towns. Therefore, a national urban strategy which sought to "strictly limit the size of large cities, rationally develop medium-sized cities and encourage the development of small cities and towns" was formulated in this conference (China, State Council 1989:14-5). This finally led to the promulgation of the Urban Planning Act of the PRC, in which is presented a revised version of the national urban development strategy, to "strictly control the development of big cities, reasonably develop the medium-sized and small cities". It is clearly stipulated in this Act that the overall plan of a provincial capital or a city with a population of more than one million should be approved by the State Council (China, Standing Committee of the NPC 1990).

As a provincial capital, Fuzhou's development has been constrained by the national urban strategy. It can be calculated from Table 5.1 that Fuzhou's total population increased at an annual average growth rate of 2.8 percent during the period of 1978-1995, not only much slower than the growth rate of the total population of cities and towns (TPCT) in Fujian (10.8 percent), which was largely caused by administrative and definition changes, but even slower than the growth rate of the non-agricultural population of cities and towns (NAPCT) in Fujian (3.4 percent). In fact, the motivation of Fuzhou municipal government to develop Fuzhou into a very large city has been very strong. This can be demonstrated by the process of re-adjustment of the overall plan for Fuzhou. The first overall plan for Fuzhou was approved by the State Council in September 1984. As the fast development of reform and open-door policies, especially the designation of Fuzhou as one of the 14 coastal open cities, had not been anticipated in this plan, the planned scales of population and land area for Fuzhou were soon surpassed by the real development. It was decided that the overall plan should be re-adjusted. In the process of the re-adjustment, it was once considered that Fuzhou should be developed into an "international metropolitan city", which would incorporate some areas of neighboring counties, with a population of three million.

This plan was not put forward in the end, because the State Council reiterated the control over the development of large cities in 1996, and made it more difficult for the approval of the city overall plan. The reason for the State's tightening control over urban planning was that in some places urban planning had been arbitrarily adjusted, and city scale had been blindly increased[36]. It is stipulated now that the overall plan of a city with a non-agricultural population of more than 500,000 should also be approved by the State Council (China, State Council 1996; personal communication, Construction Commission of Fujian Province, August 1996). Thus in the end the projected number of total population for Fuzhou in 2010 was adjusted as between 1.5 and 1.8 million, and the total built-up area as 160 square kilometers. As the State Council strictly demanded that the population size and land area should be controlled within the limit of the approved overall plan, it will be difficult for Fuzhou to develop beyond the above target.

5.2.2 HOUSEHOLD REGISTRATION MANAGEMENT

Although the official transfer of household registration status has been relaxed since the 1980s, the number of people who are eligible to benefit from this relaxation is still limited. This is particularly the case in Fuzhou. As a provincial capital there are more restrictions on agricultural household registration transferring to non-agricultural, and even on holders of non-agricultural household registration moving to Fuzhou. In fact, household registration is still regarded as the most effective way of controlling population growth in the large cities (personal communication, Provincial Construction Commission, August 1996). There has been an attempt to implement "blue seal registration" in Fuzhou, but it has not been approved (personal communication, Public Security Bureau of Fujian Province, October 1996). As to holders of non-agricultural registration status, there is a government department called the Office for Controlling Population Growth Caused by Migration in Fuzhou, which is directly under the leadership of the municipal government, and responsible for setting quotas for the number of immigrants with non-agricultural registration status. This quota is again decomposed and assigned to different government departments, who are responsible for the approval of immigration of different categories[37] (personal communication, provincial and local Public Security Bureaus, October 1996).

---

[36] Since the 1990s there has been a fashion for many Chinese municipal governments to develop their cities into very large ones. According to Xin (1996), at least 40 cities proposed to develop themselves into international cities.

[37] Basically the Personnel Department is responsible for cadres; the Labor Bureau is responsible for ordinary workers; and the Public Security Bureau for dependants and coordination.

As can be inferred from previous sections, the strict control over official household registration does not prevent potential temporary residents, who have become the main source of migrants, from entering cities. To adapt to this new situation, the focus of household registration management has been gradually transferred to the management of temporary residents in recent years. New regulations on temporary residence have been promulgated to manage temporary residents. According to "The interim procedures for fostering the management of temporary residents in Fuzhou" (General Office of Fuzhou Municipal Committee of CCP 1996), the general guidelines for the management of temporary residents can be summarized as follows: first, before leaving their original place, temporary residents older than 16 years should get an "employment card for outgoing person", which provides information about the holder's marriage, health, family planning, military service, and criminal record in the last three years. Secondly, within three days of arrival at the destination, temporary residents who intend to stay for more than one month are required to be registered by the Public Security Bureau, and obtain a "temporary residence permit". They should also obtain an "employment permit for temporary residents" from the Labor Bureau, which is responsible for controlling the number of employment permits. The principle for this control is that only when the need of employment cannot be met by the local labor force can outsiders be employed. Thirdly, neither working units nor individuals are allowed to employ those temporary residents who do not have "employment cards for outgoing person" and "temporary residence permits". Fourthly, those who rent housing to temporary residents need to go through approval procedures from both the Public Security Bureau and the local housing department and get relevant permits. And finally, those temporary residents who do not have legal permits, fixed residence, and source of income will be regarded as "blind drifters" and will be rounded up and repatriated. Obviously the government is trying to use these measures to reduce the number of unwanted temporary residents, and to avoid negative effects of temporary residents on urban development.

The effectiveness of household registration control over the increase of the NAP in Fuzhou can be demonstrated by the fact that the annual average increase rate of the NAP in Fuzhou was only 1.7 percent during the period 1978-1995, only half of that for Fujian. As for temporary residents, it is hard to say how effective the new regulations have been. As can be inferred from the data provided above, the annual average growth rate of temporary residents was as high as 22.6 percent during the period 1982-1990, suggesting an unchecked growth. But it could also be argued that without those regulations, there would have been more temporary residents in Fuzhou. In any case, temporary residents will probably remain regulated in the aforementioned way in the foreseeable future.

5.2.3 REGULATING THE INTERNAL DISTRIBUTION OF POPULATION

China's control over large cities does not mean that all development in large cities should be stopped. In fact, the main target of this control is the population size of built-up areas, where housing shortage, traffic congestion, and environmental problems are most serious (Yan 1989:53-4; Zhu 1991:493-4). This is also the case in Fuzhou. Since the 1980s some major urban developments have been taking place in this city, but not in the existing city proper, rather on the outskirts of the city.

The first such major development was the setting-up of the Fuzhou Economic and Technological Development Zone in January 1985 in Mawei, which used to be one of the suburban areas of Fuzhou city until 1982. The FETDZ is located in the Mawei port area on the north bank of the Min River on its lower reaches, 19 kilometers away from the city proper (Figure 5.1). The total area of FETDZ is 10 km^2, 14 percent of the total area (73 km^2) of Mawei. Besides being a development zone as a whole, FETDZ has a Free Trade Zone, Taiwanese Investment Zone, and Hi-Tech Industrial Development Zone inside its area. Since its establishment FETDZ has been the biggest growth pole in Fuzhou in terms of physical expansion of the city and foreign investment. In 1995 a total amount of US$ 900 million foreign investment through signed contracts was made in Fuzhou, and 73 percent (648 million) will be invested in Mawei (calculated according to Zhao et al. 1996:365). By the end of 1995 500 projects were located here, with a total amount of US$ 2,300 million investment, 1,700 million being foreign investment. Five hundred million *Yuan* have been invested for infrastructure construction. The total industrial output value has reached US$ 17,000 million (data provided by the Office of Opening to the Outside World, Fuzhou Municipal Government during fieldwork, September 1996). By the end of 1992 the 10 km^2 development zone was fully occupied, and an extension district of FETDZ with an area of 5.6 km^2 was set up to accommodate more development. The effect of the development of FETDZ on population growth is obvious. Between the 1982 and 1990 censuses the annual average growth rate of the number of permanent residents in Mawei was 3 percent, much faster than that of Fuzhou as a whole (1.8 percent). More importantly, FETDZ attracted a significant proportion of temporary residents coming to Fuzhou. At the end of 1994, 6 percent of the total number of temporary residents who had lived in Fuzhou for more than one month were in Mawei, although the number of permanent residents in Mawei accounted for only 2.9 percent of that for Fuzhou as a whole.

Figure 5.1 The location of FETDZ and GFIZ

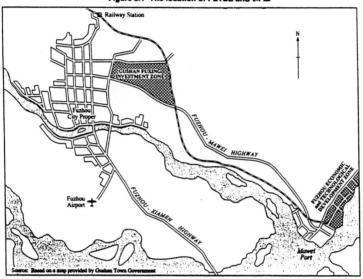

Source: based on the data in Liu et al. 1992:128-30.

Apart from the major development in Mawei, there have been more small-scale developments on the outskirts of Fuzhou. The major driving forces of these developments have mainly come from two sources: the development of TVEs, and foreign investment. Fuzhou's suburban area is one of the regions in Fujian with most developed TVEs. This development started in 1978, and has transformed the economic structure of the whole suburban area. In 1992 the gross output value of TVEs accounted for 84.4 percent of the total product of society in Fuzhou's suburban district, and 77.3 percent of the labor force here was working in the TVEs (calculated according to Statistical Bureau of Fuzhou Suburban District 1993:2, 60). In terms of economic and employment structure the suburban district of Fuzhou could not appropriately have been called an agricultural area for quite a few years. On the basis of the strengthened local economy, a new round of development characterized by the setting-up of investment zones and development zones started in the early 1990s. One typical example of this is Gushan Fuxing Investment Zone. Before this investment district was set up, Gushan town had long been famous for its fast development of TVEs. In 1993 there were 40 enterprises run by the town and 256 enterprises run by the villages, producing footwear, knitwear, garments, leather products, stone manufacture, biochemistry products, plastic products, toys, wrist watches, Shaoshan stone carving, ivory carving, and fabric woven with Chinese iris. The total product of society for this town reached 1,822 million *Yuan* in this year (Chen and Pan 1995:36-7). In the process of this development a complete set of infrastructure including water, electricity, gas, transport and telecommunication had been developed. In August 1990, approved by the municipal government, the first development zone run by a town in Fujian, the Gushan Fuxing Investment Zone, was established. This district is five kilometers away from the city center (Figure 5.1), with a total area of 5 km^2. By the end of 1995, 221 projects had been set up here, involving not only such industries as electronics, textiles, foodstuffs and toys, but also office buildings, apartments, and recreation grounds, with an amount of US$ 450 million investment through signed contracts, 420 million being foreign investment. The total investment for infrastructure had reached 380 million *Yuan*, most of it raised by the town rather than by the State. It is expected that this zone will absorb 50,000 laborers when it is finally completed (data collected during fieldwork from the Office of Opening to the Outside World, Fuzhou Municipal Government, and Gushan Town Government, September 1996).

Gushan Fuxing Investment Zone is not the only development of this kind. There are at least six smaller-scale investment zones in the suburban area of Fuzhou. These areas have already been incorporated into the overall plan for Fuzhou as the proposed new built-up areas, and corresponding residential and commercial facilities have been or are being built. Many previous farmers are now living in flats, although they still hold agricultural household registration status (*Fujian Daily* 1994). As a result of urban development in suburban areas, the administration divisions in Fuzhou were readjusted in 1995. Much of the former "suburban district" was incorporated into the districts in the city proper, and the name of "Suburban District" for the remaining area was replaced by "Jinan District", indicating the transformation from a suburb of the city to a part of the city proper. The transformation of the suburban areas has not only prevented farmers from entering the city proper and aggravating burdens on infrastructure in the areas with high population densities, but diverted many of the temporary residents, who would otherwise have migrated to the city center, to the suburban areas. The pattern of internal distribution for temporary residents in Fuzhou identified in Chapter 4 can largely be attributed to the development described above.

5.2.4 SUMMARY

The above discussion about Fuzhou's urban development seems to suggest that Fuzhou has not been exceptional in terms of the urban physical expansion which has been seen in many developing countries. Even if Fuzhou's built-up area can be restricted within 160 km^2 in 2010, as currently planned, it will still be twice as large as it was in 1990. But it must also be realized that there is a certain kind of restriction to this expansion, especially in the aspect of urban population growth. First, Fuzhou's development is constrained by the national urban strategy. Its development needs the approval of the State Council, and the number of its permanent residents is still strictly and effectively controlled by the household registration system. Administrative intervention is still used to prevent over-expansion of the city, especially the growth of the non-agricultural population. At the same time, the *in situ* transformation on the outskirts of the city has been effectively urbanizing the local population, preventing them from entering the already congested old city district. While there is no restriction on temporary residents entering the city, they are strictly "managed" and under control, and a significant proportion of them has been attracted to the outskirts of the city, which has been undergoing rapid development. In short, Fuzhou has been contributing to the overall urbanization progress in Fujian by transforming its own suburban population and absorbing some temporary residents, but at the same time special efforts have been made to prevent over-expansion of Fuzhou, and further congestion in its built-up area. These policies seem to be effective, but as will be seen later, their success should be appreciated in the context of other regional development practices.

5.3 TOWNSHIP AND VILLAGE ENTERPRISES AND THE *IN SITU* TRANSFORMATION OF RURAL AREAS: THE CASE OF JINJIANG[38]

The preceding section about Fuzhou's urban development shows that although the development of this large city is controlled by the government, there

---

[38] From 30 September 1988 Shishi Town and its three neighboring towns and one township in Jinjiang County were designated as Shishi Municipality. Except where otherwise indicated, the following discussion about Jinjiang includes Shishi if it refers to the situation before 30 September 1988 and excludes Shishi if it refers to the situation after that date.

is actually no guarantee that this policy will succeed only by implementing restrictive policies in Fuzhou. As temporary residents can move freely now, the key
for achieving balanced urbanization patterns is on the side of rural areas, where a
large number of surplus rural laborers are looking for an outlet. As has been
demonstrated in Chapters 3 and 4, the fast development of TVEs and foreign-
funded enterprises at the regional levels in Fujian absorbed a large number of
rural people, and effectively reduced migration pressure on the major cities. If
there had not been such development, it would have been much more difficult for
Fuzhou to control its urban population growth. It is the main purpose of this section to look at the development of TVEs in Jinjiang Municipality and reveal how
this development has been achieved.

Located on the southeast coast of Fujian Province, Jinjiang is 200 kilometers
south of Fuzhou, the provincial capital, and 100 kilometers north of Xiamen, the
second largest city in Fujian and one of the SEZs in China. In 1992 it was designated as a municipality, covering a total area of 649 km^2. It is one of the regions
with the highest population densities in Fujian, with a total number of permanent
residents of 977,700 and a population density of 1,506 persons per km^2 by the
end of 1995. Shishi Municipality, which was just separated from Jinjiang in
1988, has a total area of 160 km^2 and had a total number of permanent residents
of 286,100 by the end of 1995, with a population density of 1,788 persons per
km^2.

Before 1978, Jinjiang's economy was dominated by agricultural activities.
By 1978 agricultural output value still accounted for 62 percent of the total agricultural and industrial output value, and 85 percent of the labor force was engaged in agricultural activities. Farmers' average annual per capita income was
only 62 *Yuan*, about US$ 7.5 at the current exchange rate (Liu et al. 1992:54-87).
But since 1978, great changes have taken place here. As the Secretary of the Jinjiang Municipal Committee of the CCP put it:

In terms of total economic output, today's Jinjiang is 35 times that of Jinjiang
in 1978. In 1993 the gross national product of the Municipality was 6,500 million
Yuan; the national income of production was 5,200 million *Yuan*; the total output
value of industry and agriculture was 11,200 million *Yuan*; the financial revenue
was 350 million *Yuan*; the per capita average annual income for farmers[39] was

---

[39] The per capita average annual income for farmers is a statistical index to measure the income of
those people who are agricultural by household registration, rather than the income of real farmers.
In Jinjiang, there are in fact not many real farmers now.

2,121 *Yuan*. They are 51 times, 47 times, 33 times, 31 times, and 37 times those of 1978 respectively[40] (Qiu 1995:8).

The economic and employment structures of Jinjiang have also been greatly changed. The primary sector accounted only for 6.5 percent of the GDP in 1995 (Statistical Bureau of Fujian Province 1996:410), and only 16 percent of the work force was engaged in the agricultural sector in the same year, according to the 1995 one percent sample survey. The economic development in Jinjiang has been so successful that it is termed the "Jinjiang model" in China.

However, in terms of State-sponsored urban population Jinjiang seems to be predominantly rural. The non-agricultural population of cities and towns accounted for only 11 percent of the total population. This indicates that what has been happening in Jinjiang is the *in situ* transformation of the local economic and employment structure and an spontaneous urbanization process. But what have been the driving forces behind this dramatic development?

The development of Jinjiang has been caused by a series of policy changes with regard to rural development, especially the development of township and village enterprises in China. It is also closely related to some socio-economic conditions which have enabled the successful implementation of these policies. This chapter first reveals the effect of policy changes by identifying some stages of development in Jinjiang, leaving the examination of the socio-economic conditions to Chapter 6.

5.3.1 RURAL SURPLUS LABOR AND THE EMERGENCE OF TOWNSHIP AND VILLAGE ENTERPRISES

The increase in rural non-agricultural activities, especially the emergence of TVEs in Jinjiang, has been closely related to the increasingly severe problem of rural surplus labor. As one of the most densely populated counties in Fujian Province, Jinjiang had long been stranded by rapid population growth and limited arable land before the reform began. As mentioned in Chapter 2, many people in the coastal areas of Fujian migrated to Southeast Asia and Taiwan as a result of overpopulation in the Qing Dynasty, and Jinjiang was one such area (Wu 1994:28-31). Since 1949, the population pressure in Jinjiang had become even

---

[40] In the following two years these figures increased again. For example in 1995 the gross national product of the municipality was 15,791 million *Yuan*; the per capita CNP was 16,119 *Yuan*; the per capita average annual income for farmers was 4,321 *Yuan*.

more acute. On the one hand, as Southeast Asian countries became independent one after another, they began to adopt restrictive policies towards Chinese immigrants (Wu 1994:31-2). On the other hand, Jinjiang experienced rapid population growth during the period 1949-1978. As can be seen in Table 5.2, the total population of Jinjiang increased rapidly in the period, with an average annual growth rate of 2.6 percent. However, the area of arable land decreased noticeably, and the per capita arable land fell from 1.23 *mou* (0.08 ha) to 0.56 *mou* (0.04 ha). Because economic activities were strictly limited within the agricultural sector before 1978, a large number of rural laborers were inevitably surplus. According to the government statistics and accounts, there were 311,900 rural laborers in Jinjiang in 1978, but no more than 130,000 of them were needed for tilling the available land, and almost 200,000 rural laborers (58 percent of the total) needed to find jobs outside agricultural activities (Liu et al. 1992:386). The labor surplus was so obvious that farmers had to take turns to go to work (Liu et al. 1992:130).

Table 5.2 Population and arable land area in Jinjiang County, 1949-1978

Year	Area of arable land (*mou*[a])	Population	Per capita arable land (*mou*)
1949	553,003	448,486	1.23
1950	554,109	459,523	1.20
1951	554,926	470,485	1.18
1952	555,376	481,151	1.15
1953	553,851	494,128	1.12
1954	554,094	503,693	1.10
1955	550,400	517,462	1.06
1956	548,730	530,784	1.03
1957	540,814	549,080	0.98
1958	530,402	555,408	0.95
1959	521,295	561,940	0.92
1960	513,690	570,139	0.90
1961	509,664	588,876	0.87
1962	516,194	610,371	0.85
1963	515,567	634,558	0.81
1964	528,045	648,380	0.81

1965	531,491	671,915	0.79
1966	530,539	687,095	0.77
1967	529,076	705,644	0.75
1968	528,473	724,464	0.73
1969	523,065	743,264	0.70
1970	533,655	777,996	0.69
1971	530,852	802,783	0.66
1972	532,468	823,848	0.65
1973	527,822	847,121	0.62
1974	525,517	866,646	0.61
1975	526,184	889,429	0.59
1976	526,767	914,227	0.58
1977	528,243	934,191	0.57
1978	528,926	948,098	0.56

[a] 1 *mou* = 1/15 ha.
Source: Liu et al. 1992:25, 71.

But the necessity of developing non-agricultural activities did not necessarily lead to their development. As in other developing regions, it was constrained by the lack of investment and labor skills (Chen and Geng 1993:82, 113). What is more, as China adopted the stringent policies of the centrally planned economy until 1978, the development of non-agricultural activities in Jinjiang had been very much influenced by the central government policies regarding the development of rural enterprises. The predecessor of TVEs in Jinjiang as well as in China as a whole germinated from the necessity of finding outlets for surplus rural labor and rural development, but were constrained by the government policies and ideologies.

The problem of rural surplus labor and the necessity of developing rural non-agricultural activities have long been realized by China's central government. As early as in 1952 the Central Employment Committee of China pointed out that there were a large number of surplus laborers in the rural area, and proposed a range of measures to solve this problem. One of the measures was to promote sideline activities and handicraft industry (Central Employment Committee 1986:105-7). In 1958, during the People's Commune campaign, the Central Committee of the CCP put forward "the industrialization of communes", suggesting that industry should be greatly promoted in the communes, and the production of light and heavy industries such as fertilizer, pesticide, farm implements, agricultural machinery, construction materials, agricultural product processing and comprehensive utilization, sugar, textile, papermaking, mining, metallurgy, electricity etc should be developed in a planned way.

This led to the establishment of many commune enterprises (Chen and Geng 1993:266; Chen and Han 1993:54-5), which were the predecessors of TVEs. In 1972 Mao Zedong read a document about rural commune and brigade enterprises, and made the comment that the hope of rural development lay in the commune and brigade enterprises (Liu et al. 1992:387). The development of rural non-agricultural activities was certainly encouraged by the positive attitude of the Chinese leadership.

Nevertheless government policies on the development of commune and brigade enterprises had varied very much before 1978. In the early 1960s, for political reasons and because of economic difficulties, most commune enterprises were closed. Although they revived soon and developed reasonably quickly afterwards, they were still very much constrained by government ideologies and policies. First, the government gave enormous attention to the promotion of a self-reliant agriculture, especially grain production, and rural industry was treated as subordinate to agricultural development. This was encapsulated in the strategic slogan "take grain as the key link and seek all-round development". In Jinjiang a slogan "run industry around agriculture and promote agriculture by running industry well" had to be proposed to win support for and legitimize the status of rural industry (Liu et al. 1992:130-1). One reason for the relatively rapid development of commune and brigade enterprises in the early 1970s was that in 1970 the Chinese government set the target of achieving agricultural mechanization in 10 years' time, and many agricultural machinery plants and relevant industries were legitimately set up accordingly (Chen and Han 1993:56).

Secondly, given the stringent central planning of the economy, commune and brigade enterprises could only produce some "extra-plan" products, which were left out by the State plan. In fact the relatively rapid development of commune and brigade enterprises in the early 1970s could also be partly attributed to the fact that during the "cultural revolution" urban industry did not run normally, leading to shortages of daily necessities in urban areas and of some spare parts for the major industries. Under this situation commune and brigade enterprises were allowed to produce these products (Chen and Geng 1993:268). But as the production of commune and brigade enterprises was not included in the plan, they were vulnerable to being criticized as having "capitalist tendencies", and losing their legitimate status. Even as late as 1976 and 1977, during the campaign of "cracking down on the new bourgeois element" in Jinjiang, many commune and brigade enterprises suffered a major blow, and many of their managers were even arrested (Qiu 1995:10).

This was the context within which the predecessor of Jinjiang's TVEs started and developed. As shown in Figure 5.2, during the period 1949-1978 non-agricultural output value did increase, but its proportion of the total value of rural industrial and agricultural output value[41] was limited. The operating scope for commune and brigade enterprises in Jinjiang at that time was limited to those serving local agricultural activities and the local people's life, including farm implements, wood products, bricks and tiles, construction, weaving, and processing of agricultural and sideline products. In the 1960s some enterprises producing machinery, hardware, and construction materials were also established. In 1978 there were 1,141 commune and brigade enterprises, employing 51,961 rural laborers, 15 percent of the total rural labor force in Jinjiang (Chen and Zhuang 1994:304). In short, the foundation of TVEs had already been laid down before 1978, but they played only limited roles in the rural economy.

Figure 5.2 Agricultural and non-agricultural output value, Jinjiang 1949-1978

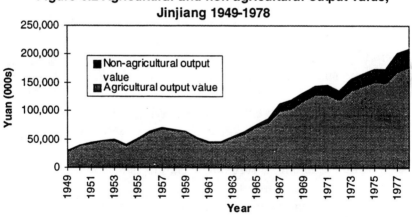

Source: based on the data in Liu et al. 1992: 128-30

---

[41] The industrial output value of the enterprises run by the State or towns is not included in this value.

5.3.2 MAJOR POLICY CHANGES TOWARDS TVE DEVELOPMENT DURING 1978-1984

The end of 1978 was not only an important political watershed in China, but also a major turning point for the development of TVEs. At the Third Plenary Session of the Eleventh Central Committee of the CCP, China adopted its economic reform and open door policies, which provided a good political and economic environment for the development of rural enterprises. More specifically, it was clearly pointed out in this meeting that "there should be a great development of commune and brigade enterprises". Later, the State Council released several documents, expounding the significance of the development of commune and brigade enterprises and stipulating policies regarding their development orientation, distribution, operating scope, and source of capital (China, State Council 1979; 1981). These documents not only gave commune and brigade enterprises legitimate status for their development, but asked "all trades and professions to actively support the development of commune and brigade enterprises", and offered preferential credit and taxation policies for their development[42].

More important changes took place in 1984. In March 1984 the Central Committee of the CCP and the State Council issued a document, transmitting "the report on creating a new situation in commune and brigade enterprises" submitted by the Ministry of Agriculture, Animal Husbandry, and Fishery (Central Committee 1984). Apart from stressing the importance of commune and brigade enterprises for agricultural development and the national economy, the importance of commune and brigade enterprises in absorbing rural surplus labor was also clearly stated:

It is predicted that by the end of the century, the number of workers in the current rural areas (including market towns) will be 450 million. According to the experience of advanced regions, after the degree of mechanization is increased, agriculture can only absorb three tenths of the labor force or their working time. Forestry, animal husbandry, fishery can only absorb two-tenths of the labor force or their working time. Only one-tenth of the labor force can enter cities or industrial and mining areas. The remaining four-tenths of the labor force

---

[42] For example, in the 1980s newly established TVEs could usually have a certain period of tax holidays or tax reduction, although such preferential treatment has been reduced since the 1990s. TVEs enjoy easy access to credits of various banks and financial institutions and working funds set up for TVEs by governments at various levels. For more detailed information see also Fujian Provincial Committee of CCP 1991; Chen and Han 1993:104.

can only find their outlets in rural (including market town) industry, construction, transport, commerce, service sectors and household industrial and sideline activities. Otherwise there would be a serious social problem. At present there are 31 million laborers (including those engaged in agriculture in the busy seasons) in commune and brigade enterprises, two million in commune member cooperated enterprises. All of them account for only one tenth of the rural labor force. Therefore commune and brigade enterprises and commune member co-operative enterprises should be multiply developed (Central Committee 1984:4).

It is also important to note that TVE development was directly related to China's urban strategy and rural development. As stated in Chapter 3, the State Council lowered the criteria for the designation of official town status, and allowed peasants to move to designated towns (excluding county seats) for permanent settlement under certain conditions, to promote the establishment of small new urban centers. TVE development played important roles in this regard:

The development of township and village enterprises will promote the development of market towns, accelerate the construction of rural economic and cultural centers, help to achieve "leaving the land but not the villages" for farmers, prevent too many farmers from migrating to cities. At the same time of planning and supervising TVE development, the party committees and governments at and above the county level should also work out comprehensive plans for market towns (Central Committee 1984:2).

Another important piece of information regarding new policies for commune and brigade enterprises in this document was that commune and brigade enterprises were renamed for the first time "township and village enterprises" (TVEs). This was caused by the fact that communes and brigades would soon be abolished and replaced by townships and villages, and more importantly, by the fact that many cooperative joint-household enterprises and individual enterprises had come into existence. This was an important change because it gave those cooperative and private individual economies (*geti Jingji*) legitimate status, encouraging individual initiatives to create new enterprises. While it was pointed out that some production of rural industry should be concentrated in towns, it was recommended that some production projects be dispersed to small household industry, because it fitted in with the situation that Chinese farmers do not give up their land easily, and because it could save a lot of investment. In the No.1 document of the Central Committee of the CCP in the same year it was also stated that "peasants should be encouraged to invest in various kinds of enterprises and become shareholders; collectives and individuals should be encouraged to collect funds on a voluntary basis to establish various kind of enterprises" (Editorial Department 1994:9). Besides, it was pointed out that the production and sales of commune and brigade enterprises were mainly regulated by the market.

All these show that the strategic importance of TVEs in China's rural development and urbanization had been established and the relevant policies had been formulated. However, while the State created a favorable political and economic environment for the TVE development, it gave little direct financial support. Later development showed that local initiatives were of vital importance: this was also one of the main intentions of the policy changes in 1984. Because of the vast geographical, social, economic, and historical variations, the paths of TVE development have been different among different regions in China. There have been at least 10 different development models for TVE development, including the "Jinjiang model" (Chen and Han 1993:66). It is not the purpose of this study to examine all these models. But the following review on the process of TVE development in Jinjiang can provide some insight into how *in situ* transformation can be achieved in rural areas without much State investment and metropolitan influence.

5.3.3 RAPID DEVELOPMENT OF TVES AND ITS IMPLICATIONS FOR RURAL-URBAN TRANSFORMATION IN JINJIANG AFTER 1978

Not surprisingly, since 1978 TVE development has entered a new era in Jinjiang. Because Shishi Municipality was separated from Jinjiang at the end of 1988, the growth of TVEs is briefly reviewed by two stages, namely before 1988 when the area of Shishi was included, and after 1988 when the area of Shishi was not included. During the period 1978-1988 the annual average growth rates of TVE numbers, employee numbers and total income were 34.8 percent, 15.2 percent, and 42.1 percent respectively. From 1988 to 1992 the annual average growth rates of TVE numbers, employee numbers and total output value were 10.4 percent, 12.1 percent, 50.7 percent respectively. In 1978 only 15.2 percent of the rural labor force was employed by the TVEs, but in 1992 58.3 percent of the rural labor force was absorbed by the TVEs. The numbers of TVE employees mentioned here do not include temporary residents working in Jinjiang, whose number also increased rapidly.

Although the policy changes described in the preceding section were an important factor contributing to the above development, a major question remains to be answered. Rural development is often constrained by the lack of investment, infrastructure, and skilled labor. Because Jinjiang is relatively far from the two major cities in Fujian, which themselves were not strong economically, its TVE development could not start by benefiting from the spread-effect of main industries from large cities, as happened in the areas around Shanghai, or by receiving large amounts of foreign investment, as was the case in the Pearl River Delta. Thus it is necessary to examine how the initial capital was accumulated to establish the earlier TVEs, and how these TVEs could have kept developing until now.

5.3.3.1 Joint-Household Enterprises and Start of TVEs

By examining Figure 5.3 some important hints can be obtained. While it can be expected that there had been some major turning points for the increase in TVE employees since 1978, corresponding to the policy changes, the composition of this increase is more noteworthy. From 1978 to 1981 there was a rapid development in township enterprises and village enterprises, but in the period 1982-1988 their number of employees declined, and the emergence and increase of joint-household enterprises was mainly responsible for the increase in the number of TVE employees. In 1988 individual enterprises also emerged and assumed a relatively important position in the employment structure in Jinjiang. In this year 66.2 percent of the total number of TVE employees were employed by joint-household enterprises and individual enterprises: the large scale of TVE development started actually on the household basis. The further development of different forms of TVEs since 1988 can be seen in Figure 5.4.

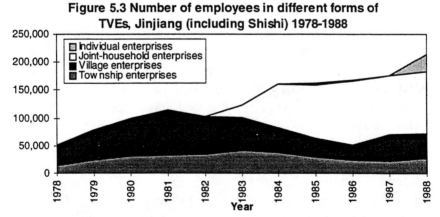

Figure 5.3 Number of employees in different forms of TVEs, Jinjiang (including Shishi) 1978-1988

Source: based on Chen and Zhuang 1994:307.

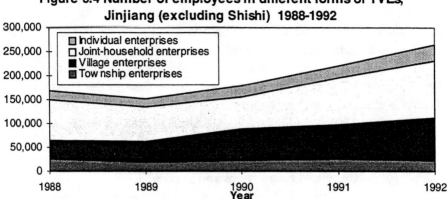

Figure 5.4 Number of employees in different forms of TVEs, Jinjiang (excluding Shishi) 1988-1992

Source: based on Chen and Zhuang 1994:1434.

This is the essence of the "Jinjiang model", which provides an example of how the constraints of lack of capital and labor skills were overcome in the early stage of rural development. First, the joint-household enterprise is a good way of accumulating initial capital for the establishment of rural enterprises. It is summarized that TVEs in Jinjiang started from "the three idles": idle laborers, idle rooms, and idle funds. Jinjiang is one of the major hometowns of Chinese overseas, many of whose dependants received overseas remittances regularly, saved some money, and built some houses. For most single families these unused funds and houses were not significant, and not enough for the establishment of enterprises. But putting them together would create a different story. Joint-household enterprises emerged for this reason. In Jinjiang this kind of enterprise started in Chendai, the most famous town for TVE development in Jinjiang, as early as in 1979, four years before joint-household enterprises were officially recognized in 1984 by the State. At the end of 1980 there were 344 rural enterprises in this town (at that time still called a commune), and 242 (70 percent) of them were joint-household enterprises. Half of the labor force in Chendai commune was employed by this kind of enterprise. The total initial capital for these enterprises amounted to about 30 million *Yuan*, of which 27 million *Yuan* (90 percent) were raised from farmers. A typical example of this was farmer Lin Tuqiu's shoe factory. In 1979 Lin established his factory in his house by raising 100,000 *Yuan* funds from 14 farmers, who also became the first group of workers in his factory. After more than 10 years development, his factory owned 2.4 million *Yuan* fixed assets and one million floating capital, and could produce 3,000 to 5,000 pairs of shoes every day in 1991 (Xu and Wang 1992:298-302). In this way the problem of capital shortage was effectively solved and the surplus labor was absorbed (Office of Jinjiang Prefectural Committee of CCP 1981).

Another characteristic of Jinjiang's TVEs was their low requirement for funds, infrastructure and labor skills, and their labor-intensive nature. In the case of Chendai town it can be calculated that the average initial capital for a single enterprise was only 87,209 *Yuan* (about US$ 10,533 at the current exchange rate). A survey on the educational attainment of employees of 152 TVEs in Jinjiang in 1987 showed that 52.4 percent of the employees were illiterate or had only primary school education, and another 30.5 percent of them had only accomplished junior middle school education (Liu et al. 1992:227). In employment structure, industrial employment accounted for 94 percent of the total employment in Jinjiang's TVEs in 1987, and the industry itself was in turn dominated by five major sectors: sewing, construction materials, machinery, food, and chemicals (Table 5.3). Obviously the sewing, construction materials, and food industries do not have high requirements for labor skill, initial funds and infrastructure. It is particularly noticeable that the sewing industry was the largest industrial sector in Jinjiang in 1987. Running this kind of industry only needs some space, workers who had some simple skills or could be easily trained for the job, and limited funds. It was this industry that experienced the most significant growth when a large number of TVEs were first established. In 1979 the output value of the sewing industry accounted for only 0.3 percent of the total output value of TVE industry in Jinjiang (Liu et al. 1992:142). But it increased steadily since then, especially after 1984, showing its key role in the early development of TVEs[43].

5.3.3.2 Further Development of TVEs and their Changing Institutional and Spatial Organization

The above analysis suggests that the "Jinjiang model" has been effective in absorbing rural surplus labor and transforming the economic and employment structure of the rural economy. But what is the spatial effect of this transformation? To answer this question three major trends of TVE development in Jinjiang are worth mentioning.

---

[43] The proportion of the total output value of the five major industries in the total industrial output value was only 60.8 percent in 1979, but increased to 88.7 percent in 1987, as shown in Table 5.3.

Table 5.3 Major sectors of TVE industry in Jinjiang, 1987

Sector	Number of enterprises		Number of employees		Total output value	
	Number	% of total	Number	% of total	Million Yuan	% of total
Total	5,348	100.0	166,464	100.0	1,014.3	100.0
Sewing	1,754	32.8	63,435	38.1	346.3	34.1
Construction materials	1,330	24.9	41,467	24.9	243.4	24.0
Machinery	849	15.9	20,242	12.2	164.7	16.3
Food	479	8.9	13,911	8.3	81.7	8.1
Chemicals	365	6.8	10,811	6.5	63.9	6.3
Sub-total	4,777	89.3	149,866	90.0	900.0	88.7
Others	571	10.7	16,598	10.0	114.3	11.3

Source: Liu et al. 1992:141

First, TVE development in Jinjiang has been increasingly connected with foreign investment. Before 1984 foreign investment had already been involved in Jinjiang's TVE development in the form of compensation trade (product buy-back) and intermediate processing of goods. In the former case foreign investors received payment in the form of the goods produced by the enterprises in which an investment was made; in the latter case foreign firms supplied materials, equipment and parts for TVEs to process or fabricate into finished products according to the foreign investors' designs and specifications. In the period 1979-1988 some 400 TVEs in Jinjiang were involved in the intermediate processing of goods, 80 percent of which was clothing, 10 percent of which was knitted sweaters. In this way not only did the TVEs increase their income and absorb more rural laborers, but they also introduced some new equipment and trained some qualified personnel (Chen and Zhuang 1994:305).

Later, some of the TVEs became foreign-funded enterprises (*sanzi qiye*). In fact, one of the major characteristics of foreign investment in Jinjiang is that most foreign-funded enterprises are TVEs as well, indicating the important role of TVEs in absorbing foreign investment. The fast development of foreign investment in TVEs began in 1988. At the end of this year there were 241 foreign-funded enterprises, among which 154 (63.9 percent) were foreign-funded TVEs, which had absorbed 45.7 million *Yuan* actualized foreign investment; the amount of total foreign investment through signed contracts for these TVEs was 177.9 million *Yuan* (Chen and Zhuang 1994:305-7). By the end of 1994 the number of foreign funded enterprises had increased to 1,805, among which 1,096 (60.7%) were foreign-funded TVEs, which had absorbed US$ 964.1 million actualized foreign investment; the total amount of foreign investment through signed contracts was US$ 1167.1 million (Statistical Bureau of Jinjiang Municipality 1995:189, 276). The establishment and development of foreign-funded TVEs have greatly improved TVEs' production techniques and equipment, and enhanced TVEs' competitiveness, especially their export capability.

Secondly, although Jinjiang's TVEs are characterized by their small scale and dispersed distribution, there has been a tendency to specialization for these enterprises and concentration of certain industries in certain areas. For example, the industries of construction materials and ceramics are concentrated in the north-east of Jinjiang, especially in Chizao town; shoe and hat industries are concentrated in the east of Jinjiang, especially in Chendai town; and the garment industry is concentrated in the south-east of Jinjiang, especially in Yinglin town. There was further division inside these specialized zones. For example in Chendai, each factory specialized in producing certain kinds of shoes, and at the same time, some 200 different kinds of shoes, including their parts, were produced and sold in this small town (Liu et al. 1992:396; Chen and Zhuang 1994:309; also personal observation during fieldwork, September 1996). This suggests that despite the dispersed nature of TVE, a certain kind of scale economy and agglomeration economy could still be achieved in Jinjiang.

Thirdly, since the 1990s attention has been increasingly paid to the scale of TVEs and relative concentration of their location. One way of doing this is to establish large group enterprises by uniting small TVEs. This is a new way of promoting further development of TVEs, and it has been actively advocated by the governments at all levels in Fujian Province (Fujian Provincial Committee of CCP 1991). In Jinjiang, many TVEs have joined enterprise groups in different ways (personal communication, TVE Management Bureau of Jinjiang Municipality, September 1996). The other way is to encourage TVEs to be located in the industrial zones, which are planned and established for TVEs with standard factory buildings. The development of industrial zones has been further facilitated by large-scale infrastructure construction, which involved 1,500 million *Yuan* investment between 1992 and 1995 and has greatly improved Jinjiang's trans-

port, communication, electricity and water supply[44] (*Fujian Daily* 1995). In Jinjiang by the end of 1992 there had been 40 industrial zones at the municipal and
town levels and 20 at the village level, with 1,000 standard factory buildings
(Chen and Zhuang 1994:1433). By the middle of 1996 about 30 percent of TVEs
had moved to various industrial zones (personal communication, TVE Management Bureau of Jinjiang Municipality, September 1996). When I visited Chendai
town in 1991, many shoe factories were still located in the family houses, but
when I revisited the same place during my fieldwork in 1996, most of those factories had moved to the industrial zones, and the houses were used for commercial purposes related to the shoe industry. When I asked why some factories still
stayed in the family house, I was told that one of the reasons was that those left
behind had not accumulated enough capital to move to industrial zones. The head
of the TVE Management Bureau of Jinjiang Municipality gave the same explanation.

These three trends seem to suggest that the transformation in Jinjiang will not
stay in the form of joint-household enterprises forever. Their institutional and
spatial organization will be changing accordingly, as the transformation progresses. It is important to note that the emergence of early TVEs in the form of
family workshops paved the way for the *in situ* transformation of the rural economic and employment structure in Jinjiang, which is the precondition for the
further spatial transformation represented by the establishment of industrial
zones. This change has been made more possible by the inflow of a large amount
of foreign capital, which has been invested heavily in land exploitation.

5.3.4 SUMMARY

As a very densely populated place, Jinjiang could have been a major source
of migration to the major cities in Fujian. But this has not happened. Rather, as
mentioned in Chapters 3 and 4, Jinjiang has attracted many migrants not only
from Fujian, but also from other provinces in China. The "Jinjiang model" provides a success story of rural development which keeps surplus rural laborers
from leaving their home. One of the key factors contributing to the transformation in Jinjiang has been the emergence of joint-household enterprises, which
were an effective way of raising initial funds for the early development of rural

---

[44] There is more discussion in Chapter 6 on the improvements in Jinjiang's transport and communication.

enterprises and very much encouraged by the government. Selecting suitable industries which fitted in with rural conditions of lack of capital and skill is also important. The development in Jinjiang is continuing its upward trend, transforming not only the economic and employment structures, but also their institutional and spatial organization, leading to the future prospect of full urbanization. Although Jinjiang's case is unusual in the speed and scale of development, it is certainly not the only such case in Fujian. TVEs in Fujian as a whole absorbed 4.7 million rural surplus laborers in 1995, who could have migrated to the major cities; this has diverted considerable potential pressure on the existing large cities. Compared with the restrictive policies for migration to Fuzhou, the successful transformation of rural areas is a more important reason why Fujian's largest city Fuzhou has not expanded very fast.

5.4 FOREIGN INVESTMENT AND RURAL-URBAN TRANSFORMATION: THE CASE OF FUQING

The economic reform and open door policies since 1978 brought about many changes in China, among which the attitude toward foreign investment is a most significant one. There is no longer any hostility to foreign investment. On the contrary foreign investment has been increasingly used as a means of overcoming the shortage of domestic funds and of improving China's management, productivity and competitiveness, and of increasing employment. Special districts like Special Economic Zones and Technological and Economic Development Zones, which offer many economic incentives for investors, have been set up to attract foreign investment (Panagariya 1995; Yeh and Xu 1996:221-30). Much of the approving authority for foreign investment projects has been delegated to local governments, and the relevant approving procedures have been greatly simplified[45]. In this section the effects of these policy changes on China's new urbanization patterns are examined by looking first at the general situation of foreign investment in Fujian, and then examining the case of Fuqing, where foreign investment has been leading to *in situ* transformation of rural areas.

---

[45] In Fujian Province prefectural governments or municipal governments at the prefectural level can approve foreign investment projects up to US$ 30 million (personal communication, Fujian Provincial Office of Opening to the Outside World, August 1996; see also Fujian Provincial Government 1991)

5.4.1 SPATIAL PATTERNS OF FOREIGN INVESTMENT AND LAND DEVELOPMENT ZONES IN FUJIAN

Section 5.3 showed the importance of foreign investment in the *in situ* transformation of rural areas. However, this transformation started on the basis of local economic activities, especially the establishment of TVEs. Foreign investment has greatly promoted the transformation process, but has not been the leading force in this process. When a large number of foreign-funded enterprises began to set up in Jinjiang, structural changes in the employment and the economy were already well under way, and most of these enterprises were established on the basis of TVEs.

But as can be seen in the case of Fuqing, foreign investment can also serve as the leading force in *in situ* transformation of rural areas. Foreign investment not only can play a leading role in changing the structure of the rural economy by investing in the secondary and tertiary sectors, but has been involved in the rural-urban transformation in Fujian Province on a much larger scale since the late 1980s and early 1990s. As shown in subsection 5.2.3, various development zones and investment zones have become important forms of land development. These kinds of development are not limited to Fuzhou; many land development zones are located in the rural towns or townships outside Fuzhou, and foreign investment is the major force driving the development of these zones. By the end of 1995 120 land development zones had been set up in Fujian, with a total developed area of 109 km^2 (Zheng 1996:101); and US$ 2,774 million, 75.7 percent of it (2,107 million) being foreign investment, had been invested in the development. By the end of the same year these development zones had attracted 1,323 projects, with a total investment of US$ 4,130 million, among which 80 percent (US$ 3,300 million) was foreign investment (Zhuang 1996:31-3).

It can be easily appreciated that foreign investment is an important factor contributing to the growth of spontaneous urbanization. Foreign investment provides the bulk of funds needed for new urban development in the land development zones. In fact it accounted for 51.6 percent of the total societal fixed assets investment in Fujian in 1995 (Yan 1996:61). It had created 703,905 non-agricultural employment opportunities by the end of 1995 in the form of foreign-funded enterprises (Statistical Bureau of Fujian Province 1996:331). The advantage of these is that they make few demands on the State budget, but contribute to the increase in TVE employees and temporary residents.

The spatial effect of foreign investment on Fujian's urbanization patterns is a more important problem to be addressed here. Detailed and systematic data on the spatial distribution of foreign investment in Fujian are not available, but by combining information from different sources, a broad picture can be drawn. First, as can be seen in Table 5.4, there are three major regions for foreign investment in Fujian: Fuzhou, where the provincial capital is located; Xiamen, one of China's Special Economic Zones; and Quanzhou, the area with most developed TVEs. These three municipalities stretch from the middle coast of Fujian to the south coast, covering a large area. As a result, since the 1980s Fuzhou's development has been overshadowed by Xiamen and Quanzhou. The case of Xiamen is particularly worthy of mention. As one of the Special Economic Zones in China, it enjoys more preferential policies, and is more attractive to investment, especially foreign investment. As can be seen in Table 5.4, Xiamen Municipality attracted an amount of foreign investment which was close to that attracted by Fuzhou Municipality through signed contracts, and even more actualized foreign investment than Fuzhou Municipality, although its population is only one-fifth of the latter. Xiamen's social and economic development has also been faster than Fuzhou's since the 1980s. The per capita GNP was 27,406 *Yuan* in Xiamen in 1995, compared to 18,029 *Yuan* in Fuzhou. Obviously Xiamen's faster development than that of Fuzhou has had a counterbalancing effect on the attractiveness of Fuzhou as the provincial capital. The stable and slightly downward trend of the two-city primacy index, and the important role of Xiamen in absorbing temporary residents mentioned in Chapter 4, clearly demonstrated this effect. As to the case of Quanzhou Municipality, foreign investment mainly serves as a contributing factor to the development of TVEs, which has been shown earlier in the case of Jinjiang.

Secondly, the amount of foreign investment in Fuzhou shown in Table 5.4 includes the foreign investment made to the counties and municipalities at the county level, which are administered by Fuzhou. If these counties and municipalities are excluded, the share of foreign investment absorbed by the core area of Fuzhou (Fuzhou city, including its suburban areas) will be much smaller. One statistic shows that only 52.4 percent of foreign investment through signed contracts in Fuzhou in 1995 was in Fuzhou's core region, its city districts (*Shiqu*) (Zhao et al. 1996:365). The other statistic about the foreign investment through signed contracts in Fuzhou's development and investment zones shows that 62.6 percent of foreign investment by the end of 1995 had been in the core area of Fuzhou (data provided by the Office of Opening to the Outside World, Fuzhou

Municipal Government during fieldwork, September 1996). If it is assumed that 55 percent of foreign investment in Fuzhou municipality has been located in Fuzhou city, then only about 17 percent of the total foreign investment in Fujian has been invested in Fuzhou city. Because Fuzhou is the only large city in Fujian, this means that more than 80 percent of the foreign investment in Fujian has been invested in places which are at the level of or lower than medium-sized cities in the residential hierarchy. This result bears some similarity to the situation in Guangdong Province, but is in sharp contrast to the concentrated spatial distribution of foreign investment in many other countries[46] (Fuchs and Pernia 1987:97-8; Sit and Yang 1997:659).

Table 5.4 The amount and percentage distribution of foreign investment by prefectures and municipalities[a] in Fujian

| | Foreign investment through signed contracts | | | | Actualized foreign investment | | | |
| | 1979-1995 | | 1991-1995 | | 1979-1995 | | 1991-1995 | |
	Million US$	% of total	Million US$	% of total	Million US$	% of total	Million US$	% of total
Fuzhou	12,348.1	31.2	10,896.7	30.6	4,162.8	28.3	3,343.6	25.7
Xiamen	10,177.0	25.7	8,549.1	24.0	4,906.7	33.3	4,474.8	34.4
Putian	2,815.5	7.1	2,678.7	7.5	830.5	5.6	739.1	5.7
Sanming	508.4	1.3	446.2	1.3	181.2	1.2	160.1	1.2
Quanzhou	8,371.7	21.1	7,873.5	22.1	2,669.8	18.1	2,466.1	19.0
Zhangzhou	3,448.9	8.7	3,289.2	9.2	1,143.3	7.8	1,065.3	8.2
Nanping	890.3	2.2	862.5	2.4	397.0	2.7	347.0	2.7
Ningde	475.0	1.2	437.6	1.2	179.2	1.2	161.2	1.2
Longyan	571.0	1.4	547.0	1.5	248.0	1.7	242.2	1.9
Total	39,605.9	100.0	35,580.5	100.0	14,718.5	100.0	12,999.4	100.0

[a] The municipalities in this table refer to so-called "municipalities at the prefectural level", which administer several counties or municipalities at the county level.
Source: Yan 1996:295-6.

---

[46] For example, the proportions of Japanese investment in the center of the metropolitan capitals in Taiwan, South Korea, Malaysia, Philippines, Thailand and Indonesia in 1978 were 81 percent, 90 percent, 61 percent, 24 percent, 99 percent, and 98 percent respectively. In the case of the Philippines, the other 76 percent of the investment was still distributed in the recently added cities and towns within the metropolitan area (Fuchs and Pernia 1987:98).

The distribution of land development zones, which transform many rural areas into urban or urban-like ones, can be regarded as a major reflection of the spatial effect of foreign investment on Fujian's urbanization. Table 5.5 shows the distribution of land development zones in Fujian Province. While it can be identified that the developed area of these zones is concentrated in four coastal municipalities in south-east Fujian, its distribution among these four municipalities does not exhibit much concentration in Fuzhou city either. The developed area of land development zones in Fuzhou city accounts for 21.2 percent of the total in Fujian, which is similar to Fuzhou's share in the total foreign investment in Fujian: nearly 80 percent of the developed area is dispersed in widespread regions. When the area of land development zones is compared with the built-up area of Fuzhou, their significance is more evident. The total developed area of land development zones outside Fuzhou was 85.9 km^2, 1.3 times the current built-up area of Fuzhou city. This implies that another Fuzhou has been built in a dispersed way.

Table 5.5 The distribution of land development zones by prefectures and municipalities in Fujian, 1995

	Number	% of the provincial total	Developed area (km^2)	% of the provincial total
Fuzhou Municipality	20	16.7	45.64	41.9
Xiamen	15	12.5	9.57	8.8
Putian	15	12.5	8.62	7.9
Sanming	0	0.0	0	0.0
Quanzhou	30	25.0	15.02	13.8
Zhangzhou	24	20.0	14.89	13.7
Nanping	4	3.3	7.73	7.1
Ningde	6	5.0	6.35	5.8
Longyan	6	5.0	1.13	1.0
Total	120	100.0	108.95	100.0
Fuzhou City	13	10.8	23.1	21.2

Sources: Zheng 1996:101; data provided by Fuzhou Municipal
Office of Opening to the Outside World.

After examination of the macro-effect of foreign investment in Fujian, a closer look at the micro-level is needed. The following section examines the case of Fuqing, a newly designated city well known for foreign investment and land development zones, to study more closely what changes foreign investment has brought to this place.

5.4.2 FOREIGN INVESTMENT AND RURAL-URBAN TRANSFORMATION IN FUQING

Located on the middle coast of Fujian Province, Fuqing is one of the municipalities at the county level under the administration of Fuzhou, the provincial capital, and 60 kilometers south of it. It is also one of the regions with high population densities in Fujian. In sheer population size it ranks fifth among counties and municipalities (at the county level) in Fujian Province, with a total number of permanent residents of 1,142,300 by the end of 1995. Its total land area is 1,519 km^2, with a population density of 752 persons per km^2. It was granted municipal status at the county level at the end of 1990.

Like most counties in Fujian, Fuqing was predominantly rural before 1978. In 1978 agricultural output value accounted for 72.5 percent of the total agricultural and industrial output value (Zhang and Lu 1986:116-7). Changes have begun since then, but unlike in Jinjiang, they started much later and proceeded much more slowly in Fuqing before the 1990s. By the end of 1990 TVEs alone employed almost half of the rural labor force in Jinjiang, but in Fuqing only 36.1 percent of the rural labor force was employed in the non-agricultural sectors (calculated according to Statistical Bureau of Fuqing Municipality 1991:12-3; Chen and Zhuang 1994:1432). At the end of 1990 the value added of the primary sector still accounted for half of the GDP in Fuqing (Guo et al. 1994:163), while in Jinjiang the value added of the primary sector only accounted for 24.8 percent of the GDP (Statistical Bureau of Fujian Province 1991:465). The difference in the structural change between the two places could be partly attributed to the difference in the development of TVEs. Whereas half of the rural labor force was absorbed by TVEs in Jinjiang in 1990, in Fuqing only 30.4 percent of the rural labor force was employed by TVEs. Four years later Fuqing's TVEs absorbed 34.8 percent of the total rural labor force, indicating only moderate progress.

But around the end of the 1980s Fuqing found its own way of development. As in Jinjiang this development had much to do with Chinese overseas, but in a very different way. Similar to Jinjiang, Fuqing is also one of the famous hometowns for Chinese overseas. Some Chinese overseas from Fuqing are very successful in business, and among these one prominent figure, Liem Sioe Liong, is particularly worth mentioning. Born in Fuqing in 1917, Liem migrated to Indonesia in 1938. There he successfully established and developed his business empire, the Salim Group. It was estimated that Liem's net assets are worth at least US$ 3 billion, and Liem is second only to the Sultan of Brunei as South-East Asia's wealthiest individual. His Salim Group has more than 400 affiliated companies, employing at least 135,000 people. In 1993, group sales were estimated to be approximately US$ 9 billion, accounting for approximately 5 percent of Indonesia's GDP (East Asia Analytical Unit 1995:163).

Liem is only one of the successful Chinese overseas from Fuqing, although he is certainly the most successful. These Chinese overseas still have many connections with their hometown, and are willing to help their hometown's economic development. Before making large-scale investments they had donated a lot of money to help develop public undertakings and industry in Fuqing. Gradually they realized that donation, like "blood transfusion", is not the best way of helping the economic development of their hometown; investing in the hometown is a far better way, because this will help the hometown to develop and strengthen the ability of "blood creation". In October 1986, the State Council promulgated "the regulations encouraging foreign investment", which further stimulated the enthusiasm of Chinese overseas to invest in their hometowns (Cao et al. 1994:482, 948-51). In April 1987, invited by the leaders of Fuqing County and initiated by Liem Sioe Liong, a "Fuqing overseas Chinese inspection delegation" visited Fuqing, and decided to establish the "Rongqiao Industrial Development Zone"[47]. This was the prelude to large-scale foreign investment in Fuqing (Cao et al. 1994:482; personal communication, Fuqing local officials, October 1996).

5.4.2.1 Characteristics of Foreign Investment in Fuqing

Since the 1990s foreign investment has increased sharply in Fuqing. As Table 5.6 shows, in the period 1990-1995 the average annual growth rate of foreign investment through newly signed contracts was as high as 82.7 percent, while that of actualized foreign investment was 58 percent. By the end of 1995 the total actualized foreign investment in Fuqing amounted to US$ 941 million, 83.5 of

---

[47] In Chinese "*Rongqiao*" means Fuqing's overseas Chinese.

which was made in the period 1990-1995 (calculated according to Table 5.6 and Zhao et al. 1996:201).

Table 5.6 Foreign investment in Fuqing, 1990-1995

	1990	1991	1992	1993	1994	1995	Average annual growth rate during 1990-1995 (%)
Foreign investment through newly signed contracts (Million US$)	28.1	108.4	404.9	578.3	452	572	82.7
Actualized foreign investment (Million US$)	28.1	49.5	59.2	83.4	231	277	58.0

Source: Fujian Provincial Urban and Rural Planning and Design Institute 1995:63; Zhao et al. 1996:201.

Several characteristics of foreign investment in Fuqing are important. First, compared with the foreign investment in other regions of Fujian, the average single-project amount of foreign investment is higher in Fuqing. While the average single-project amount of foreign investment through signed contracts was US$ 2.4 million in Fujian Province in 1994, that in Fuqing was US$ 3.5 million (Fujian Provincial Urban and Rural Planning and Design Institute, 1995:63; Statistical Bureau of Fujian Province 1995:419). There have been 52 projects with a total investment of US$ 10 million each and two projects with a total investment of 100 million each. This is in sharp contrast to Jinjiang, which had received even more foreign investment than Fuqing by the end of 1995 (US$ 1139.6 million in terms of actualized foreign investment), but had achieved this mainly by absorbing foreign investment in small amounts. In 1994 the average single-project amount of foreign investments through signed contracts in Jinjiang was US$ 0.96 million (calculated according to Statistical Bureau of Fujian Province 1995:373), which was much smaller than the provincial average[48].

This characteristic of foreign investment in Fuqing has much to do with the way foreign investment was introduced in Fuqing. Big consortiums run by Chi-

---

[48] This observation was also confirmed by personal communications from the officials in the Foreign Economic and Trade Commissions of both Fuqing and Jinjiang Municipalities, September to October 1996.

nese overseas from Fuqing took the lead in investing in Fuqing. This is quite different from the situation in Jinjiang where small business owners dominate foreign investment. Furthermore, through their business network all over the world, Chinese overseas from Fuqing help to attract more foreign investors, some of which are big consortiums and had no previous connection to Fuqing, to invest in Fuqing. Such big international consortiums include Samsung from Korea, Siemens from Germany, Toyota from Japan, Shell from Britain, and BHP from Australia. The fact that Liem Sioe Liong invested in Fuqing also serves the purpose of increasing the confidence of other foreign investors to invest here (personal communication, Foreign Economic and Trade Commission of Fuqing Municipality, October 1996).

Secondly, related to the source of investment, the industry structure of foreign-funded enterprises in Fuqing seems to be more advanced than that of TVEs in Jinjiang. This can be demonstrated by Table 5.7. While textiles and sewing, and food and beverages are two main industries attracting foreign investment, it is important to note that the industry of electronics, clocks and watches, and communication is the biggest industry in terms of the output value. This seems to suggest that although industry in Fuqing still features some labor-intensive sectors, it is more advanced in techniques than the industry in Jinjiang. Correspondingly the educational requirements for employees are also relatively high. Employees in the foreign-funded enterprises in Fuqing should have at least completed junior middle school education, in some enterprises even high school education. In Guanjie electronic enterprise 15 percent of employees are graduates of universities and colleges (personal communication, municipal government and managers of the enterprises in Fuqing, October 1996).

Thirdly, most foreign investment is concentrated in the major development, investment and industrial zones, which has led to large-scale landscape transformation of the rural areas. As can be seen from Table 5.8, by the end of 1994 84.2 percent of the total investment for foreign-funded enterprises had gone to six major development, investment and industrial zones, in which 91.3 percent of the total output value was produced. The first development zone in Table 5.8, the Rongqiao ETDZ, was established on the basis of the Rongqiao Industrial Development Zone mentioned earlier. It was later approved by the State Council as an Economic and Technological Development Zone at the national level in 1992. Yuanhong Investment Zone was also established in the same year and approved by the State Council. Other industrial zones were approved by the relevant provincial or municipal authorities. Foreign investors in these zones can enjoy preferential treatment such as tax holidays and low fees. Land price is also a factor attracting foreign investors. A hectare of land costs 2,000-2,667 *Yuan*, only one-fourth of the land price in the FTEDE of Mawei in Fuzhou. In addition, foreign investors are allowed to use their own capital, techniques, equipment, raw materials and markets, and can decide by themselves on the choice and design of project, factory location, choice of project contractor, business partners, recruitment of employees, and project management, so long as they conform to China's sectoral policies and Fuqing's urban planning (personal communication, Foreign Economic and Trade Commission of Fuqing Municipality, October 1996; unpublished documents of Fuqing Municipal Government).

Table 5.7 Industry structure of foreign-funded enterprises[a] in Fuqing, 1994

	Number of enterprises		Total investment[b]		Total output value	
	Number	% of total	Million US$	% of total	Million *Yuan*	% of total
Electronics, clocks and watches, communication	18	9.9	60.9	9.0	1,790.6	28.4
Food and beverages	25	13.8	131.3	19.5	1,397.8	22.2
Textiles and sewing	27	14.9	189.3	28.1	452.3	7.2
Plastic and leather products	8	4.4	6	0.9	214.6	3.4
Construction materials, glass and other non-metal materials	14	7.7	41.6	6.2	285.0	4.5
Aquaculture, fodder	5	2.8	14	2.1	176.0	2.8
Plastic cement, shoe industry	18	9.9	67.2	10.0	1,489.8	23.7
Paper products, printing	7	3.9	9.4	1.4	20.5	0.3
Renovating, decorating, and packaging	8	4.4	6.7	1.0	10.8	0.2
Products of light industry	14	7.7	28.4	4.2	411.9	6.5
Chemical industry	7	3.9	28.6	4.2	48.4	0.8
Real estate	18	9.9	76.1	11.3		0.0
Service industry (hotel and restaurant)	6	3.3	5.3	0.8		0.0

| Others | 6 | 3.3 | 17.9 | 2.7 | | 0.0 |
| Total | 181 | 100.0 | 673 | 100.0 | 6,297.7 | 100.0 |

[a] Including only those enterprises that had gone into operation.
[b] Including investment by Chinese parties in the case of Sino-foreign joint ventures.
Source: Fujian Provincial Urban and Rural Planning and Design Institute, 1995:80.

Table 5.8 The distribution of foreign funded enterprises[a] in Fuqing, 1994

	Number of enterprises		Area		Total investment[b]		Total output value	
	Number	% of total	km²	% of total	Million US$	% of total	Million Yuan	% of total
Rongqiao ETDZ	62	34.3	18.0	14.9	398.4	59.2	4,285.2	68.0
Hongkuang industrial zone	16	8.8	10.0	8.3	35.8	5.3	413.2	6.6
Yuanhong investment zone and Yuanzai industrial zone	11	6.1	50.0	41.3	56	8.3	452.6	7.2
Yuxi industrial zone	15	8.3	6.0	5.0	37.6	5.6	113.3	1.8
Jinyang industrial zone	6	3.3	6.0	5.0	22.4	3.3	423.2	6.7
Shangjing industrial zone	6	3.3	4.0	3.3	16.7	2.5	59.2	0.9
Subtotal	116	64.1	94.0	77.7	566.9	84.2	5,746.7	91.3
Fuqing city	35	19.3	0.0	0.0	69.8	10.4	358.8	5.7
Others	57	31.5	27.0	22.3	113	16.8	787.9	12.5
Total	181	100	121.0	100.0	673	100	6,297.7	100

[a] Including only those enterprises that had gone into operation.
[b] Including investment by Chinese parties in the case of Sino-foreign joint ventures.
Source: Fujian Provincial Urban and Rural Planning and Design Institute 1995:79.

5.4.2.2 Implications of Foreign Investment for the Rural-Urban Transformation in Fuqing

The transformation brought about by foreign investment in Fuqing is tremendous. First, in a few years Fuqing's economic structure has been greatly changed. In 1990 the primary sector, secondary sector and tertiary sector accounted for 51.7 percent, 27.3 percent and 21.0 percent of the GDP respectively, but in 1994 these figures changed to 27.7 percent, 50.7 percent, and 21.6 percent respectively (calculated according to Fujian Provincial Urban and Rural Planning and Design Institute 1995:62). During the 1990-1994 period the average annual growth rate of the value added of the primary sector was 17 percent, whereas for the secondary and tertiary sectors it was 60 percent and 38 percent. Obviously the industrial sector contributed most to the economic growth in Fuqing, and foreign-funded enterprises, which produced 75.2 percent of the total industrial output value in Fuqing in 1994, were the main contributors to this growth (Fujian Provincial Urban and Rural Planning and Design Institute 1995:76). This indicates clearly the significance of foreign investment in the structural change of the economy.

Secondly, perhaps the most noticeable change since the inflow of foreign investment in Fuqing is the landscape transformation of the previous rural areas where development zones, investment zones, and industrial zones are located. As analyzed above, foreign investment in Fuqing is more capital-intensive and technically more advanced; it tends to concentrate in the development zones, investment zones, and industrial zones. Therefore the physical transformation it brought to those zones is quite significant. In Rongqiao Development Zone an area of 10 km^2, which used to be farmland and farm houses, has been developed into an industrial area with standard factory buildings, roads, and residential and commercial centers. A further 8 km^2 are to be incorporated into the existing area. This development zone alone is already three times the size of the built-up area of Fuqing City in 1987, when the development zone had just been set up (6.2 km^2). Because the development zone is directly connected to the old city, it has greatly extended the built-up area of Fuqing city. Similar changes can be found in other investment zones and industrial zones to a different extent.

Some further explanation should be made on Yuanhong Investment Zone. In terms of planned area this is the largest zone for foreign investment in China. Its establishment and development are closely related to the construction of the harbor to the south of this zone. As the first stage of the harbor construction has just been completed and large-scale infrastructure construction, which is mainly funded by the Salim Group, is still going on, the development of Yuanhong Investment Zone has been relatively slow. According to Fuqing's urban planning only 10 km^2 of the total planned area will be developed before the year 2000. But in the future, as the infrastructure continues to be improved and more foreign investment goes in, another urban center will emerge here, attracting light and medium industries from Taiwan, Hong Kong, Singapore and Japan, as well as multinational corporations (East Asia Analytical Unit 1995:170). According to the new urban planning there will be a small city in the year 2000 and a medium-sized city in the year 2010[49].

Figure 5.5 shows the distribution of development zones, investment zones and industrial zones in Fuqing. It is not hard to imagine that a dramatic rural-urban landscape transformation has been going on in those areas. As can be seen in Table 5.8 they cover a total area of 94 km^2 (planned area), which is much larger than the current built-up area of Fuzhou. Although Jinjiang also has these kinds of development zones, the biggest of them has only a total area of 2.5 km^2; in fact in Quanzhou Municipality, which administers eight counties, city districts, and municipalities at county level including Jinjiang, the total area of such zones was only 29.5 km^2 by June 1995 (data provided by the Institute of Geography, Fujian Normal University during fieldwork, September 1996). Obviously large-scale land development is one of the most distinctive characteristics in the rural-urban transformation in Fuqing.

Thirdly, foreign investment certainly also promoted rural-urban transformation in the employment structure, especially in the development, investment and industrial zones. In Honglu town, where Rongqiao Development Zone is located, the proportion of the rural labor force engaged in agricultural activities declined from 60.5 percent in 1990 to 41.3 percent in 1994. Foreign-funded enterprises also attracted many temporary residents. It was estimated that there were 50,000 temporary residents distributed in the development, investment and industrial zones and Fuqing City in 1994 (Fujian Provincial Urban and Rural Planning and Design Institute 1995:37).

---

[49] In the recent Asian financial crisis and Indonesian political and social turmoil, the Salim Group suffered a major blow (*Global News Digest* 1998). This may have some effect on the development of Fuqing, especially Yuanhong Investment Zone. Nevertheless, how serious this effect will be remains to be seen. Since Liem Sioe Liong took the lead in investing in Fuqing, the sources of foreign investment here have been gradually diversified. This may cancel some of the effect caused by the difficulties of the Salim Group. In the first three months of 1998, foreign investment through newly signed contract and actualized foreign investment in Fuqing still amounted to US$ 51.9 million and US$ 35.1 million respectively (*Fujian Today* 1998).

But compared with the landscape transformation, and the changes in the employment structure in other areas of Fujian Province with well developed TVEs, changes in the employment structure in Fuqing do not seem to be very impressive. In those areas not covered by the development, investment and industrial zones, structural change in employment has not been very fast. While in 1990 63.9 percent of the total rural labor force in Fuqing was engaged in the agricultural sector, this percentage still stood at 60.7 in 1994, only 3.2 percentage points lower. By the end of 1994, 49.7 percent of the economically active population in Fuqing was still engaged in agricultural activities (calculated according to Statistical Bureau of Fuqing Municipality 1991:12-5; 1995:26-9; Fujian Provincial Urban and Rural Planning and Design Institute 1995:66).

Figure 5.5 A sketch map of development, investment and industrial zones in Fuqing

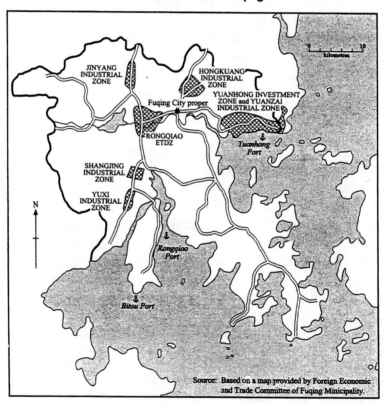

Interviews with local officials, managers of foreign-funded enterprises, and local residents in Fuqing suggest that foreign investment in the development, investment and industrial zones has not been very effective in providing non-agricultural employment opportunities for the local and nearby residents. As mentioned earlier, foreign-funded enterprises have the autonomy to recruit their own employees, for whom relatively high educational attainment and labor skills are required. Besides, foreign-funded enterprises usually employ only young people (not older than 35 years). These preconditions preclude many local residents in Fuqing from being employed by foreign-funded enterprises[50]. Moreover, when farmers' land is taken for use by the foreign-funded enterprises, neither the government nor the investor is responsible for providing jobs for those farmers. They can get some lump-sum compensation for the loss of land, and some of them have used this capital to run businesses, mainly concentrated in the tertiary sector, such as transport for foreign-funded enterprises, restaurants, shops and recreational places catering for employees in the development, investment and industrial zones. In Honglu town, most farmers have transferred to the non-agricultural sectors in this way. But not all the local residents have the ability to run a business, and some of them are living on the limited compensation fees, and worrying about their future. It seems that apart from foreign investment, Fuqing still needs to find a way to absorb its own surplus agricultural labor force.

5.4.3 SUMMARY

This section mainly looked at the role of foreign investment in Fujian's urbanization. Foreign investment appears to be another factor leading to the rural-urban transformation and the decentralized patterns of urbanization in Fujian. Closer examination of the case in Fuqing reveals more about the changes brought by foreign investment. It seems that the development driven mainly by foreign investment is more capital-intensive, technically more advanced, and concentrated in the development, investment and industrial zones. Foreign investment effectively transformed the economic structure and much of the rural area in physical terms in a very short time, and also brought about changes in the employment structure. Nevertheless, compared with the development model of TVEs represented by Jinjiang, foreign investment itself is not as effective in providing employment opportunities as TVEs. But there is no doubt that foreign in-

---

[50] In the late 1980s when the development zone first came into existence in Fuqing, local residents enjoyed the privilege of having priority for employment by the foreign-funded enterprises using their land. But this priority was soon abolished.

vestment is a counterbalancing force to the development in the major cities, and the physical transformation of the rural area may be the prelude for large scale transformation of the employment structure.

5.5 CONCLUSIONS

This chapter examined three major factors contributing to the development of urbanization in China and its patterns by using three cases in Fujian Province. These three factors are related to three different types of urbanization: urbanization from above, that is, sponsored by the State; urbanization from below, that is, driven by local economic activities; and urbanization from outside, that is, driven by foreign investment. The relative importance of these three factors and of the corresponding types of urbanization related to them has greatly changed since 1978. As pointed out in Chapter 3, the urbanization process before 1978 was dominated by the first type, government-sponsored urbanization. The analysis in the first part of this chapter reveals that the State mainly took a restrictive approach to this kind of urbanization by using effectively the stringent household registration system, together with controls over urban employment, grain supply, and urban housing. But since 1978 this mechanism for regulating urbanization has greatly changed. The State is still using the household registration system to control State-sponsored urbanization, and check the growth of large cities. The national urban strategy was enacted to encourage the growth of small and medium-sized urban places and prevent large cities from over-expansion. While these measures still seem to work in a way, economic reform has undermined the State control over urban employment, grain supply, and urban housing, making it possible for farmers to enter freely into cities. It can be seen in the case of Fuzhou that a series of measures has been taken to adapt to this new situation, but they provide no guarantee that farmers will be excluded from the major cities. Examining the cases of Jinjiang and Fuqing reveals that it is the *in situ* transformation of the rural areas, in the form of urbanization from below and urbanization from outside, that keeps many farmers in their hometowns and even attracts many migrants from other regions, and thus is more important for achieving the government's goal of balanced urbanization.

Although the cases of Jinjiang and Fuqing seem to be quite different in their ways of transforming rural areas into urban ones, they are actually mutually complementary. In fact, there is a tendency to convergence of the two models.

The model of Jinjiang started from dispersedly distributed joint-household enterprises engaged in some preliminary production. It particularly fits the situation where initial capital and labor skills are lacking in the rural areas, and is very effective in the transformation of rural employment structures. However, the physical transformation of the landscape lags behind. On the contrary, in Fuqing we have seen a tremendous physical transformation of the previous rural landscape, driven by intensive foreign capital inflows into the various zones, leading to the emergence of large-scale areas with urban-like landscape. But this type of development is not as effective as the one in Jinjiang in creating non-agricultural employment opportunities. Interestingly, leaders in both Jinjiang and Fuqing have realized the shortcomings of their development models, and what they propose to do in the future in each case is to try to draw on the strength of the other model. In Jinjiang, TVEs are encouraged to move to the industrial zones, which will lead to more physical transformation of the rural areas. In Fuqing, the municipal government has begun to pay increasingly more attention to TVE development. The government has also realized that while it is important to introduce and develop big foreign-funded enterprises, more attention should be paid to the introduction and development of medium and small projects. A metaphor in Fuqing regards big foreign-funded enterprises as the moons and the suns, and the small TVEs as the stars. Fuqing's leader proposed that while we had had already the big moons and suns, we should also have the sky full of stars (speech of an official of Fuqing Municipal Government collected during fieldwork, October 1996). If this is achieved, it will certainly help to create more non-agricultural employment. The strong industrial bases built up in recent years through foreign capital inflow should be conducive to this effort. Thus Fuqing and Jinjiang may have chosen different ways of rural-urban transformation, but ultimately they will lead to the same final result of rural-urban transition.

An indirect assessment of the three factors influencing Fujian's urbanization can be made as follows. As "the underlying explanation of urbanization has to do with changing employment opportunities as structural change takes place in the economy" (Jones 1991:10), the relative importance of the above three factors in creating non-agricultural employment can be regarded as major proxies of their effects on Fujian's urbanization. Table 5.9 provides some information in this regard. The share of employment created by the State and urban collective economic units declined noticeably during the period 1985-1995. On the other hand, employment opportunities created by TVEs and foreign funded enterprises greatly increased, accounting for 66.1 percent of the total in 1995. The average annual growth rates for the above three forms of employment show further that the employment opportunities provided by the State and urban collective sector almost ceased to grow, whereas extraordinarily high growth rates of employment opportunities were recorded in TVEs and foreign-funded enterprises, especially the latter. This analysis clearly shows that the State was not in the position of serving as the locomotive for urbanization in Fujian. The urbanization process has been mainly propelled by local and foreign forces. Given the spatial patterns and functions of TVEs and foreign investment in the rural-urban transformation, as analyzed in this chapter, it is not surprising that Fujian's urbanization has been characterized by a spontaneous and dispersed process.

Table 5.9 Three different kinds of employment and their relative importance in Fujian, 1985-1995[a]

	1985		1995		
	Number of employees	% of total	Number of employees	% of total	Average annual growth rate in between (%)
State and urban collective economic units	2,723,000	57.1	2,773,600	33.9	0.2
Foreign-funded enterprises	13,643	0.3	703,905	8.6	48.3
Township and village enterprises	2,036,363	42.7	4,709,956	57.5	8.7
Total	4,773,006	100	8,187,461	100	

[a] There may be some slight overlapping between the employment of foreign-funded enterprises and that of the State and urban collective units, and that of township and village enterprises.

Sources: Foreign Economic and Trade Commission 1994:74; Statistical Bureau of Fujian Province 1996:58, 186, 331.

CHAPTER 6

EXAMINING CHINA'S NEW URBANIZATION PATTERNS FROM AN INTERNATIONAL AND HISTORICAL PERSPECTIVE

So far China's new urbanization patterns have been analyzed within the context of its socio-economic changes, using Fujian as an example. As pointed out in Chapter 1, a deeper understanding of China's urbanization can be achieved if this analysis is placed in an international and historical context. This is particularly necessary in the assessment of the desirability and applicability of China's new urbanization patterns. This chapter will tackle this issue.

The analysis in this chapter will focus on the decentralized nature of China's urbanization, which, although strongly promoted by both the Government and many academics, also attracts much criticism. Efforts will be made to assess this dispute by drawing on urbanization experience in other parts of the world, and to reveal other contributing factors to this decentralized urbanization. This will also help to explain why the new urbanization and regional development policies reviewed in Chapter 5 were able to be successfully implemented.

6.1 THE ASSESSMENT OF CHINA'S URBANIZATION IN THE CONTEXT OF DEVELOPED COUNTRIES' EXPERIENCES

China's new urbanization patterns have to be examined in the context of developed countries' experiences because two major "rules" regarding the urbanization experience of developed countries have been accepted by some Chinese scholars. First, the industrialization of an agricultural society is, among other things, a process of the migration of rural people into cities to work in the secondary and tertiary sectors. As Liao (1995) states, this is a general rule for the industrialization and modernization of various countries in the world, and is confirmed by the history of the social and economic development of developed countries. Second, at the initial and middle stages of urbanization, the population growth of large cities is faster than that of medium-sized and small cities, and this rule is also confirmed by the experience of various countries in the world (Liao 1995; Wang 1995). Most criticism of China's recent urbanization patterns is based on the judgement that according to these two rules, the experience of China's rural-urban transformation is abnormal, because it has been dominated by the dispersed development of TVEs and small towns and cities.

When the experience of developed countries is examined, things do not seem to be so straightforward. The two rules mentioned above seem to oversimplify the process of industrialization and urbanization in developed countries, neglecting some important stages of development. In fact, some experiences of developed countries suggest that China's new patterns of rural-urban transformation, as demonstrated in Fujian's experiences, are the necessary transitional forms in the whole process of industrialization and urbanization. This can be seen from two aspects.

6.1.1 PROTO-INDUSTRIALIZATION IN DEVELOPED COUNTRIES' PAST, AND ITS IMPLICATIONS FOR THE ASSESSMENT OF TVES

The first problem of these two "rules" is their neglect of proto-industrialization, which was an important stage of development in developed countries. This is perhaps a common phenomenon in social science studies, because since the Industrial Revolution the main interest of social scientists has focused on factory industry, not paying much attention to a large number of traditional industries existing before the Industrial Revolution (Kriedte, Medick and Schlumbohm 1981:1; Chen and Han 1993:69). Nevertheless, in the process of social and economic transition from an agricultural to an industrial society, these small-scale, dispersed traditional industries played very important roles. This important stage of development was first named by Franklin Mendels "proto-industrialization".

Mendels defines proto-industrialization as the rapid growth of traditionally organized but market-oriented, principally rural industry (Mendels 1972:241). This kind of industry existed in many regions of Europe well before the beginning of machine industry. According to Kriedte, the first regions of relatively dense rural industry developed in England, the southern Low Countries, and southern Germany in the late Middle Ages, and at the end of the sixteenth and in the seventeenth centuries came the phase of proto-industrialization (Kriedte 1981:23). The small workshops of the rural industry created more value and employed more people than the centralized and mechanized production units in most European countries until well into the nineteenth century (Kriedte et al. 1981:1). In the process of proto-industrialization, "urbanization was less important than the increasing concentration of an industrial population in the countryside". In fact, "it was typical of the population development in proto-industrial regions that the growth of its urban population lagged behind or even stagnated, in comparison with its overall growth or the growth of proto-industrial villages" (Medick 1981:84).

Proto-industrialization arose from a set of socio-economic conditions. This is not the place to review all these conditions, but two of them are particularly worthy of mention. First, as pointed out by Medick, the dynamic of population development provided an essential impetus to proto-industrialization. Regions with strong concentration of rural industry usually had higher population growth than agrarian regions. This population growth assured a large labor-supply, which caused underemployment and frequently initiated the emergence of mono-industrially concentrated districts (Medick 1981:74-82). Mendels (1981) also found that rural industry resulted from the population pressure in eighteenth-century Flanders. Medick pointed out further that "long-distance migration played a minor role, although the in-migration from neighboring agrarian regions was not an unimportant factor in the growth of proto-industrial population" (Medick 1981:83). Second, among other factors, the demand for industrial products generated by foreign markets created much demand for industrial labor. "These prevented industrial population from reaching the limits to growth that existed in agrarian society in which the demand for artisanal labour depended on local and regional agrarian booms and crises" (Medick 1981:78).

It is important to note that the growth of proto-industrialization is regarded as a first phase which preceded and prepared for modern industrialization proper (Mendels 1972:241). The connections between the two phases are manifold. Proto-industrialization created an accumulation of capital, which was needed for the adoption of machine industry. A group of merchant-manufacturers, middlemen, and sometimes small artisans, with capital and entrepreneurial skills, emerged in this process and became the agents of industrialization. A broad stratum of skilled handicraft-workers was formed, providing a reserve of labor power for the next phase of industrialization. A network of local, regional, national, and international markets developed during the process of proto-industrialization, creating the current of demand which helped give rise to the new system of production. The putting-out system[51], which was popular in the period of proto-industrialization, brought advances in the organization of production, because under the putting-out system the production of petty producers could be more responsive to market demand. The development of proto-industrial regions also helped increase the efficiency and specification of agricultural production. In short, proto-industrialization laid the foundation for capitalist industrialization (Mendels 1972:244-6; Kriedte 1981:141-2).

When proto-industrialization is compared with the rural industrialization characterized by TVE development in Fujian described in the preceding chapters, it is not hard to find similarities between them. Both developments started in the form of small workshops of rural industry, and were market-oriented; population pressure was a major cause for both of them; migration played only a secondary role in the growth of the industrial population; and the results of their development, such as the accumulation of capital, the connection to the market, and the emergence of entrepreneurial classes and skills[52], are also similar. These results of development laid the foundation for the modern industrialization in developed countries' past, and paved the way for the transformation of family industry to factory industry in the industrial zones in the field site of this study. These similarities suggest that some aspects and stages of proto-industrialization have been repeating themselves in Fujian Province. If proto-industrialization can be regarded as a first stage of industrialization which preceded and prepared for modern industrialization proper, then there is no reason to see TVE development in Fujian as an abnormal process. Given the fact that China's industrialization between 1949 and 1978 was actually confined to the existing urban areas (Chen and Han 1993:1-3), it follows that the *in situ* transformation of China's rural areas is a necessary stage in the process of full transition from agricultural, rural to in-

---

[51] Putting-out system (*Verlagssystem* in German) is a system of production where the producer works only upon being commissioned by a merchant or trader. Often in the putting-out system part of the means of production (e.g. the raw materials) are owned by the merchant (*Verleger*) (Kriedte et al. 1981:xi).

[52] Some of the consequences of TVE development in Jinjiang can be seen in Chapter 5 (for example the capital accumulation and the emergence of the industrial zones). Later this chapter looks at the effect of TVE development on the market connections.

dustrial, urban society. This is not saying that there is no difference between proto-urbanization in European history and the *in situ* transformation of the rural areas in current China. Nor does it ignore the different paths of transition from proto-industrialization to modern industrialization proper in European history itself. The main point is that in the process of rural-urban transition, the role of a transitional form of dispersed rural industrialization and quasi-urbanization should be recognized, and not be regarded as "against the rules".

6.1.2 RELATIVE IMPORTANCE OF LARGE AND SMALL CITIES IN THE PROCESS OF URBANIZATION IN DEVELOPED COUNTRIES AND ITS IMPLICATIONS FOR CHINA'S URBANIZATION

The second oversimplified "rule" of urbanization in developed countries relates to the relative importance of large and small cities. It is asserted that in the early stage of industrialization and urbanization, large cities grew faster than small cities, and that this rule should not be violated in the current stage of urbanization in China (Cui et al. 1992:12-3; Liao 1995; Wang 1995). In fact, this kind of assertion on the relative importance of large and small cities in the industrialization period can be traced back to Adna Weber's pioneering analysis of urbanization published in 1899 (Weber 1968), which argues that modern urbanization is characterized by population concentration in large cities. But this proposition should be appreciated in perspective, especially when it is applied to the analysis of developing countries.

First of all, the population size of large cities in the industrialization period of developed countries was so different from that of large cities in the current developing countries that one should be very careful in inferring the development of developing countries' large cities directly from the past experience of developed countries. As pointed out in Chapter 1, in the industrialization period of developed countries, cities with populations of 100,000 or more were already referred to as large cities (Weber 1968; de Vries 1984), many of which would be classified only as small or medium-sized cities in today's developing countries. The large cities talked about now in China are those with populations of more than 500,000, which were rare 200 years ago. So we cannot infer that cities with populations of more than 500,000 in today's China should grow faster on the basis that past developed countries' cities with populations of 100,000 grew faster than smaller cities. The problems arising from the growth of today's large cities in developing countries are also very different from those in developed countries in the past: both the sheer population size of individual large cities and their un-precedented predominance in the urban system in developing countries are more responsible for these problems[53]. Secondly, if we accept a population of 100,000 or more as the lower threshold of large cities in the industrialization period of developed countries, their relative growth rate with relation to other cities is much more complicated than the "rule" and Weber's proposition suggest. In fact, de Vries's study shows that the industrial age was inaugurated by an interval in which urban growth assumed a form that was the opposite of the conventional assumption that modern urbanization is characterized by population concentra-tion in large cities (de Vries 1984:260; also see Skeldon 1990:39). His estimation suggests that in the century of 1750-1850 - the century of the Industrial Revolu-tion - there was a period of "urban growth from below" (de Vries 1984:259) in which "the relative importance of smaller cities improves as the number of such cities grows for the first time since the middle ages", and "this is partly the result of the creation of new factory towns", but more importantly "is the impact of demographic and economic trends on the many hundreds of long-existing rudi-mentary urban settlements", elevating them to a level meeting the urban criterion (de Vries 1984:69-73)[54]. Since 1850 there had been an era when, according to Weber's pioneering work, "the large cities are growing more rapidly than the small cities and absorbing the bulk of the urban increase" (Weber 1968:446), but de Vries warns that the extent of this urban concentration should not be exagger-ated and that it was more a legacy of large-city development in the seventeenth century than a result of the Industrial Revolution (de Vries 1984:101-2). Moreo-ver, there is some conflicting evidence from Weber's own data showing that in this period of time, in some cases smaller cities grew faster than the large cities (Weber 1968:34-5; 48-50).

Thus even if we accept the proposition that large cities grew faster than smaller cities after 1850 in the history of European countries, we have also to recognize the fact that before 1850 there had been a period in which "urbaniza-tion takes the form of changing the functional character of hitherto non-urban or quasi-urban places" (de Vries 1984:264), leading to the emergence of many new

---

[53] For more discussion on this point see also Brockerhoff and Brennan 1998:77-82.

[54] According to Yan (cited in Zhu 1991:46-7), in the period of 1800-1900, in the total urban popu-lation of the world, the proportion of population in the cities with populations of less than 20,000 and of 20,000-100,000 increased from 20 percent to 32 percent and from 23 percent to 27 percent respectively, while the proportion of population in the cities with populations of more than 100,000 decreased from 57 percent to 41 percent.

small urban centers. This emergence, as a result of elevation of "the long-existing rudimentary urban settlements" in the residential hierarchy, shows further that this urbanization process was to a certain extent the continuation of the development of proto-industrialization, which created many quasi-urban settlements. Only after this did the process of consolidation and concentration get under way. Here we can see that urbanization in the developed countries took two mutually-related forms in the two sub-phases of industrialization: first, the city-creation mode, and then the urban-concentration mode (de Vries 1984:264). While we recognize "the urban concentration mode", which is perhaps more noticeable in the urbanization process, we should not neglect the city-creation mode. The definition of urbanization given by Hope Eldridge Tisdale illustrates this issue from another perspective. As she pointed out, "Urbanization is a process of population concentration. It proceeds in two ways: the multiplication of points of concentration and the increase in size of individual concentrations" (Tisdale 1942, cited in de Vries 1984:10). It seems that in the early stage of industrialization and urbanization in developed countries, the "multiplication of points of concentration" prevailed at first, then there was a period in which "the increase in size of individual concentrations" was more important.

The above analysis on the relative importance of large and small cities in the industrialization period of developed countries does not support the assertion that China's recent urbanization patterns violate the "rules" of urbanization based on the experience of developed countries. Rather, many characteristics of China's urbanization demonstrated in the experience of Fujian Province, such as the development of dispersed, labor-intensive rural industry, the emergence of a large number of small towns on the basis of TVE development, the trend of increasing importance of small urban places, and the sequence of their emergence, resemble the industrialization and urbanization process in European-American history. A corollary of this comparison is that at the early stage of urbanization, rural industrialization and the creation of new urban centers is a necessary process, and the much criticized TVE and small town development in China just serves this purpose. At least in this sense, China's new urbanization patterns have not been undesirable so far.

However, if one infers further the future development of China's urbanization from the experiences of developed countries, it would be reasonable to assume that after the periods of rural industrialization and city-creation, there will be a period of more concentrated urban development in China. Nevertheless, forecasting the timing, degree, and concrete form of this development may be difficult. In fact, as pointed out earlier, there are many differences between the urbanization experiences of developed countries and that of China so that it is difficult to make such kinds of prediction based only on the experience of developed countries. Taking the case of Fujian as an example, one of such differences is that while it took several hundred years for developed countries to complete the process of proto-industrialization and Industrial Revolution, it has taken only 20 years for Fujian Province to go through a similar process. This leads to the consequence that in the case of Fujian, the division of different developmental stages is not as clear-cut as it was in the developed countries' history. A major manifestation of this is that after only a very short period of growth of more traditional industry, the growth of factory industry and new urban centers began in Fujian. The growth of these two kinds of industry has been proceeding concurrently, contributing to a much more complicated spatial organization. How China will further complete the transition from the traditional rural industrialization to modern urban industrialization remains to be seen. We can draw some hints from the past experience of developed countries, but the final answer to this lies in the analysis of China's socio-economic development itself.

6.2 EXAMINING CHINA'S URBANIZATION IN THE CONTEXT OF DEVELOPING COUNTRIES

In the context of developing countries, China's new urbanization patterns are unusual. The analysis in the preceding chapters shows that in Fujian the dilemma of developing countries' urbanization mentioned in Chapter 1 has been largely avoided: as urbanization has been taking the form of *in situ* transformation of rural areas, the potentially rapid and highly concentrated urban population growth has been diverted into many urban and quasi-urban centers; because most rural-urban transformation has been happening in the densely populated rural areas, a large rural population has benefited from the widespread regional economic development, and this has helped to reduce rural-urban disparities[55]; as most local rural populations, and even a large proportion of migrants from other

---

[55] This can be confirmed by the fact that while the per capita annual income of urban residents was 2.5 times that of rural residents in Fujian Province in 1978, this difference was reduced to 2.1 times in 1995. In Jinjiang, the per capita annual income of farmers was 4,321 *Yuan*, almost equivalent to that of urban residents in Fujian Province (4,326 *Yuan*) (Statistical Bureau of Fujian Province

provinces have been absorbed in the new urban or quasi-urban centers, urban problems have at least not been intensified in the urbanization process; and most importantly, as shown in Chapter 2, Fujian has been experiencing its fastest economic growth since 1949, suggesting that these urbanization and regional development patterns are compatible with rapid economic development. These results seem quite desirable.

The tremendous socio-economic changes in China described in Chapter 5, especially those policies adopted by the Chinese Government since 1978, can explain to a certain degree Fujian's urbanization patterns. However, as described in Chapter 1, similar rural-urban transformation patterns, although much less developed in terms of both geographical area and degree of industrialization, also exist in some other developing countries. The role of policy changes in Fujian's *in situ* rural-urban transformation should be appreciated in this context. Efforts should be made to determine whether there are certain enabling factors which make feasible the implementation of policies favoring dispersed rural-urban transformation. Looking at Fujian's urbanization in the context of developing countries with similar experience will be helpful in this aspect.

It is noticeable that in almost all the cases of dispersed urbanization mentioned in Chapter 1, high population densities and improved transport and communication facilities are two common conditions. As shown in Chapter 5, both Jinjiang and Fuqing have very high population densities. Their transport and communication facilities, as will be examined later in this chapter for the case of Jinjiang, are also well-developed. Taiwan is widely regarded as a successful case of decentralized industrialization (Ho 1979; Jones 1983:26; Tsai 1987; Speare, Liu and Tsay 1988). It also has a very high population density, which had reached 559 persons per km^2 by 1989. Because most of Taiwan's population is distributed on the western coast of the island, the population density in this region is even higher. The transport system has received a great deal of attention since the beginning of this century and is well-developed, especially in densely populated western Taiwan. This is widely regarded as a major contributing factor to the decentralized development in the island (Ho 1979:94-5; Tsai 1987). McGee's concept of "settlement transition", which involves "the urbanization of the countryside without massive rural-urban migration", covers a wide range of

---

1996:135, 144). Please note that urban and rural distinction here is made according to household registration status (see also footnote of Chapter 5).

areas in Asia[56]. Although he restricts his conceptualization within the areas of "extended metropolis", the characteristics of those areas to which he refers, such as the development of village and small town industries, and the high shares of non-agricultural income and employment in the agglomerated villages which are not officially recognized as urban places, resemble very much what has been happening in Fujian. More importantly, high population densities and the advance in transport and communication technology play crucial roles in the settlement transition in these areas (Ginsburg 1991; McGee 1991). Similar assessments regarding population density and transport facilities can also be found in Hackenberg's (1980) study.

Thus it seems that there is a need to examine what roles are played by high population density and improved transport and communication facilities in developing countries' rural-urban transformation. In the following two sections this will be attempted by examining the cases of Fujian Province, especially that of Jinjiang, compared with other regions of the world.

6.2.1 RE-EXAMINING THE EFFECTS OF HIGH POPULATION DENSITY ON URBANIZATION PATTERNS

Compared with developed countries in the past, rapid population growth is the most distinctive condition under which developing countries have been urbanizing. This difference is magnified by the fact that developing countries have little opportunity to export people to the new world, as countries such as Ireland, Germany, and Italy did over the nineteenth century (Beier 1976:4; Todaro 1981:12)[57]. This unprecedented population growth is commonly regarded as leading to faster population increase within developing countries' cities and

---

[56] This includes Japan, South Korea, Nanjing-Shanghai-Hangzhou region, Central Plains of Thailand, the Taipei-Kaohsiung corridor, the Calcutta region, Jabotabek in Java, the Jogjakarta region in Java, Kerala in South India, Bangladesh, and the Sichuan basin in China (McGee 1991).

[57] The effect of long-lasting international migration in European history should not be underestimated. It absorbed a large proportion of population increase. In fact, as Bähr (1983, cited in Zhu 1991:48) argued, in the period of industrialization in Germany, international emigration was the main way of reducing population pressure until 1870. He added that several decades of population migration overseas played an important role in Germany's development into the largest industrialized country in the Europe-Asia continent because it liberated German's economy from the population which it could not employ and which could have hindered social change and industrial development.

larger population movement to existing cities (Beier 1976:4), presenting an overwhelming challenge to developing countries.

While this is true if we look at the prevailing situation in the developing world as a whole, the cases of dispersed urbanization mentioned above suggest that there could be another effect of the unprecedented population growth on urbanization patterns in the developing world. To reveal this effect, it will be helpful to return to Tisdale's definition of urbanization. As mentioned before, urbanization can be achieved by either "the multiplication of points of population concentration" or "the increase in size of individual population concentrations" (Tisdale 1942, cited in de Vries 1984:10). If one looks only at the increase in size of individual population concentrations, it follows that high population growth will inevitably lead to the expansion of existing cities and highly concentrated urban population. Nevertheless, it should not be neglected that a high population growth rate also affects "the multiplication of points of population concentrations". While a significantly higher population growth rate can lead to much faster expansion of existing cities in developing countries, it can also greatly facilitate the creation of new urban-like settlements in rural areas, reducing the proportion of urban population living in the existing cities.

The increase in population density of rural areas plays a key role in the creation of new urban-like settlements. Corresponding to the unprecedented population growth within generally fixed territorial boundaries, the population densities in many rural areas of the developing world are also unprecedentedly high. The comparison between Fujian Province and some European countries in the past can illustrate this point. By the 1990 population census, the population density of Fujian Province, which has a total area of 121,400 thousand km^2, had reached as high as 248 persons per km^2. The 27 coastal counties and municipalities at the county level[58] have a total area of 29,266 km^2, similar to the area of Belgium (29,456 km^2) or Holland (32,538 km^2) (Weber 1968:182), and the average population density of this area is as high as 595 persons per km^2. Such high population densities are not easy to find in the history of developed countries for a geographical unit with a similar land area. According to Weber's data on the population densities of some currently developed countries (or regions) at the end of the last century (Table 6.1), Saxony had the highest population density, followed by Belgium. But this population density is lower than the 1990 population density of

---

[58] The scope of the coastal area mentioned in Chapter 2 is based on the administrative boundary of prefectures and prefecture-level municipalities and therefore includes some non-coastal counties and municipalities.

Fujian as a whole, and less than half of the population density of the coastal area of Fujian Province[59].

Table 6.1 Population density of Fujian in the 1990 census compared to those of developed countries at the end of the 19th century (persons per km^2)

Saxony	234
Belgium	206
England and Wales	192
Netherlands	139
Italy	107
Japan	107
Germany	92
France	73
United States	8
Fujian Province	248
Coastal area of Fujian Province	595

Source: Weber 1968:147; Zhu 1994b:188.

The high population density in the rural areas leads to the emergence of rural settlements which have the population size and density of an urban or semi-urban place. In Fujian Province, especially in the case study sites of this study, rural settlements with a population of 2,000 are not unusual. In Jinjiang and Fuqing, the average population sizes of villages in 1995 arc 2,345 and 2,310 persons respectively. They are far above the criterion of 2,000 persons for the designation of town status in China, and close to the criteria of population size for qualifying as an urban place in many countries in the world both at present and in the past, including Germany and France (Weber 1968:14-5; United Nations 1995:33-50)[60].

---

[59] Even today the population densities in many developed countries are still lower than that of Fujian. For example, the population densities of Germany, Italy and France were 222, 189, and 103 in 1990 respectively (Heilig 1997:151). See also the relevant discussion about the roles of TVEs in Fujian's urbanization in Chapter 3.

[60] de Vries (1984:22) holds that a serviceable definition of urban population in early modern Europe is the inhabitants of densely housed settlements of at least 2,000 or 3,000 population.

The agglomeration degree of these villages' populations can be shown by the following comparisons: In Fuqing, the average land area of villages is 5.4 km^2; in Jinjiang, it is only 1.7 km^2. As can be seen in Table 6.2, these are much smaller than the average size of the basic urban unit in several currently developed countries or regions at the end of the nineteenth century. The rural population agglomeration in the coastal area of Fujian Province is so evident that many villages have encroached on each other's land and become joined, forming bigger incorporated villages (Chen and Huang 1991:43). Thus, although many settlements in Fuqing and Jinjiang are still regarded as rural or quasi-urban, they have populations as large as, and areas smaller than, some urban settlements in developed countries in the past. Such rural settlements with "demographic densities similar to urban areas" have also been identified by McGee (1991) in many parts of Asia, although they are located adjacent to urban cores. These densely populated settlements are the places where most of the *in situ* rural-urban transformation has been happening.

Table 6.2 Average size of basic urban unit for selected countries and regions, the end of the 19th century

Country/region and unit	Average size of area (km^2)
Massachusetts, Town or City	61.4
Spain, *Ayuntamiento*	54.0
Netherlands, *Gemeënte*	28.7
Hungary, *Gemeinde*	22.0
France, Commune	14.6
Switzerland, Commune	12.6
Belgium, Commune	11.4
Austria, *Gemeinde*	10.6
Germany, *Gemeinde*	7.0
Prussia, *Gemeinde*	6.3
Fuqing's villages (1995)	5.4
Jinjiang's villages (1995)	1.7

Source: Weber 1968:142-3; Cao et al. 1994:87;
Statistical Bureau of Jinjiang Municipality 1995:24;
Statistical Bureau of Fujian Province 1996:399.

The above analysis suggests that compared with developed countries in the past, densely populated, agglomerated rural settlements are much more likely to emerge in many rural areas of developing countries on a widespread basis just as the consequence of local population growth. If there is no industrialization in the rural areas, these rural settlements will remain rural in their functions, and many of their residents will leave their homes for the existing cities, causing highly concentrated urbanization patterns commonly seen in the developing world today. However, if policies favoring dispersed patterns of industrialization are adopted and consequently the economic and employment structures are changed, these rural settlements will more readily become urban or urban-like centers. Migration will help, but is not necessary for this process. Unlike in the conventional patterns of urbanization, structural changes in the economy and employment do not serve so much to attract migrants to increase these settlements' population size and densities, as to transform their functions. The rural-urban transformation of these settlements creates more "points of population concentration", diverts much urban population growth into new small urban centers, and reduces the degree of urban concentration. Therefore in the developing world, when certain suitable policies are adopted in the rural areas with very high population densities, high population growth rate can have an effect on the spatial patterns of their urbanization opposite to what is conventionally imagined.

6.2.2 THE ROLES OF IMPROVED TRANSPORT AND COMMUNICATION FACILITIES IN DEVELOPING COUNTRIES' URBANIZATION PROCESS

Widespread, better transport and communication facilities in today's developing countries are further factors distinguishing the urbanization in developing countries from that of developed countries in the past. They have the effects of stimulating rural-urban migration (McGee 1971:54; Beier 1976:4, 10; Todaro 1981:42-3), because they facilitate the accessibility of both cities and information about urban amenities and opportunities. However, more and more observers have noticed that they have even stronger decentralizing than centralizing effects on the urbanization process in the developing world today. In the period of industrialization in developed countries, and even in the middle of the twentieth century when many cities evolved in developing countries, widespread motor transport was still not available, and dense settlement near the center was required so that workers could walk to work and goods could flow easily between manufacturers, wholesalers and retailers, causing huge concentrations of persons in small areas (Hackenberg 1980:404; Speare et al. 1988:193). But the transport revolution later on, especially the increased availability of relatively cheap transport such as two-stroke motorcycles, buses and trucks, greatly facilitates the circulation of commodities and people. This not only makes the concentration of population in large cities unnecessary, but more importantly, extends the scope of urbanization deep into the countryside (Jones 1983:25; Brookfield et al. 1991:1). The decentralizing process takes two forms: on the one hand, the improvement in transport gives rural laborers the option of commuting to urban jobs without moving permanently to existing urban areas; on the other hand, it increases the accessibility of rural areas to external resources and markets, making it more feasible for non-agricultural activities to be located in the rural areas (Jones 1991:12). While there are a number of studies on the first decentralizing form of transport and communication[61], empirical research on the second decentralizing form is still rare. Evidence from Fujian Province shows that the second kind of decentralization plays an important role in *in situ* rural-urban transformation, and can provide more insight into the effects of transport and communication on developing countries' urbanization.

The case of Jinjiang can be used to illustrate how transport and communication facilities, together with the unique market system corresponding to these facilities, make possible *in situ* rural-urban transformation. First, although Jinjiang is geographically not close to large cities, its business links with them are not necessarily weak. These links are not limited to Fujian; they extend far away to major business centers in China, even in the world. This is made possible by several factors. Highways seem to be particularly important in connecting Jinjiang with other places: several important highways, including the Fuzhou-Xiamen expressway, go through Jinjiang, connecting it to the two major cities. Regular bus service and lorry transport connect Jinjiang not only to the major cities in Fujian, but also to other major Chinese cities such as Guangzhou, Shenzhen, Shanghai, and Wenzhou, with which Jinjiang has major business relations. In Shishi alone, which separated from Jinjiang in 1988, there are 1,100 bus services every day, transporting 30,000 to 40,000 persons to the neighboring towns as well as cities in other provinces (data collected during fieldwork, September 1996). Modern communication technology is also important. Jinjiang was the second county in China to introduce the program-controlled telephone exchange system. The volume of its telephone service is at the top of all counties and cities at the county level in Fujian Province, with the IDD telephone services

---

[61] Hugo's (1980) research on rural-urban commuting and circular migration in West Java gives good examples of this aspect.

reaching every part of the world. Fax is widely used in business activities. Among counties and cities at the county level, Jinjiang's volume of communication ranks first in Fujian and fourth in China. This obviates the need for much face-to-face contact, which is an important reason for many businesses to be located in large cities (Button 1976:22; Renaud 1981:85-6). Moreover, it greatly broadens the information sources with regard to both the supply of raw materials and the sales of products. In fact, convenient communication is one of the major factors attracting investors, especially those from abroad, to do business here (Liu et al. 1992:185).

Secondly, the shortcomings of dispersed internal distribution of enterprises are also compensated by a well-developed road network inside the territory, and flexible, practical means of transport run mainly by private enterprises. By the end of 1992, basically every village in Jinjiang was connected to the road network. The total length of road was 599.6 km, and the road density was 0.9 km per km^2, the highest in China[62]. As a result of local economic development since 1978, local governments have been able to raise their own funds for the development of the road network. For example, among the total investment of 2.25 million *Yuan* in village-township road construction in 1986, 74 percent was from the relevant townships and towns, with the rest coming from the transport department of higher-level government (Liu et al. 1992:177). Correspondingly the number of motor vehicles increased dramatically. In 1978 there were only 706 motor vehicles in Jinjiang. Before Shishi was separated in 1988, this number had increased to 25,688, 36 times the former figure. By 1992, in the territory of Jinjiang (excluding Shishi) alone, there were 63,220 motor vehicles, indicating another big increase. The characteristics of the composition of the vehicles and their ownership are noteworthy. Among 63,220 motor vehicles, 72 percent were motor cycles. They are not only the major means of personal transport, but also an important way of cargo transport, as many industries in Jinjiang involve only light raw materials and products. Most of these vehicles were privately owned and run. Almost all motorcycles and 63.2 percent of 2,538 buses and trucks running for business in 1992 were run privately (Xu 1996:192; 242). Personal transport is so convenient that one can go to any of the main town centers without waiting for more than fifteen minutes (personal observations in the field site, September 1996). In a way Jinjiang Municipality operates like a polycentric ur-

---

[62] Roads in Shishi Municipality are not included. It is noteworthy that this road density is higher than that of most cities and prefectures in Taiwan in 1983 (see Tsai 1987:220).

ban area connected by multiple means of transport. The distance between those centers, which can cause diseconomies according to the conventional wisdom, seems to be overcome by the transport system to some extent. As Jinjiang is small in area, and the means and organization of transport are of "informal" nature, this transport system does not seem to increase the cost of production much.

Thirdly, a unique aspect of Jinjiang's development is its market system. On the one hand, Jinjiang has built a sales network, which involves 6,000 sales places and more than 10,000 sales personnel all over China (data from an unpublished document of Jinjiang municipal government, 1996). These sales personnel work not only for particular industries or enterprises, but also for all kinds of businesses. They are responsible not only for promoting sales, but also for purchasing supplies, which is as important as sales of the products because most of the raw materials used in Jinjiang cannot be provided locally. They also provide business information and consultation for the development of enterprises. In fact, they constitute a unique industry in Jinjiang, which effectively connects Jinjiang's production to the markets and resources all over China. This connection is further extended to the world by foreign investors. On the other hand, Jinjiang is not only a base for industrial production, but also an important market for some products, especially for those in which Jinjiang specializes. For example, there is a specialized shoe and hat market in Chendai town, a construction materials market in Cizao town, and a clothes market in Shishi City. As mentioned in Chapter 5, each place is also famous for the production of the commodities in which its market specializes. These markets attract both tourists and travelling traders from all over China to buy the local products. It is estimated that in Shishi alone, there are tens of thousands of travelling traders doing business, and more than 6,000 local traders provide services for them (data collected in the field site, September 1996). Thus, although Jinjiang itself was not an important market place, and not even close to markets when the development began, it successfully built up a close link to the markets in its unique way, and eventually established its own local markets. This is another way for Jinjiang to overcome the geographical distance to large cities, and convenient transport and communication services greatly facilitated this development.

6.3 THE EFFECTS OF THE "CHINESENESS FACTOR" ON CHINA'S RURAL-URBAN TRANSFORMATION FROM AN INTERNATIONAL AND HISTORICAL PERSPECTIVE

So far China's new urbanization patterns have been examined in the context of either developed or developing countries. In addition to this, the effects of the "Chineseness factor" (Wong 1997:6) should also be added to this examination in such a broad context. This factor relates to the roles of Chinese overseas, Hong Kongers, Taiwanese and Chinese culture in China's rural-urban transformation. Although it is unique to China, it originated from a historical and international background as a result of international migration, and is functioning in an international context as there are ethnic Chinese all over the world. Its effects on China's rural-urban transformation can be examined in the following two aspects by using Fujian as an example.

6.3.1 THE CONNECTIONS OF CHINESE OVERSEAS[63] TO THEIR ANCESTRAL REGIONS AND THE SPATIAL PATTERNS OF THEIR INVESTMENT

As can be seen in Chapter 5, foreign investment is an important factor influencing Fujian's urbanization patterns. Such foreign investment has been actually dominated by the capital of Chinese overseas. The connections of these Chinese overseas to their ancestral regions, and the distinctive mode of their business organization and operation deeply influenced by their cultural background, are important factors contributing to the decentralized characteristics of rural-urban transformation in Fujian.

Table 6.3 provides data on the main sources of foreign investment for Fujian Province, Jinjiang Municipality, and Fuqing Municipality. Caution should be exercised in interpreting this table, because there are distortions in the real distribution of the sources of foreign capital, with Hong Kong's contribution overstated and those for other countries and regions, especially Taiwan and Southeast Asia, considerably understated. The reason for this is that many Chinese overseas and Taiwanese tend to route their China investments through Hong Kong and to form a company there for that purpose. This is especially the case for Taiwanese

---

[63] For the sake of simplicity, in this chapter the term "Chinese overseas" includes Chinese in Taiwan and Hong Kong unless otherwise indicated.

investment because there are government restrictions on direct investment in Mainland China, although the restrictions have been relaxed recently[64] (Tracy 1996). Nevertheless, despite all these problems, the fact that investments from Hong Kong and Taiwan account for 57.2 percent and 27.9 percent of the total investment respectively can already confirm the dominance of the capital of Chinese overseas in the foreign investment in Fujian Province.

Table 6.3 Major sources of actualized foreign investment in Fujian, Jinjiang and Fuqing

Fujian Province (1979-1996)			Jinjiang Municipality (1979-1995)			Fuqing Municipality (1979-1994)		
Sources of foreign investment	Amount (US$ 000s)	% of total	Sources of foreign investment	Amount (US$ 000s)	% of total	Sources of foreign invest-ment	Amount[a] (US$ 000s)	% of total
Hong Kong	9,241,350	57.2	Hong Kong	933,270	81.9	Hong Kong	306,530	57.5
Taiwan	4,500,290	27.9	Taiwan	69,870	6.1	Indonesia	70,710	13.3
Singapore	565,960	3.5	Philippines	62,360	5.5	UK	52,670	9.9
USA	342,900	2.1	Macau	50,910	4.5	USA	45,780	8.6
Japan	300,680	1.9	Singapore	8,060	0.7	Taiwan	25,270	4.7
Others	1,194,700	7.4	Others	15,090	1.3	Others	32,480	6.1
Total	16,145,880	100.0	Total	1,139,560	100.0	Total	533,440	100.0

[a] Including only investment for those enterprises that had gone into operation.
Sources: Foreign Economic and Trade Commission of Fujian Province 1998; Statistical Bureau of Fuqing Municipality 1995:178-9; Yan 1996:366.

In addition to the general feature of the dominance of Chinese overseas capital in foreign investment in Fujian, Table 6.3 suggests that at the regional level, the sources of foreign investment in each region are closely related to the distribution of Chinese overseas originating from it. This can be seen by examining the sources of foreign investment in Jinjiang and Fuqing. According to the statistics provided by Fuqing's Overseas Chinese Affairs Department, there were 268,365 Chinese overseas (excluding those in Hong Kong and Taiwan) who were from Fuqing or of Fuqing origin at the beginning of the 1980s, and 72.6 percent of them were living in Indonesia (Cao et al. 1994:943). As can be seen in Chapter 5, these Indonesian Chinese have been making a major contribution to the devel-

---

[64] For more detailed information on this issue see Tracy (1996). It is estimated that the reported level of Taiwanese investment in Mainland China may be as little as one quarter to a third of the actual total (East Asia Analytical Unit 1995:108).

opment of their ancestral region since the late 1980s. Although it is not clear how much of their investment came through Hong Kong and was included in the investment from Hong Kong, it is still identifiable that investment from Indonesia accounted for 13.3 percent of the total, ranking as the second largest source of foreign investment.

The sources of foreign investment in Jinjiang are also closely related to the distribution of Chinese overseas originating from it. According to 1987 statistics, there were 944,500 Chinese overseas (excluding those in Hong Kong and Taiwan) from Jinjiang or of Jinjiang origin, and 68.8 percent of them were living in the Philippines (Wu 1994:35). Obviously this contributes to the fact that the Philippines is the third largest source of foreign investment in Jinjiang, ranking only behind Hong Kong and Taiwan. As with Fuqing, the figure for investment from Hong Kong is overstated, which may result from the fact that many foreign investments were made through Hong Kong. But the dominance of Hong Kong in the foreign investment in Jinjiang is associated with Hong Kong being another major destination of out-migration from Jinjiang. According to the same statistics mentioned above, there were 298,500 persons from Jinjiang or of Jinjiang origin in Hong Kong and Macau (about 20,000 in Macau), constituting 6 percent of Hong Kong's total population. In the periods 1953-1965 and 1976-1986 alone, 60,234 migrants were officially approved to leave Jinjiang for Hong Kong and Macau[65] (Wu 1994:35; 229-33). Interviews in the field confirmed that these migrants are important sources of investment later on. According to the officials responsible for foreign investment, Hong Kongers originating from Jinjiang invested more than Filipino Chinese originating from Jinjiang, because the former left their hometown much later than the latter, and have more connections with their hometown (personal communication, Department of Foreign Economy and Trade, Jinjiang Municipality, September 1996). The strong presence of Taiwanese investment in Jinjiang can also be explained by the fact that there were one million Taiwanese with Jinjiang origin (Chen and Zhuang 1994:1224).

All this suggests that Chinese overseas tend to choose their ancestral regions as the destination of their investment. The reason for this can be partly explained by their willingness to contribute to the development of their ancestral homes, but there is another important Chinese business characteristic leading to this

---

[65] Owing to the Cultural Revolution there were no statistics on migration to Hong Kong during this period. Nevertheless, there was much illegal migration from Jinjiang to Hong Kong at this time. This was also the case for the periods when there were official statistics. If these illegal migrants are included, the figure will be even higher.

situation, which has more profound effects on rural-urban transformation in Fujian.

This characteristic involves the construction of personalized business networks based on friendship and trust. It is seen as one of the major factors explaining the ethnic Chinese business success (East Asia Analytical Unit 1995:2, 123-4; Tracy 1996:8). These networks originated from the formation of mutual help societies in the settlements of early Chinese migrants. Because most ethnic Chinese came to the new settlement through chain migration, kinship (clan), place of origin, dialect or sub-dialect, or the combination of these, were important bases for these mutual help societies, which helped new arrivals to settle and lent money to members for specific purposes (East Asia Analytical Unit 1995:2). On the basis of this, the ethnic Chinese created personal connections, business associations and financial and distribution networks (Wong 1997), which enable business opportunities to be quickly and efficiently exploited in an environment of mutual trust and benefit. The particular importance of dialects is central in the operation of ethnic Chinese business networks, and often partly explains who does business with whom and what is traded (East Asia Analytical Unit 1995:19). This is not surprising, as speaking the same dialect not only means the convenience of mutual communication[66], but also suggests a common place of origin or even blood relationships.

Understandably, this culturally-underpinned business practice has been inevitably extended to Mainland China since China opened to the outside world. This is because on the one hand, Chinese overseas investors tend to employ their old practices in their new business in Mainland China; on the other hand, the ethnic, historical and cultural links make this very easy. Moreover, in Mainland China where market mechanisms and institutional frameworks are not well developed, building connections and dealing with local government are vital for investors, and this mode of operation in China closely resembles the normal business practices of Chinese overseas (East Asia Analytical Unit 1995:195; Tracy 1996:8). Thus it has been found that the business expansion of Chinese overseas into China frequently uses old family and dialect ties and newly forged political connections (East Asia Analytical Unit 1995:176), and business networks are also seen as an essential part of the Chinese overseas success in China, as in other parts of the world (Tracy 1996:8). The Chair of the Hong Kong Trade

---

[66] In China, especially in its southern part, many dialects are mutually unintelligible. For example the dialect spoken in northern Fujian is not intelligible in southern Fujijan.

Development Council also pointed out that "because of ethnic, historical and cultural links there is already an established network of highly effective business connections among Chinese throughout greater China", and this is the "natural advantage" enjoyed by Hong Kong and Taiwan (*China Business Review*, May/June 1992:39; cited in Lever-Tracy and Tracy 1993:21). As China is so big and there are many regional differences in dialects and cultural customs, investing in the ancestral region is the best way for Chinese overseas to use their language, culture and paramount skill in making connections and networking (East Asia Analytical Unit 1995:6).

This at least partly explains the fact that Liem Sioe Liong's Salim Group invests in Liem's hometown Fuqing. Another such example in Fujian is Mochtar Riady of Indonesia, who invests in several projects in his birthplace Putian (East Asia Analytical Unit 1995:235-6). In Jinjiang, 95 percent of foreign investors are from Hong Kong. Most of them migrated to Hong Kong from Jinjiang only a few decades ago, accumulated some capital, and came back to their ancestral region to invest so that they could take full advantage of their connections and dialects (personal communication, Department of Foreign Economic and Ttrade, Jinjiang Municipal Government, September 1996). A survey conducted in Quanzhou, Jinjiang's direct neighbor, shows that 99 percent of the investors speak the local dialect, 88 percent of them are of local origin, and 86 percent of them have local kin (Tracy 1996 Table 18). Li (1996:218) identifies personal connection as still a major factor influencing the location decisions of Hong Kong's industrial enterprises intending to invest in Mainland China. As most Chinese overseas with Fujian origin came from small places, investing in their home region means investing in small cities and rural places, thus facilitating the decentralized urbanization patterns. Because domestic reform is at its strongest in smaller cities and rural areas in China, these investors can further benefit from avoiding much bureaucracy, hard bargains, and the inflexibility and potential risk involved with cash-strapped State sectors (Tracy 1996:7). This increases the decentralizing trend.

6.3.2 CHINESE CULTURE AND THE DOMINANCE OF SMALL AND MEDIUM-SIZED BUSINESS UNITS IN CHINESE COMMUNITIES

As can be seen in Chapter 5, individual and joint-household enterprises have been the dominant forms of TVEs in Jinjiang. This implies that most TVEs in Jinjiang are small business units. In 1994 the average number of employees for Jinjiang's TVEs was only 13 persons. The size of foreign funded enterprises in

Jinjiang is bigger, but their average number of employees was still only 60 persons, well within the range of small and medium sized business according to most criteria in Table 6.4.

Table 6.4 Selected size criteria for business categories

	Persons employed		
	Small	Medium	Large
Japan	<100	100-299	300+
Malaysia	<50	50-199	200+
Thailand	<50	50-199	200+
Indonesia	<20	20-99	100+
Hong Kong	<50	50-199	200+
Taiwan	<10	10-49	50+

Sources: Tsai 1987:221; Sit and Wong 1989:7.

An important point arises if the small size of business units in Jinjiang is examined in the context of Chinese communities throughout the world. Evidence from many studies shows that the dominance of small and medium-sized business units is not a unique characteristic of Jinjiang's enterprises, rather it is a common phenomenon in most Chinese communities no matter where they are. When Fukuyama discusses his ideas on community trust, he regards China as a low-trust society where small scale family firms tend to dominate the industrial landscape (Fukuyama 1996, cited in Sorensen 1997:4). In Taiwan, over two-thirds of manufacturing establishments were small (with fewer than 10 workers) in 1971 and in 1981, and about one-fourth were of medium size (with 10 to 49 workers) (Tsai 1987:221-3). Even in the recent period 1987-1989, the number of factories employing fewer than 30 persons still accounted for 82.0 to 85.2 percent of the total number of manufacturing factories in Taiwan (Li 1994:53). In Hong Kong, in 1985 99 percent of all manufacturing establishments, employing 72 percent of all workers and producing 65 percent of output, had fewer than 200 employees. Ninety-two percent, employing 41 percent of workers and producing a third of gross output, had under 50 employees (Sit and Wong 1989:29). In East Asia, the vast majority of ethnic Chinese businesses are small to medium-sized (East Asia Analytical Unit 1995:3). In the Philippines' Iloilo city for example, it was found that Chinese business was proportionately strongest in middle sized businesses with 10-50 employees (Omohundro 1981:49).

The importance of small and medium-sized business in Chinese communities is further intensified by the fact that the growth of the economy in Chinese communities is often achieved by multiplication rather than consolidation. In Jinjiang, there were only 1,141 TVEs in 1978, employing 51,961 persons. The two figures increased to 22,650 and 530,860 respectively in 1995 (including those in Shishi Municipality), with the number of enterprises increasing much faster than the number of employees, suggesting a growth process by multiplication. Similarly, Sit and Wong found that in the latter and maturing stages (post-1970), Hong Kong's industries were moving towards smaller firm size instead of growing in average firm size (Sit and Wong 1989:27). In their study of migrant Chinese businesses in Australia, Lever-Tracy and Tracy also found that many of these businesses are of small and medium size. But this is not because they failed to grow, rather it is because their mode of growth is by multiplication (Lever-Tracy and Tracy 1993:4).

Given the dominance of small and medium-sized businesses in Chinese communities all over the world, it seems that this is a culturally-related phenomenon. Familism, which lies at the heart of Confucianism and has much influence in all Chinese communities in the world, may partly explain this phenomenon. Under the influence of familism people tend to put the interest of the family (sometimes its extended form, i.e. clan) in the first place, and pay much attention to the reputation and social status of the family or clan. Close blood relationship is the most important criterion in establishing relationships among both individuals and social groups. As a reflection of this familistic behaviour, business is often run on the basis of family or clan, with most important management positions held by family or clan members. Most small and medium sized businesses in Hong Kong and Taiwan are organized in this way (Li 1994:55). In his study about a Chinese merchant family in Iloilo in the Philippines, Omohundro also found that there were concentric circles of decision-making and earning power in a Chinese family business, with the inner circle composed of members of the family of the owner who held the money, made the decisions, and took the responsibilities. Trusted managers or accountants, salesmen, and poor relatives belonged to the second circle, and the Filipino employees and the new Chinese recruits were in the third circle (Omohundro 1981:141-5). Wong also points out that the essence of Chinese economic organization is familism: "There is little doubt that family firms have been prevalent in Chinese commerce and industry operating on capitalistic principles", an assertion supported by studies on Chinese business in both mainland China in the late 1940s and a Chinese community in the Philippines in the early 1960s (Wong 1985:59-60). In my study in Jinjiang on fertility transition, it was found that one of the important motivations for the interviewed families to have a son was that most business and production were organized on the basis of families (Zhu Y. 1997:54).

If the family firm is a major form of business organization, it is generally believed that the growth of the enterprises will be hindered[67] (Omohundro 1981:142; Wong 1985:60-1;). There are two reasons for this. The first is the self-evident fact that "there is only a finite number of members in a family. Thus expansion would quickly exhaust the supply of managerial competency, and the firm cannot grow any further." The other is that the family enterprise is "intrinsically conservative in its financial policy because it is particularly wary of external interferences or takeover" (Wong 1985:60-1). This situation is intensified by the subdivision of the firms when managers and skilled workers from outside the family (if there are any) depart to set up their own firms. Furthermore, it is difficult for these firms to combine with each other even it is necessary. In my fieldwork in Jinjiang, many local officials mentioned that one of the factors hindering the consolidation of TVEs was that people prefer being owners or managers of their own firms to being employed by a larger enterprise, even as senior executives. Wong found a similar situation in his study of Hong Kong's cotton spinners (Wong 1988:143).

All this seems to suggest that the Chinese culture favors the development of small and medium sized enterprises. If the preceding analysis of the mechanism of smallness of Chinese business is true, it will have two major implications for the development of enterprises in China: first, as Chinese overseas are the main foreign investors, they are more likely to create small and medium sized enterprises than other foreign investors in China; secondly, local businesses are also more likely to emerge and develop in the form of small and medium enterprises. Compared with large enterprises, small enterprises are less likely to locate in

---

[67] Exceptions such as the Salim Group and as given by Wong (1985:61-2) can certainly be found, but they can only be considered as "exceptions which prove the rule" rather than as falsifying the generalization mentioned above. It should also be noted that as a result of the influence of familism, "usually ethnic Chinese family businesses expand by acquiring an ever-increasing number of companies rather than by expanding existing companies", so that "the overall business group may be large, but its individual component companies may be relatively small" (East Asia Analytical Unit 1995:153).

large cities (Fuchs and Pernia 1989:389-401)[68], thus will favor the development of decentralized urbanization. This culturally-related factor seems to contribute much to Fujian's pattern of rural-urban transformation examined earlier, especially in the case of Jinjiang. Even in the case of Fuqing where a large Chinese family business plays an important role, the average number of employees of the enterprises (176 persons for 1994, Statistical Bureau of Fuqing Municipality 1995:180) is still considerably smaller than that of Japanese firms in Indonesia, South Korea, Malaysia, Philippines, Taiwan and Thailand (409 persons for the period 1978-1980, Fuchs and Pernia 1989:389-401). More studies comparing Chinese businesses and the businesses of other ethnic groups are still needed to reach conclusive understanding in this aspect, but the above evidence and analysis provide at least a new perspective from which to examine China's new urbanization patterns.

6.4 CONCLUSIONS

This chapter has served two main purposes: first, to understand more deeply why the rural-urban transformation examined in the previous chapters has taken its current forms by looking at it in an international and historical context, and secondly, to assess the new urbanization patterns from an international and historical perspective.

The examination of Fujian's experience in the context of developed countries suggests that instead of violating any "rules", relatively dispersed rural industrialization and urban development are necessary steps in the whole process of rural-urban transformation. This process can be greatly promoted by government policies favoring decentralized rural-urban transformation, as has been shown in Chapter 5, and the implementation of these policies has been made possible by several factors. Quasi-urban population density brought about by high population growth ensures that a certain degree of agglomeration and scale economy can still be achieved without much geographical relocation of the population in the structural economic change, and creates an important basis for the emergence of new small urban centers in the previous rural areas. Widespread better transport and communication facilities are also important factors facilitating *in situ* rural-urban transformation. Changes in these aspects in developing countries make

---

[68] Fuchs and Pernia's study on Japanese overseas firms in Pacific Asia shows that firms in the metropolitan areas are substantially larger than those outside the metropolitan areas.

geographical proximity to large cities and internal agglomeration of enterprises less important than formerly. The "Chineseness factor" enhances the decentralized nature of rural-urban transformation in China, especially in areas like Fujian Province.

The assessment of Fujian's urbanization in the context of developed countries suggests that there is no reason to regard China's new urbanization patterns as abnormal. Furthermore, Fujian's urbanization patterns not only avoid many problems common to developing countries, but also are compatible with rapid economic development. At least in this sense, China's new urbanization patterns are not undesirable, although they are not without problems. The applicability of Fujian's experience to other parts of the developing world is a more complicated issue. On the one hand, as there have already been several similar cases in other parts of the developing world, and high population density and the advances in transport and communication are helpful rather than detrimental to decentralized urbanization patterns, it is reasonable to assume that similar patterns of rural-urban transformation can be adopted in more developing regions, if there are suitable conditions, especially suitable government policies. On the other hand, the function of the "Chineseness factor" makes its experience seem less transferable. Nevertheless, how unique this "Chineseness factor" is remains to be examined further. Interestingly, in a recent study Portes also spoke of immigrant networks not related to ethnic Chinese. He found that "in the Dominican Republic today there are hundreds of small and medium enterprises founded and operated by former immigrants to the United States" (Portes 1997:249-53), a phenomenon resembling the situation for Chinese overseas. Therefore, as more research is conducted in developing countries, it may be found that the "Chineseness factor" is not unique as is assumed, and that more developing countries can share a similar experience. In any case, Fujian's experience should not be taken as random or even abnormal, and can be taken by other developing regions as a reference point in their policy making.

CHAPTER 7

THEORETICAL AND POLICY IMPLICATIONS

After having revealed the characteristics of China's new urbanization patterns and examined them in the context of domestic socio-economic changes and from an international perspective, this chapter explores their theoretical and policy implications. The articulation of China's urbanization into existing theories, and their revision and expansion, require much more empirical and theoretical research and are far beyond the scope of a single study; but the following analysis may pinpoint some major inadequacies of the existing theories and suggest ways to improve them, and it may contribute to the solution of some practical issues in urban and regional development in developing countries, especially China.

7.1 THEORETICAL IMPLICATIONS

7.1.1 CONCEPTUAL REVISION OF URBANIZATION STUDIES AND ELABORATION OF RELEVANT THEORIES

As reviewed in Chapter 1, existing urbanization theories are deficient in explaining the flexible relationship between urbanization and structural economic change under changing social and economic conditions in developing countries. A major implication of this study is that the conventional conceptual framework in urbanization studies needs to be modified to tackle this problem. Its inadequacy is demonstrated below.

First, as can be seen in Chapter 1, most conventional theories of urbanization assume a rigid rural-urban dichotomy in the urbanization process. Under such a conceptual framework, rural areas are identified with the traditional, agricultural sector with low productivity, while urban areas are identified with the modern, non-agricultural sector with high productivity. Rural non-agricultural activities as an aspect of the overall development process have been much neglected (Ranis and Stewart 1993). As shown in the previous chapters, this kind of dualistic conceptual framework cannot cover the *in situ* rural-urban transformation, where non-agricultural activities are prevalent in the rural areas. Such activities are not unique to the study areas of this book; they have also been increasing universally in East and Southeast Asia[69] (Jones 1983).

Therefore "the rural-urban dichotomy, so clear-cut in the medieval fortress towns of Europe, begins to lose its meaning" (Jones 1983:25). It must be replaced by a rural-urban continuum in urbanization studies, if one wants to articulate new realities of rural-urban transformation in developing countries. Some efforts have already been made in this respect. McGee and Ginsburg's "extended metropolis" mentioned in Chapter 1 is an example of this. They argued that in certain areas of these regions agricultural and non-agricultural activities are juxtaposed adjacent to and between urban cores, and an intense mixture of land use has developed (Ginsburg 1991; McGee 1991). In China, some economists proposed a three-sector model to accommodate the fact that the rural industrial economy is so important that it can no longer be treated as subsidiary to either the rural-agricultural or the urban industrial sector (Chen and Hu 1994). These are certainly major steps in conceptualizing the quasi-urban nature of rural-urban transformation in many developing regions.

Nevertheless, this kind of research is still rare. The blurring of the rural-urban divide is still a fact "so widely recognized but so little studied" (Brookfield et al. 1991:vi). More often than not, "rural-urban" is only proclaimed as a continuum, but applied as a dichotomy (Koppel 1991:50). In addition, evidence from previous chapters suggests that quasi-urban economic structure and landscape are not necessarily results of interaction between rural areas and the core cities close to them. In fact the major cities in Fujian are still not strong enough economically to function as major growth poles (Zhou 1991:107). The transformation of economic structure and landscape in this study is very much a result of rural local initiatives and foreign investment coming from far away, and is beyond the coverage of the paradigm of "extended metropolis". As to the "three-sector model",

---

[69] As will be seen later, what is unique to the *in situ* rural-urban transformation in Fujian is the exceptional scale of non-agricultural activities.

it seems that treating the rural non-agricultural sector as an independent sector is not enough. The transformation of rural areas from agricultural to non-agricultural should be treated as a gradual and multidimensional process.

Secondly, corresponding to the problem of rural-urban dichotomy, urbanization is too often treated as a leap rather than a gradual transformation process from rural to urban. This has much to do with the criteria used to make rural-urban distinctions. As can be seen in Chapter 3, these criteria are difficult to define and often controversial. A more serious problem is that studies on urbanization based on these criteria often oversimplify the process of rural-urban transformation[70]. People tend to concentrate their attention on the changes close to the critical points where the urban criteria are met, neglecting the long process leading to the changes. In this way the connections between rural development and urbanization are often ignored. This is why TVE development, which has been so important in China's rural-urban transformation since the 1980s, has been neglected in urbanization studies. Such neglect would lead to ignorance of the continuity from TVE development to urbanization in Fujian Province shown in the previous chapters. More importantly, the neglect or inclusion of this kind of development has a major effect on our assessment of China's urbanization trend and its spatial patterns, and on our understanding of China's urbanization process and its driving forces. In fact, if this study had ignored TVE development because it does not qualify as conventionally understood urbanization, the essence of the new paths to urbanization would have been missed. The continuity from proto-industrialization to urbanization shown in the review on proto-industrialization in developed countries also supports the necessity of treating urbanization as a long-term transformation process. Thus the increase of rural non-agricultural activities should be seen as a component and a stage of such a transformation process, assuming a more important position in urbanization studies.

Thirdly, urbanization is often treated as identical with migration from rural areas to existing cities (e.g. Todaro 1969; Chen and Geng 1993:128-30). In contrast, the role of reclassification in the urbanization process is often ignored or mixed with migration, and there is no theoretical foundation from which to consider this issue (Skeldon 1990:153-7; Wei 1990; United Nations 1993:2-21). A related problem is that while much attention is paid to the expansion of existing

---

[70] This is not to deny the necessity for having such criteria; from the statistical viewpoint they are still useful to catch certain aspects and stages of the urbanization process, but there are limitations to their usefulness in urbanization studies.

cities, the process of city-creation is neglected. This may not be a big issue in the cases of developing countries where the urbanization process is dominated by the growth of primary cities and rural-urban migration. But evidence from this study suggests that under certain conditions, the city-creation process and reclassification may become more important in the urbanization process than city-expansion and rural-urban migration. As can be seen in Chapter 4, reclassification and very short-distance migration accounted for 53 percent of the growth of State-sponsored and spontaneous urban population in Fujian Province. In fact, urbanization there has been to a great extent a process of transforming local rural communities into more urbanized ones, with an ultimate result of more new urban centers. When Jones (1997:241) comments on this analysis, he suggests that what is said of Fujian above "could be repeated for many densely settled regions of Asia". Therefore, more studies oriented to reclassification and city-creation processes are needed to accommodate this kind of reality. This is consistent with the previous point, as evidence from this study suggests that the increasing importance of reclassification and city-creation is a result of the increase in non-agricultural activities in the rural areas.

Fourthly, some characteristics of many developing regions are not well articulated in the existing theories. As analyzed in Chapters 5 and 6, the increasing possibility of non-agricultural activities in rural areas has much to do with these characteristics. High population density, advances in transport and communication techniques, government policies, and cultural factors such as the "Chineseness factor" are some of such characteristics examined in this study. More enabling factors for *in situ* rural-urban transformation could be identified if more research could be conducted. The incorporation of these factors into urbanization theories will modify our understanding about the role of spatial clustering in economic development, and help us to understand the flexible relationship between structural economic change and urbanization.

In summary, the above points are possible directions in which future research could go to solve the problem in the existing urbanization theories mentioned at the beginning of this section. They provide a framework for the existing theories to incorporate the kinds of rural-urban transformation examined in this study, and to become closer to reality. The conventional view that with economic development, rural labor will be gradually transferred from the traditional agricultural sector to the modern non-agricultural sector, still holds true in this new framework. Economic factors and employment opportunities are still foremost among reasons for this transfer. Rural-urban migration and the expansion of existing cities are still important forms of this transition. Nevertheless, non-agricultural activities are not regarded as necessarily dominated by the existing cities, rather increasingly possible in rural areas as well, forming a parallel process leading to the transformation of rural areas and the creation of new cities without much rural-urban migration. High population densities and advances in transport and communication technologies in many developing regions make possible these new patterns of urbanization, as they make it less necessary than suggested by the conventional wisdom for those regions to achieve agglomeration economies through massive migration, and to locate non-agricultural activities in big existing cities for easier access to markets and resources. Government policies and some cultural factors can promote or undermine such patterns of rural-urban transformation, as shown by the example of this study. It seems that with the help of this conceptual framework, a more complete picture of urbanization can be drawn in the future. However, such a complete picture can only be achieved on the basis of extensive regional studies, as the concrete relationship between urbanization and economic development is contingent upon regional conditions, and cannot be generalized though a single study.

7.1.2 INCORPORATING NON-POLARIZED SPATIAL PATTERNS IN A BROADER REGIONAL DEVELOPMENT PARADIGM

Another theoretical aspect of this study is the issue of polarization in regional development. To start with, a few words have to be said about the appropriateness of using Fujian Province as an example to discuss the primacy issue. Although in most cases primacy is regarded as a national issue, as pointed out by Jones (1990:3), it may also be observed at the provincial level. For populous countries like China and Indonesia with a large land area, primacy at the provincial level may even be more relevant than that at the national level, as the former is usually not a serious problem, but the latter tends to be more marked (Kim 1989:4; Jones 1990:3). In addition, as can be seen in Chapter 2, Fujian is a relatively independent geographical unit, isolated and remote from other provinces of China. This makes its primacy issue similar to the one at the national level to a certain extent. In the following I will explore the theoretical implications of Fujian's development patterns for this issue by looking at Fujian's development mainly in the context of the traditional center-down development paradigm, as this paradigm has dominated spatial planning theory and practice in developing countries and newer "bottom-up" alternatives remain relatively undeveloped

(Hansen 1981; Stöhr 1981:47; Brohman 1996:1). I will also draw complementarily on the perspective of world system-dependency theory, as this theory offers its explanation for the issue of polarization more adequately from an international perspective. It is hoped that this will contribute to formulating a more adequate regional development paradigm in developing countries.

As can be seen from the preceding chapters, the fast economic development in Fujian since the 1980s has not led to urban primacy in either State-sponsored or spontaneous terms. The absence of polarization at so early a stage of regional development is abnormal according to most conventional theories. This gap between the theories and Fujian's reality can be attributed to the following reasons.

7.1.2.1 The Existing Theories do not have enough Appreciation of the Characteristics such as High Population Density in many Developing Regions

In Friedmann's center-periphery model for example, a sparsely populated country -Venezuela - is taken as a prototype. The population density of this country was only about 11 persons per km^2 around 1945-50 when the economic "take-off" occurred (Friedmann 1966:129), and is still only about 24 per km^2 today. This is very different from the realities in Fujian with an average population density of 248 per km^2, and of 595 per km^2 in its coastal area. In fact, Fujian's population density is not particularly high, compared with the areas where most Chinese live. As analyzed by Heilig, roughly one billion Chinese live in only a little more than 30 percent of the country's land area. The population density of this area is 354 per km^2, greater than that of Belgium. Thus the extremely high density of China's very large population is a critical factor in the country's future development (Heilig 1997:149-51), including its spatial process. As analyzed before, high population density, together with the improvement of transport and communication technologies, makes in situ rural-urban transformation more possible. Viewed from the perspective of spatial process of development, this means that the advantage of agglomeration economy for the center region in relation to the periphery is not as great as traditionally suggested, and the centripetal force of development may not be as strong as conventionally believed. High population densities and the advances in transport and communication have further important roles in the generation and diffusion of innovation in the development process, as will be analyzed later. Thus more attention should be paid to these backgrounds of development.

7.1.2.2 The Center-Down Paradigm Neglects the Independent Role of the Periphery in Originating and Transmitting Innovation

The center-down paradigm gives a central role to external innovation impulses in regional development (stöhr and taylor 1981:1). Nevertheless, Fujian's experience suggests that while the importance of innovation is fully justifiable, innovations are not necessarily created and diffused in a center-down manner. The neglect by the center-down paradigm of the importance of the periphery in originating and transmitting innovations may be another important reason for the disconformity between the theory and Fujian's reality.

Friedmann's center-periphery model reflects the view of the center-down paradigm on innovation. Friedmann holds that "economic growth can be analyzed by the impact that new knowledge and new values have on observed behavior", and as generators and consumers of new information, cities have a key role in the increased flow of information among all points of the location surface (Friedmann 1966:64). Thus population migration to cities is "one of the ways to assure an adequate circulation of ideas" (Friedmann 1966:65). Later in his "general theory of polarized development" (Friedmann 1972:82-107), he simply treats development as an innovative process. Core regions are the centers of innovative change, and large city size is especially favorable for innovation. Innovations originate from a relatively small number of such centers and diffuse downwards and outwards to the periphery. Core region growth will tend to promote the development process of the relevant spatial system. But after a certain point in time the self-reinforcing character of core region growth will become dysfunctional, and the dominance of core regions will eventually be challenged through the establishment of new core regions in the periphery and the gradual linkage of core regions into more encompassing spatial systems[71].

Fujian's experience does not challenge the importance of innovation in development. As can be seen in Chapter 5, the emergence of joint-household enterprises was an important institutional innovation, which played a key role in Jinjiang's development. There have been other important innovations such as new techniques which have accompanied foreign capital. In fact, innovation is an effective conceptualization to account for Fujian's experience since the 1980s. Nevertheless, the facts that innovations originated at a very early stage in a peripheral area like Jinjiang and that this process was relatively independent of the development in the core regions like Fuzhou, are obviously at odds with Fried-

---

[71] A similar view can also be seen in Richardson 1980:276.

mann's idea. These innovations not only have not led to polarization, but have been very much responsible for the dispersed patterns of Fujian's development.

Two explanations can be given for the important role of the peripheral area in generating innovation in Fujian. The first explanation is related to the possibility of the periphery generating innovation. As mentioned in Chapters 2 and 5, the shortage of land and the surplus of labor, the long tradition of trading with and migrating to other countries and regions, and the long history of continuous adjustment of economic structure, cultivated the entrepreneurship displayed in the regional development of Fujian's coastal area, especially in a place like Jinjiang. Thus the innovations in this region are the responses of local people to the unfavorable population-land ratio and the legacies of people's ability to create new development opportunities in the historical development. In Jinjiang, innovation has even become a geographically and historically determined local cultural identity described as "Jinjiang spirit" (Qiu 1995). Thus under certain conditions, even at an early stage of development, periphery regions do not only passively accept the diffusion of innovation from the core regions. Their geographical, historical, and cultural conditions may lead to the generation of innovation on their own.

The second explanation for the innovation in the periphery is related to the role of the periphery in receiving and transmitting innovation. Fujian's experience seems to suggest that innovation can be propagated in and between the spatial systems much more flexibly than suggested by Friedmann's model. Both Jinjiang and Fuqing received a number of technical and institutional innovations through joint-ventures and foreign investment. These innovations were transmitted directly from the core regions outside China, bypassing many vertical and lateral links suggested in Friedmann's model. As can be seen in Chapter 5, this greatly enhanced Jinjiang's and Fuqing's position in the spatial system. Again the regional history of development may be made responsible for this way of innovation diffusion. As can be seen in Chapter 5, Chinese overseas, Hong Kongers and Taiwanese originating from Fujian are the major sources of foreign investment, and hence also of the innovations. The cultural links of those Chinese overseas, Hong Kongers and Taiwanese to their ancestral home seem to overcome the hindrance created by the urban hierarchical orders and geographical distance. This is further facilitated by the advances in transport and communication technologies, which make the interaction of people and information increasingly easy and frequent. In this way, some peripheral areas in Fujian Province were not only the major sources of innovation, but also major receivers and transmitters of innovations from outside of China.

The above analysis provides further evidence to support the feasibility of *in situ* rural-urban transformation and dispersed spatial patterns of development in certain densely settled developing regions. Since there are conditions under which innovations can originate in, or be received and transmitted by periphery areas at the early stage of development, then population migration is less necessary to "assure an adequate circulation of ideas". On the contrary, innovation can come to where the population is and start the development there. This is not to deny the roles of core regions and migration in the development process, but regional development theories should at least recognize the independent roles of the periphery in the development process and should be more sensitive to those geographical, historical and cultural factors leading to innovations in periphery regions.

7.1.2.3 The Third Factor Leading to Fujian's Development without Polarization is Related to the Spatial Patterns of Foreign Investment

To examine this issue one needs to draw on the conceptual framework of world system-dependency theory. This is not to say that the traditional development paradigm is irrelevant here, but it is less useful because the role of foreign influence, especially foreign investment in developing countries' regional development process, does not seem to have been adequately addressed in this kind of paradigm (Fuchs and Pernia 1987:89-90)[72]. Although regional economies are regarded as subject to external influence and regional economic growth is thought to be externally induced, there does not seem to be enough analysis of the effects of foreign investment on the spatial restructuring in regional development[73]. In fact, this is a problem in conventional regional development studies in general (Fuchs and Pernia 1989:387; Sit and Yang 1997:648), and it has become increasingly problematic as a result of dramatic "globalization" of production, finance and other businesses since the 1980s. As world system-dependency theory views developing countries' internal spatial structure as part of a world sys-

---

[72] Such criticism of Friedmann's model can also be found in Gilbert and Gugler 1982:34, though focusing on the model's neglect of foreign influence in developing countries' political and economic decision making.

[73] Nevertheless it can be inferred from Friedmann's model that foreign investment will follow the general trend of concentration in the core regions in the period of incipient industrialization (Friedmann 1966:17; Fuchs and Pernia 1987:90), which is not the case in Fujian's development.

tem of production and consumption, it may offer a complementary framework to look at this issue.

From the perspective of world system-dependency theory, Fujian's development without polarization may be attributed to the absence of some factors which could lead to urban primacy in developing countries. As critically reviewed by Smith, colonial exploitation, export dependency, and rural collapse are three dominant theoretical explanations for urban primacy in developing countries (Smith 1985). However in Fujian Province, not only was colonial penetration limited, but its effects had almost been eliminated, when China adopted open-door policies in 1978, after 30 years of isolation from the outside world. The land reform in the 1950s, and rural reform and development in the 1980s, combined with the continued household registration system, also prevented the permanent migration of a large number of peasants to major cities[74]. These may have removed some conditions which could have led to urban primacy in Fujian's development since the 1980s.

Nevertheless, Fujian's condition does not preclude the functioning of export dependency[75]. In fact, one of the major characteristics of Fujian's development since the 1980s has been its increasing involvement in the world economy, which can be seen in Chapter 5. This would have been a factor favoring the development of urban primacy from the standpoint of world system-dependency theory. Empirical studies in other countries suggest that foreign investors have generally preferred to invest in the economic core regions (Fuchs and Pernia 1989:388; Xu and Li 1990:50; Sit and Yang 1997:648-9), which is in line with the implication of world system-dependency theory. Obviously Fujian's experience is at variance with these conclusions.

Several reasons have been given for the spatial patterns of foreign investments in Fujian's development in the preceding chapters. Their theoretical impli-

---

[74] Similar explanations for the absence of urban primacy in China as a whole in the 1980s can be found in Chen 1991:347-53. Tao (1995:44) also argues that the absence of extremely unequal land and income distributions in the population and the existence of the household registration system are important in holding potential migrants in the rural areas.

[75] It is recognized here that the export dependency in Fujian's development, which is related to industrial production, is different from the export dependency suggested by dependency theory, which emphasizes primacy caused by export-oriented production of primary goods (Smith 1985:102; Chen 1991:346). Nevertheless, the dependency upon the external consumer and capital market, which is the cause of distortions in local economies according to the export dependency theory (Smith 1985:102), also exists in Fujian's development, although such dependency may not be as strong as in many other developing countries because of China's large domestic market.

cations can be further explored here. First, the increasing involvement of Fujian in the globalization process suggests a more important role for foreign influence, especially foreign investment in developing countries' development process. Furthermore, Fujian's experience, especially that of Jinjiang, challenges the view of world system-dependency theory on the consequence of the penetration of developing-country economies by foreign elements. It also suggests that the necessity of "selective spatial closure" (Stöhr 1981:44-6) in the "development from below" strategy needs to be re-assessed, as such a strategy is not necessarily incompatible with the openness of local economies. These realities should be incorporated more fully in the relevant theories, and more attention should be paid to the research in this area.

Secondly, both regional development theories and world system-dependency theory need to incorporate more factors at the local level in explaining the spatial patterns of foreign investment in Fujian. As analyzed in Chapter 6, the dispersed spatial patterns of foreign investment are closely related to the connections of Chinese overseas, Hong Kongers and Taiwanese to their ancestral home and the business characteristics of Chinese communities. Instead of the destruction of local industry suggested by export dependency theories (Smith 1985:103), TVEs have played important roles in absorbing the foreign investment at the local level and their development has been greatly enhanced by the foreign investment in Jinjiang[76]. These analyses suggest the important roles of local historical, cultural and institutional backgrounds in affecting the spatial patterns of foreign investment. The deficiency of relevant existing theories in explaining Fujian's development may lie in their neglect of these important regional, historical and cultural settings. It seems that these theories should draw on the approach of "locality studies", a new research area in geography and related fields which "focuses on the ways in which the general dynamics of development are conditioned by local context" (Brohman 1996: 246-7, 342). In this way the effects of those local historical, cultural and institutional backgrounds on the regional development can be revealed. This is in line with the preceding point regarding the role of innovation in the patterns of regional development.

---

[76] Nevertheless, the effect of foreign investment on the local economy of Fuqing in employment creation is not as ideal as in Jinjiang, as analyzed in Chapter 5. The comparison between Jinjiang and Fuqing emphasizes the importance of TVEs in the effect of foreign investment on local economy.

7.1.2.4 The Unique State Roles in Facilitating Fujian's Development Patterns are not well Integrated in the Existing Theories

Views of different theories on the role of the State in achieving balanced development are various and controversial. Some theorists see regional convergence as an automatic process, but others stress the necessity of State intervention (Friedmann 1966:14; Gilbert and Gugler 1982:176-7). In world system-dependency theory, periphery states are usually assumed to be dominated by a small elite, and relatively weak both in relation to core states and in their ability to implement domestic policy, implying unwillingness and limited roles of the State in promoting balanced patterns of regional development (Shannon 1989:94). In the cases where State intervention is recognized, little is known about the ideal way it is exercised. There is much criticism on the "tendencies to impose inappropriate top-down projects without much public input from the affected communities themselves", the State domination and the lack of local participation in the management of development programs, although more balanced and equitable development is the goal of these programs (Brohman 1996:217-25).

Fujian's experience may provide some new insights into these issues. As can be seen in Chapter 5, State intervention certainly exists in Fujian's development. But the State restricts its direct intervention to controlling excessive expansion of large cities and rural-urban migration; it is only indirectly involved in local development programs. Instead of running projects and providing investment, which are usually the case in other bottom-up development strategies, the State has relaxed control over the rural economy since 1979 (Ma and Lin 1993:602; Lin and Ma 1994:80), and focused its role on stimulating local initiatives, and creating favorable policy and economic environments for those initiatives. These are reflected in a series of policy changes regarding the relaxation of urban criteria and of restriction on migration to small towns, the status and regulation of TVEs, the establishment of development, investment and industrial zones, and the provision of infrastructure through active participation of local authorities. The unique form of TVEs such as joint-household enterprises, which are encouraged and supported by the State, ensures wide participation of local people in economic development. At the same time the importance of regional characteristics is well recognized by the State, and different regions are encouraged to adopt different development strategies. This is reflected in the fact that there are at least 10 TVE development models, among which the major differences lie in the nature of local participation. Such roles of the State and their effectiveness are consistent with the preceding analyses on the role of periphery regions in generating and transmitting innovations, and absorbing foreign investment, and on the importance of local geographical, historical and cultural conditions, and therefore have their theoretical foundations. Thus Fujian's experience seems to provide a reference case for regional development theories and practices to redefine the role of the State in development.

In summary, the above analysis suggests that under certain conditions, periphery regions can play important roles in generating and transmitting innovations and in absorbing foreign investment, and thus have much stronger positions in relation to the core regions in the spatial system of regional development than conventionally believed. The conditions facilitating a more important role of periphery regions are related to the local geographical, demographic, historical, and cultural factors, and the unique State roles. Regional development studies should be more sensitive to these conditions of development, and recognize the roles of periphery regions in the development. As the case of Fujian has some unique characteristics, the fact that Fujian's situation is not well captured by existing theories does not necessarily undermine their fundamental basis. Nevertheless, careful study of the way in which existing theories fail to come to grips with Fujian's situation may help in modifying these theories to make them more adequate and closer to the reality.

7.2 POLICY IMPLICATIONS

7.2.1 IMPLICATIONS FOR URBAN AND REGIONAL DEVELOPMENT POLICIES

The important roles of China's urban and regional development policies in promoting the new rural-urban transformation patterns, and the feasibility and desirability of such policies, have been discussed from different angles in this study. On the basis of the preceding analysis, I now reassess two important aspects of these policies, and discuss a new policy issue arising from this study.

7.2.1.1 Two Important Aspects of China's Urban and Regional Development Policies

The **first** important aspect of China's urban and regional development policies is that they emphasize small towns and rural industrialization as a means to achieve many development goals (Chang and Kwok 1990:140). This is reflected in the government's strict control over large city development[77], its cautious attitude towards the development of medium-sized and small cities, and its vigorous promotion of small towns and TVE development. Thus, small town development and rural-urbanization has become the main element of urbanization in China.

The feasibility and desirability of emphasizing small towns and rural industrialization as the main element of urbanization have been addressed in the preceding chapters. Nevertheless, it is necessary to reassess this issue by relating it to the role of large cities in China's development, an issue which has reappeared in China since the 1990s, when some major metropolitan cities such as Shanghai began to show accelerated growth. Since large cities seem to play increasingly important roles in China's development, should China switch its urban development emphasis from small town development and rural-urbanization to the development of large cities[78]?

This question reflects a major problem of China's urban strategy: the strategy, especially relating to the development of large cites, was not based on a sound analysis of the roles of large cities in regional development. In fact, the formation of the strategy of "strictly control the development of large cities" can be traced back to the 1950s. It had much to do with China's heavy-industry-oriented industrial development strategy and the rigid planned economic system adopted before the 1980s, which led to serious infrastructure problems in large cities and restricted their ability to provide employment and daily necessities for their populations, and the strong State role in sponsoring urban population, causing "urban fear" in the Chinese leadership[79]. Since China has adopted market-oriented reform and adjusted its industrial strategy, large cities should now be able to play bigger roles in regional development. Thus it is fully justifiable to reassess the policy of "strictly control the development of large cities" and to a certain extent to loosen control over the development of large cities.

---

[77] As mentioned in Chapter 5, the control over the development of large cities should be appreciated in perspective. Obviously the development on the outskirts of large cities is less constrained by this control, as can be seen in the case of Fuzhou.

[78] The position of the Chinese government on this issue does not seem to have changed. A high-ranking official from the Ministry of Construction said recently that the Chinese government would continue to give priority to developing towns to boost the overall socioeconomic development in rural areas (*Economic Information* 1997:20).

[79] For detailed discussion on this point see Kirkby 1985:10-8; Wang 1995:17-9; Chen W. 1996:16-7.

Nevertheless, two important issues need to be fully appreciated in reassessing this urban strategy. First, given the vast labor resources in China, large cities' capacity to absorb potential labor resources, especially rural migrants, should not be overestimated. It is true that large cities have strong growth potential at the moment, as analyzed by Wang (1995:21-3); the increasing number of temporary residents in large cities in recent years has reflected this potential. However, it should be questioned whether this growth potential is enough to absorb hundreds of millions of surplus labor released from rural areas, which is the central issue for China's spatial planners (Kirkby 1985:243). Estimates about the number of rural surplus labor in China range from Mao's 120 million to Hu's 175 million (Mao 1996:8; Hu 1997:12). Even if the low estimate is taken, it means that more than 200 one-million cities (6.3 times the number of existing one-million-plus cities) are needed to absorb these surplus laborers and their dependants. What is more, the existing cities themselves are facing serious unemployment problems. Hu estimates that the number of urban unemployed workers is 15.5 million, accounting for 7.5 percent of the total. There are still 22 million underemployed urban workers[80] (Hu 1997:12). Obviously, a considerable part of large cities' growth potential will be used for coping with their own unemployment problems. Thus, even if the latent potentialities of existing cities are fully tapped, the employment opportunities they provide will still be inadequate to accommodate a much larger number of surplus laborers. Therefore, the emphasis on small town development and rural industrialization is still needed in China.

Second, the adherence to small town development and rural industrialization can be justified by the development experiences of China's rural areas, such as those in Jinjiang, and the relevant theoretical analyses of preceding chapters and sections. Unlike the strategy to "strictly control the development of large cities", the strategy of emphasizing small town development and rural industrialization appeared almost concurrently with the market-oriented reform, and was formulated on a sounder basis, as can be seen in Chapter 5. In fact, doubts about the feasibility and desirability of small-town development and rural industrialization are long-standing (for example see Kirkby 1985:230-44), but later results of the development turned out to be much better than the critics had expected. Thus the recognition of the development potential of large cities and the loosening control

---

[80] The urban definition used here is the State-sponsored one based on the household registration system.

over large city development should not lead to abandoning the strategy of small town development and rural industrialization.

The **second** important aspect of China's urban and regional development policies is that while they incorporate some key elements of a "development from below" strategy, "its strong emphasis on industry to create job opportunities for surplus rural labor is striking" (Chang and Kwok 1990:142-3). In doing so, many important goals of "development from below" can be achieved, but its limitations are overcome. As stated by Stöhr and Taylor (1981:1), development "from below" considers development to be based primarily on maximum mobilization of each area's natural, human, and institutional resources with the primary objective being the satisfaction of the basic needs of the inhabitants of that area.

Such development "must be motivated and initially controlled from the bottom", and should be labor-intensive, small-scale, and rural-centered, and use "appropriate" rather than "highest" technology (Stöhr and Taylor 1981:1-2). The real situation of this study's field sites, especially that of Jinjiang, is consistent with this. The joint-household enterprises examined in Chapter 5 have most of the abovementioned characteristics. They were indeed motivated and controlled from the bottom, and are successful. Thus Fujian's experience seems to prove the feasibility of some essential components of "development from below" strategy.

Nevertheless, there are some important differences between the conventional strategy of "development from below" and Fujian's experience, especially that of Jinjiang. Some rural development strategies, such as the "integrated rural development" and "the territorial approach" advocated in the 1970s, emphasized agricultural development and attached relatively limited importance to rural industry, which was closely tied to agriculture (Todaro 1981:46; Brohman 1996:216, 232-6); but in Fujian urban-like industrialization has predominated in rural development[81]. Instead of "selective spatial closure" (Stöhr 1981:45; Brohman 1996:232-6), Fujian's rural industry has been widely connected to both domestic and international economic systems. Fujian's experience is also different from the kind of rural self-employment and "cottage" industry in many East and Southeast Asian

---

[81] But this does not mean that agriculture is unimportant in rural development. In fact, in the first few years of the reform (1978-1982), agricultural production in Jinjiang also increased noticeably (Liu et al. 1992:81-3). The overall increase in agricultural production in China also relieved Jinjiang from the concern about food shortage. In fact, as analyzed by Chen and Han (1993:61-2), the dramatic agricultural development in China in that period provided a fundamental material basis for the transfer of rural population from agricultural to non-agricultural in China. Nevertheless, the rapid industrial development certainly brought about a sharp conflict between agriculture and industry, especially in land use.

countries, which in the case of Indonesia serves very small market areas within the village and does not foster the growth of towns in rural regions (Douglass 1991:248). It is noticeable that while such large-scale industrialization with increasing involvement in the world economy has been pursued in Jinjiang, the goal of full utilization of the labor force has also been achieved[82]. Such experience certainly challenges the orthodox models of urban-based development; but more than that, it suggests that if properly combined, a much larger scale of rural industrialization and some key elements of "development from below" are compatible and that such a combination can achieve more than traditional "bottom-up" development strategies, whose results generally failed to meet expectations (Brohman 1996:224), and provide a new alternative.

The above analysis has important policy implications for many other developing countries, especially those with high population densities and good transport and communication conditions. As stated before, the conditions enabling Fujian's *in situ* rural-urban transformation also exist in many developing countries. Non-agricultural activities in rural areas, and even dispersed urbanization patterns, are not unique to Fujian either. What make Fujian unusual are the exceptional scale of non-agricultural activities and *in situ* rural urban transformation, and the most likely reasons for this are China's policies promoting small town development and rural industrialization, which are seldom implemented outside China (Chang and Kwok 1990:140). The restrictive policies towards the growth of big cities and the migration to them in China are also contributing factors, but as shown before, they have been playing a diminishing role in Fujian's urbanization, if temporary residents are taken into account. Fujian's experience seems to provide a relatively successful case of "restraining" policies, which focus on the rural areas and attempt to hold potential migrants there (Skeldon 1990:193), and a workable model of such policies. Developing countries concerned about their over-concentrated urbanization patterns may take Fujian's experience as a reference, and make policies in which rural development assumes a more important role in regulating urbanization patterns.

---

[82] From the perspective of "development from below", the less ideal result of the development in Fuqing in terms of employment may be attributed to the fact that the development was less locally motivated, less labor-intensive, larger in scale and higher in technology. This suggests the necessity of combining the industrialization strategy with some of the important elements of "development from below".

7.2.1.2 The Role of Temporary Residents in their Hometowns: A New Policy Issue in China

The new policy issue arising from this study is the role of temporary residents in regional development. It is clear that temporary residents have played important roles in destination areas, but less attention has been paid to their contribution to their home areas. Recent evidence suggests that this issue needs to be looked at seriously, and it may have important implications for China's regional development as a whole, and its regional disparity problems.

A major concern about China's recent development model is that while urban-rural differences have narrowed in a few favorable areas, including Fujian, total regional disparity throughout China has probably widened. Coastal regions have gradually shifted to industry and service, but the subsistence economy of inland provinces has changed little (Chang and Kwok 1990:151-2). Such a situation is the most important reason for many migrants to move from inland to coastal areas, living and working there as temporary residents.

Nevertheless, evidence shows that these temporary residents may contribute to overcoming the difficult situation of increasing regional disparity in China. First, these migrants send back a significant amount of remittances to their home regions. In 1994, the total amount of remittances sent back by rural migrants in China was 83.17 billion *Yuan* (Chen H. 1996:6). In Sichuan, China's most populous province and biggest source of migrants, the amount of remittances sent back by out-going laborers in 1997 was 20.2 billion *Yuan*, equivalent to the province's financial revenue in the same year (Chen 1998). Such remittances are an important source of investment for both agricultural and non-agricultural sectors, and for creating employment opportunities.

Secondly, a large number of migrants have returned to their home regions and are directly involved in the development of their hometowns. These returned migrants learned new techniques and ideas, accumulated capital and managerial experience, established market connections, and cultivated risk-taking mentalities, through migration experience. They are taking these advantages to create development opportunities for their hometowns. Recent statistics show that among 6.5 million rural migrants from Sichuan Province, 340,000 have already returned to their hometowns and established their own enterprises, absorbing 750,000 local surplus rural laborers. Many more have shown their intention to return to initiate their own businesses in their hometowns (Chen 1998). In fact, contrary to the common belief that floating populations tend to become permanent residents in their destinations (e.g. Laquian 1996:28), B. S. Zhu's analysis

(1997) suggests that most migrants will eventually return to their hometowns. Thus returned migrants will be an important driving force for the regional development of China's inland areas, just as Chinese overseas, Hong Kongers and Taiwanese have been for the coastal areas of China.

Interestingly, in some inland areas, returned migrants are already treated as a new kind of "foreign investors". There is a "returned migrant investment zone" in Jintang County of Sichuan Province; furthermore, some preferential policies for encouraging returned migrants to establish enterprises in their hometowns will soon be promulgated in Sichuan Province (Chen 1998). In fact, as the ties between returned migrants and their hometowns are much stronger than those between Chinese overseas and their ancestral regions, returned migrants may be even more active in initiating "bottom-up" development like that of Jinjiang. It is still too early to assess how large a role return migrants will play in the regional development of their hometowns, but this is certainly an important trend in China's regional development. The implication of such a trend for China's policy makers is that they not only need to pay attention to the management of temporary residents in their destination areas, as shown in the case of Fuzhou, but also need to develop policies on returned migrants and their part in their hometown development.

7.2.2 IMPLICATIONS FOR URBAN PLANNING

Although I regard the new rural-urban transformation patterns as generally positive, I do not intend to encourage the neglect of problems arising from them. Inadequate scale and agglomeration economies, arable land losses, agricultural production declines, and degradation of the environment, are the most evident examples of such problems (Chang and Kwok 1990:148-51; Gu 1991:158-63; Zhou 1991:98). It is beyond the scope of this study to discuss these problems in detail, but inadequate planning is certainly a factor responsible for such a situation. As these rural-urban transformation patterns are new in both theoretical and practical terms, and is spontaneous, China's urban planning policies and practices have not incorporated them adequately, especially at the micro-level, and further exploration in this area will contribute to solving the above problems, and enrich urban planning theories and practices.

7.2.2.1 *In Situ* Rural-Urban Transformation and Urban Planning

The biggest and most urgent planning problem has arisen from the *in situ* rural-urban transformation associated with TVE development. As mentioned before, such a proccess was rarely regarded as urbanization and not well-researched
from an urbanization perspective. Thus, the theoretical foundation for its planning is weak. In addition, the *in situ* rural-urban transformation has been happening at the administrative level of towns or townships, and even at the village
level. Such places are not covered by the Urban Planning Act of the PRC (China,
Standing Committee of NPC 1990; Lin and Ma 1994:77), as the Act regulates
urban planning only at the level of designated towns, or higher. There are other
regulations on the development of villages (Mao 1996:7), but in such regulations
the relationship between the TVE development and the rural-urban transformation process is not well reflected. Thus, little planning regulation has been implemented in the *in situ* rural-urban transformation.

A conceptual framework reflecting the nature of *in situ* rural-urban transformation is needed to solve this planning problem. As analyzed before, the *in situ*
rural-urban transformation in Fujian is an intermediate stage in the whole urbanization process. A planning approach, which is suitable for rural settings but will
introduce and adapt elements of urbanism, is most needed in this situation. More
than two decades ago, the idea of "agropolis" or "city in the fields" was proposed
for such a need. As Friedmann and Douglass (1975:40) stated, "instead of encouraging the drift of rural people to cities by investing in cities", such an approach would encourage rural people "to remain where they are, by investing in
rural districts, and so transmute existing settlements into a hybrid form of agropolis, or city in the fields". The "city in the fields" accommodates both the *in situ*
and the quasi-urban, quasi-rural natures of *in situ* rural-urban transformation, and
can be taken as the framework for its planning.

Nevertheless, as the rural-urban transformation described in this study is different from the traditional models of rural development, many of the details of
the "city in the fields" should be understood on the basis of the new situation. On
the basis of analysis on the *in situ* rural-urban transformation in Jinjiang, some
major aspects of the planning of the "city in the fields" can be described below.

On the one hand, the spatial structure of such cities will carry on many features of the existing residential system. The seat of the county or municipality
will be the largest center of the residential system; but unlike conventionally con-
ceived cities, there will be many sub-centers developing on the basis of market
towns and seats of towns and townships. Even some big villages can also become

sub-centers. The population and settlements in such cities are relatively dispersed compared with traditional cities. As arable land is so precious in China, highly productive land will be retained and used both for agriculture and as open space. Such a spatial structure bears some similarities to the polycentric urban form appearing in developed countries described in Pfister (1997).

On the other hand, the development of such cities at the micro-level should be guided to meet the requirements of large-scale rural industrialization. This is particularly necessary for the location of TVEs and rural settlements. As analyzed before, the industrialization in Jinjiang started in the form of joint-household enterprises. There is still much room for more concentration of enterprise to make use of scale and agglomeration economies, so that there will be more efficiency in the administration of enterprises, land and infrastructure uses, and control on environmental problems. Such concentration has already begun, but the potential is still great, as only 30 percent of TVEs have been involved so far. One reason for this is the lack of capital, as mentioned in Chapter 5; but another important reason is the lack of regulation for the location of TVEs, according to the head of the TVE Management Bureau of Jinjiang Municipality and the head of the Chidian Town government in Jinjiang. The industrial zones are planned by the government, but whether TVEs should be located there is basically up to the individual enterprises. Many proprietors are not willing to move to the industrial zones because according to tradition, family properties should remain at home rather than being moved elsewhere. Thus, much effort is still needed to formulate a workable planning practice to cope with such situations (personal communication, Jinjiang Municipality, September 1996).

Another micro-planning problem for the *in situ* rural-urban transformation is the re-organization of old rural settlements. In recent years, merging small villages into bigger ones (*Qianchuan Bingdian*) has been given much importance by China's urban planners (Li and Wang 1996:12). In Jianggsu Province, it is planned to merge 280,000 small villages into 50,000 bigger ones (*People's Daily* 1997). The purpose of this is to save land and to provide rural residents with urban-like facilities in a more efficient way. This is of great significance for promoting the transformation of rural communities into more urban-like ones. Such planning also urgently needs to be introduced in Fujian, because an increasing number of new houses have been built in recent years as a result of economic development. In Jinjiang a new house usually occupy a land area of 200 m^2, making the problem of land shortage even more acute (Liu et al. 1992:74-5), and the provision of infrastructure difficult. Because of the strong role of the household in the rural-urban transformation, it is more difficult to implement the merger of villages in Fujian than in Jiangsu where collective enterprises pre-dominate in the rural economy. Nevertheless, efforts have to be made to find a workable solution.

Planning problems also exist in the *in situ* rural-urban transformation where foreign investment plays the major role, as in Fuqing. The spatial structure of such cities will be similar to that described above; however the micro-planning problems are different. In such cases the development zones themselves are much better planned than in the case of industrial zones for TVEs, and most enterprises are located in these zones. New settlements replacing the old ones, whose land has been taken for the needs of development, are usually concentrated in the planned residential areas. However, the location of those zones has not been well justified from the perspective of overall planning of newly emerged urban areas, as there is no sound theoretical foundation and practical experience to guide such location. Thus the planners' role in deciding the location of development zones was relegated to the production of blueprints according to the decisions made behind closed doors by cadres, who in turn often accommodate themselves to the intentions of foreign investors (Ng and Wu 1995:288-9, 292; personal communi-cation, Fujian Provincial Urban and Rural Planning and Design Institute, Sep-tember 1996). There is urgent need to conduct research on the principles of such planning.

In summary, the *in situ* rural-urban transformation has raised many new planning issues for Chinese urban planners. New planning ideas are needed to solve these issues. Such new ideas should take the spatial structure of the existing residential system as the planning framework, and promote more concentration in the distribution of both enterprises and settlements. Regulations in these respects are also urgently needed.

7.2.2.2 Temporary Residents in Urban Planning
The emergence of temporary residents also poses new planning problems. For one thing, it is obvious that China's traditional urban planning, which is based on the State-sponsored urban population, that is the non-agricultural population of cities and towns, needs to be expanded to include temporary resi-dents. So far China's urban planning has not been well prepared to cope with the need arising from the inflow of temporary residents, especially in making popu-lation projections and planning for the adequate provision of physical and social infrastructure (Ng and Wu 1995:289). In Guangdong, the province having the

largest floating population, the planning of new services and facilities such as housing, transport, education, health care and welfare does not even take the migrants into account. Moreover, "Chinese cities have gradually witnessed the rise of temporary settlements mainly at the edge of the central city" (Chang 1996:208-13). If they are not dealt with seriously, the troublesome squatter problem in many developing countries will soon be a major urban problem in China too.

Recognizing the need for planning for temporary residents is not enough. More planning problems arise from the status of temporary residents. As mentioned in Chapter 3, temporary residents frequently change their working and living places; this makes their integration into urban planning difficult. Furthermore, there is controversy on whether temporary residents will become permanent urban residents in the long run. The common belief is that most temporary residents tend to stay forever in cities and towns, and China's household registration system is often blamed for their temporary status. But there is much evidence suggesting that this is not the case for most temporary residents, especially those in large cities. Some observers argue that even if there were no restrictions on temporary residents' obtaining official urban household registration status, most of them would still not settle in the cities because they do not have the necessary economic capabilities. Therefore old temporary residents will eventually return to their hometowns, and will be replaced by new temporary residents, forming a "permanent sector of the urban population" (Chen H. 1996:7; Skeldon 1997:4; Zhu B. S. 1997). Such evidence is consistent with Hugo's finding in Indonesia that most temporary movers had no intention of eventually settling in the cities (Hugo 1980:83). In fact, Hugo suggests that temporary migration should be favored over permanent migration, as the former does not further strain the inadequate urban services and housing as much as the latter (Hugo 1980:106-7).

This suggestion should also be considered by Chinese planners. Thus while the needs of temporary residents should be taken into account in urban planning, their floating and temporary nature and their intention of returning to their home areas should still be fully recognized. Planning for the temporary residents based on such recognition will be in the best interests of both the temporary residents and the urban areas. It will also benefit the sending areas of the temporary residents because of the contributions returned migrants can make to their hometowns. Such planning may be more complicated than the planning which simply treats temporary residents as normal residents, but it is more realistic and should be seriously studied. In Mawei of Fuzhou, the place where FETDZ is located, there are settlements specially planned and established for temporary residents (Fujian TV news, November 1996 and personal observation in Mawei during fieldwork, October 1996). In Beijing, it is proposed to plan city districts where temporary residents live in compact communities (Li 1997:20). These are possible solutions for the problems brought about by temporary residents, but much more effort is needed to formulate planning theories and practice for this issue.

Another issue to be noted is that temporary residents' tendencies to settle in the cities of different sizes are different. As can be seen in Chapter 4, long-term migrants tend to concentrate in small towns and rural centers. Such a trend will probably intensify, as the Chinese government recently launched a pilot plan regarding the reform of the household registration system in small towns and cities, reducing further the restrictions on temporary residents' obtaining official household registration status (Zhang 1997). Thus in small cities and towns, the proportion of temporary residents settling in will probably be higher than in medium-sized and large cities, and a different planning approach should be adopted to deal with them.

CHAPTER 8

SUMMARY AND CONCLUSIONS

In most parts of the developing world, urbanization has been characterized by unprecedented urban population growth and highly concentrated urban population distribution. This in turn is closely associated with serious urban problems and regional disparities (United Nations 1980:7; 1993:2-8; 1995:6-10, 86-7; Rondinelli 1983:28-32; Bronger 1993:35; Brockerhoff and Brennan 1998:77-82). These problems offset or reduce the benefits of urbanization, and therefore there is an urgent need to seek more balanced urbanization patterns in developing countries.

China's experiences since the 1980s seem to suggest this is possible. The urbanization patterns in China's Fujian Province examined in this book are in sharp contrast to the experiences of most developing countries. The existing conventional theories regarding urbanization and regional development do not articulate this new reality very well. This study has been conducted against these theoretical and practical backgrounds.

In accordance with the objectives of the book proposed in Chapter 1, the preceding chapters have addressed issues relating to the temporal and spatial features, underlying causes, international and historical comparison, and theoretical and policy implications of the urbanization patterns. On the basis of the findings obtained in the previous chapters, this chapter is an attempt to draw some important conclusions from a comprehensive perspective.

8.1 THE TRANSITION FROM STATE-SPONSORED TO SPONTANEOUS URBANIZATION AND THE NEW URBANIZATION PATTERNS

The first important finding of this study is that the emergence and development of the new urbanization patterns have been closely related to the transition from the dominance of State-sponsored to spontaneous urbanization, which is analyzed in Chapter 3.

Before 1978, urbanization in China was mainly State-sponsored urbanization. The State was the major driving force of urbanization at that time, took full responsibility for looking after all the State-sponsored urban population, that is, the non-agricultural population of cities and towns, and firmly controlled rural-urban migration after the 1950s.

Nevertheless, since the 1980s China's urbanization has been proceeding along two different tracks: one is the conventional urbanization sponsored by the government; the other is the spontaneous urbanization driven by local economic development and market forces. Although the State-sponsored urbanization has proceeded at a faster rate than it did before, it has been greatly overshadowed by the newly emerged spontaneous urbanization. The spontaneous urbanization has been mainly achieved in three ways: first, the creation of many small urban centers promoted by the change in criterion for the designation of official town status, and the relaxation of restrictions on peasants' movement to small designated towns; second, the development of township and village enterprises, which has been the major driving force of the transformation of employment structure in rural areas and has greatly promoted rural economic growth and spread the urban way of life; and third, the rapid increase in temporary residents in urban places and those areas with well-developed TVEs, who cannot have official urban household registration status and are not entitled to the privileges and benefits of the normal urban residents.

This new track of urbanization is not covered by the official urban definitions. Nevertheless, analysis of Fujian's urbanization trend taking into consideration such spontaneous urbanization shows that it has been the main element of urbanization since the middle of the 1980s. Given that the number of TVE employees had reached 129 million by the end of 1995 (China, State Statistical Bureau 1996:388), and that there were 80 million floating population in China (Chen H. 1996:1), to a great extent such conclusions could be made about urbanization in China as a whole. This is of great significance for our understanding of China's urbanization, as it suggests that the characteristics of China's urbanization can only be fully revealed, and its theoretical and policy implications fully appreciated, through the incorporation of spontaneous urbanization in the study of China's urbanization.

8.2 SPATIAL EFFECTS OF SPONTANEOUS URBANIZATION

Chapter 4 reveals the importance of spontaneous urbanization in the formation of the more balanced new urbanization patterns. Although the analysis based on State-sponsored urbanization already suggests that the economic development since the 1980s neither altered the basic characteristics of the urban system nor led to an increase in urban primacy, it is important to note that spontaneous urbanization has contributed much more than State-sponsored urbanization to the more balanced spatial patterns of urbanization. The development of township and village enterprises has played the biggest role in this regard. It has significant effects on the creation and growth of new towns and small cities on a widespread geographical basis, leading to a much more decentralized urban system. The spatial effects of temporary residents are more complicated. While the distribution of long-term temporary residents tends to correspond to that of the non-agricultural population, that of the short-term temporary residents tends to strengthen the medium-sized cities. Nevertheless, there is no evidence that temporary residents, whether short-term or long-term, will increase the urban primacy, as their proportion in the largest city is very similar to that of the non-agricultural population. As the number of TVE employees and their dependants is much larger than the number of temporary residents, the effects of township and village enterprise development on the evolution of the urban system are much stronger than those of the temporary residents; therefore on the whole spontaneous urbanization will lead to a much more decentralized urban system than suggested by the analysis based on State-sponsored urbanization. Because rural-urban transformation has been increasingly driven by the development of TVEs and the increase in temporary residents, as revealed in Chapter 3, the evolution of the urban system will be dominated by the decentralizing effects of spontaneous urbanization.

Analysis of the proximate causes of urbanization reflects the decentralizing effects of spontaneous urbanization from another angle. It suggests that reclassification and short-distance migration have been vital in Fujian's urbanization process, and the urbanization in Fujian has been to a great extent a process of transforming local rural communities into more urbanized ones. All this suggests that China's success in achieving a more balanced urbanization should be more adequately attributed to the spontaneous urbanization, which has been neglected in relevant studies.

8.3 POLICY CHANGES AND THE ROLES OF STATE, LOCAL AND FOREIGN FORCES IN THE URBANIZATION PROCESS

The transition from State-sponsored to spontaneous urbanization has been closely related to a series of policy changes, and the corresponding changes in the roles of State, local and external forces, in the urbanization process. Three case studies presented in Chapter 5 demonstrate these changes and their roles in achieving the more balanced patterns of urbanization.

The reform and open-door policies adopted in China since 1978 have greatly changed the State role in the urbanization process. While the State still sponsors the urban population with official non-agricultural household registration status and controls its growth, it is in a position neither to sponsor the urbanization of rural people released from the agricultural sector, nor to control their possible migration into large cities. Although a series of measures in relation to temporary residents have been taken to adapt to this new situation, they provide no guarantee that farmers will be excluded from the major cities. However, the State has adopted a series of policies to promote the development of locally-based township and village enterprises and foreign investment, facilitating the *in situ* transformation of rural areas, keeping many farmers in their hometowns, and even attracting many migrants from other regions. Thus, local economic activities and foreign investment have replaced the State as the dominant force in sponsoring and regulating the urbanization process.

Case studies in Jinjiang and Fuqing further illustrate how the *in situ* transformation of rural areas, which is neglected by conventional urbanization studies, has been achieved in these two places. It is concluded that the development of Jinjiang was initially based on the abundant labor force and limited capital, starting from dispersed joint-household enterprises engaged in some preliminary production. This development model particularly fits the situation where initial capital and labor skills are lacking in the rural areas, and is very effective in absorbing rural surplus labor and the transformation of rural employment structures. However, the physical transformation of the landscape lags behind. In contrast to Jinjiang, the development in Fuqing has been mainly driven by intensive foreign capital inflows into the development, investment and industrial zones. Tremendous physical changes have been brought to the previous rural landscape by the development, nevertheless it is not as effective as that in Jinjiang in creating non-agricultural employment opportunities. Interestingly, a tendency to convergence of the two development models has been identified in the study. Thus TVEs in Jinjiang are increasingly concentrated in the industrial zones, while the development of locally initiated TVEs is encouraged in Fuqing. It seems that these two models are complementary, and the combination of them could provide a better way to promote *in situ* rural-urban transformation. The successful rural-urban transformation in both Jinjiang and Fuqing has not only benefited the rural areas, but also diverted a lot of pressure from the existing cities. This has been decisive in achieving more balanced urbanization patterns in Fujian. Such rural-urban transformation is not unusual in China, especially in provinces like Jiangsu, Zhejiang, Fujian and Guangdong, although different regions have their own characteristics in development. Thus it seems that those local and foreign forces affecting regional (especially rural) development are increasingly important in understanding China's urbanization patterns, and more research is needed to obtain more insight into the functions of those forces in different regions in China.

8.4 THE UNDERLYING CONDITIONS FOR THE FEASIBILITY OF THE MORE BALANCED PATTERNS OF URBANIZATION

The policy changes did not work on their own in achieving the more balanced urbanization patterns. The implementation of the policies has been facilitated by some underlying conditions, which are examined in Chapter 6.

First, the developmental stage in the rural areas has been suitable for the implementation of such policies. As China's industrialization between 1949 and 1978 was actually confined to the existing urban areas, industrialization in the rural areas was still in a preliminary stage in the early 1980s, and relatively dispersed rural industrialization and urban development are necessary in this stage, as suggested by the experiences of developed countries.

Secondly, high population density and improved transport and communication further facilitate the implementation of the policies favoring more balanced urbanization patterns. High population growth rates lead to the emergence and development of densely populated rural settlements, and make it easier for the rural population to be urbanized on the spot. Widespread, better transport and communication facilities make geographical proximity to large cities and internal agglomeration of enterprises less important than it used to be, and increase the accessibility of rural areas to external resources and markets, making it more feasible for non-agricultural activities to be located in the rural areas.

Thirdly, the "Chineseness factor" enhances the decentralized nature of rural-urban transformation. The connections of Chinese overseas, Hong Kongers, and Taiwanese to their ancestral regions and the Chinese business network encourage them to invest in their ancestral regions, and the Chinese culture favors the development of small and medium-sized enterprises. Both factors are favorable for investment and business to be located in small cities and rural areas.

Thus the decentralized patterns of urbanization are not purely artifacts created by the policy makers in China. Rather, such urbanization patterns are the combined effects of government policies and the above socio-economic conditions. As these conditions also exist in other developing countries to different degrees, it is reasonable for them to consider similar policies, if they are concerned with their highly concentrated urbanization patterns. In fact, decentralized urbanization patterns already exist in some other developing countries as a result of these socio-economic conditions, although less developed in terms of both geographical area and degree of industrialization.

8.5 THEORETICAL IMPLICATIONS

The new urbanization patterns, especially the *in situ* transformation of the rural areas demonstrated in this study, cannot be well explained by the existing theories regarding urbanization and regional development. Chapter 7 compares the realities examined in this study and the relevant theories, and reveals some of their major inadequacies.

One major gap between the realities and the relevant theories lies in the increasing prevalence of rural non-agricultural activities and their important part in rural-urban transformation on the one hand, and the insensitivity of urbanization studies to these changes on the other hand. Some conceptual revisions are suggested to bridge this gap. A rural-urban continuum is proposed to replace the rigid rural-urban dichotomy commonly assumed in urbanization studies. Urbanization should be treated as a gradual transformation process, and the increase in rural non-agricultural activities should be seen as a component and a stage of this process, assuming a more important position in urbanization studies. The role of reclassification and city-creation in the urbanization process should be paid more attention in urbanization studies, and finally, some characteristics in many developing regions, such as high population density and advances in transport and communication, should be more adequately addressed. Extensive regional studies based on this new conceptual framework will enable urbanization theories to better accommodate the kind of new realities revealed in this study.

From the perspective of regional development, the biggest theoretical challenge emerging from this study is to explain the absence of polarization in the early stage of the regional development. The inability of existing theories to account for such a fact has several reasons. First, like urbanization theories, regional development theories do not have enough appreciation of the characteristics in many developing regions, such as high population density and advances in transport and communication. Secondly, while conventional regional development theories correctly give central importance to innovations in regional development, and to core regions in the creation and diffusion of such innovations, they neglect the independent roles of the periphery in originating and transmitting innovations under certain conditions. Such neglect is further related to the insensitivity of these theories to local geographical, historical, and cultural conditions, which are found to be important in Fujian's development. Thirdly, the existing theories either inadequately address the effects of foreign investment on the spatial development in developing countries, or neglect the important regional, historical and cultural settings in which foreign investment functions, and thus cannot capture the unconventional spatial effects of foreign investment examined in this study. Fourthly, the State plays a unique role in China's development, but the existing theories are weak in explaining State roles in the development process. The identification of these inadequacies in the existing theories would not undermine their fundamental basis, but would help to indicate the future direction of regional development studies, and to make existing theories more adequate and closer to the reality.

8.6 POLICY IMPLICATIONS

China's experiences in achieving more balanced urbanization patterns, especially those of Fujian demonstrated in this study, have also important implications for urban and regional development policies and for urban planning.

Regarding urban and regional development policies, Fujian's experiences seem to provide a relatively successful case of development policies focusing on rural industrialization and small town development, as an alternative to large-city-based development models. The analysis in Chapter 7 suggests that not only does China need to adhere to such policies, but other developing countries, especially those with high population density and good transport and communication, can also take reference from such policies to promote the development of their rural areas. Fujian's experiences further suggest that large-scale, market-oriented rural industrialization is compatible with some key elements of "development from below", and this combination can achieve more than traditional "bottom-up" strategies. Locally motivated, labor-intensive, small-scale, and low-technique rural industries play a key role in achieving an ideal result of such development strategy in both economic growth and the distribution of its benefits. Evidence presented in Chapter 7 suggests further that returned migrants may be important in initiating similar development to that in Fujian in inland areas of China, and reducing China's regional disparity; and policies on returned migrants and their role in their hometown development need to be developed.

Regarding urban planning, Fujian's experiences suggest that new planning ideas are urgently needed to deal with the planning problems arising from spontaneous urbanization in China. The increase in temporary residents has already caused major concerns, and requires China's urban planning to be expanded to include these temporary residents, and more importantly, to recognize their characteristics in urban planning. The effects of *in situ* rural-urban transformation on urban planning are also enormous, especially when one considers the need for urban planning in a large number of new urban places. There is a need for new planning approaches, which take the spatial structure of the existing rural or quasi-rural residential system as the planning framework, and promote more concentration in the distribution of both enterprises and settlements. Such new urban planning approaches are unconventional, but they seem to best fit the situations emerging from spontaneous urbanization in Fujian, and perhaps in China as a whole.

CHINA'S ADMINISTRATIVE HIERARCHY

China's administrative hierarchy is divided into six levels (Figure A1.1). At the top of the hierarchy is the national government; at the bottom are the residents' committees or villagers' committees. While a town as an administrative unit is at the second lowest administrative level, a city can be a provincial-level city, a prefectural-level city, or a county-level city, depending on its position in the administrative hierarchy. It is important to note the distinctions between the prefectural-level cities and the county-level cities, their administrative structures and the corresponding urban-rural compositions of their populations. A prefectural-level city is subdivided into several urban districts, which compose the *shiqu* (the city proper and its suburbs), and it administers several counties. It should be noted that these counties, except for their designated towns, are not included in the urban areas under any statistical criterion. It is also important to note that a name of a prefectural-level city can refer to either the *shiqu* of the city, or its whole administrative area, depending on the context. In the case of a county-level city, there is no further subdivision of the urban areas and it does not administer other counties, but when using urban statistics, caution should still be taken, as a county-level city is composed of city streets, towns and townships and its urban population can be counted differently according to different criteria. See also Appendix 2.

Figure A1.1 China's administrative hierarchy

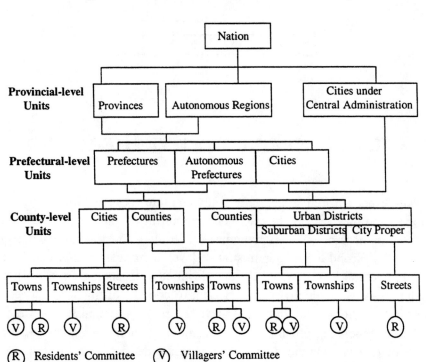

R Residents' Committee   V Villagers' Committee

Source: Chan 1994:250, slightly revised.

SOURCES AND DEFINITIONS OF THE DATA ON URBANIZATION IN CHINA[83]

1. Urban definitions and their changes

In China there were no official urban definitions until 1955. Since then there have been three major changes.

1.1 1955 definitions

The first urban definition after the establishment of the PRC was promulgated in 1955 by the State Council (China, State Council 1986a:91; 1986b:92). According to its stipulation, places that met any of the following criteria could acquire urban status:
  (1) localities with 100,000 or more permanent residents;
  (2) localities with 20,000 or more permanent residents where local administrative offices at the county level or higher were situated;
  (3) localities that had 2,000 or more permanent residents, 50 percent of whom were non-agricultural;
  (4) localities with 1,000 to 2,000 permanent residents, 75 percent of whom were non-agricultural.

---

[83] For a better understanding of the following please read Appendix 1 first.

The stipulation made a distinction between cities and towns. Places fulfilling criterion (1) or (2) were defined as officially designated cities, while places fulfilling criterion (3) or (4) were defined as officially designated towns.

1.2 1963 definitions

In 1963 the Central Committee of the CCP and the State Council issued a directive in order to reduce the number of designated cities and towns and the scope of suburban areas of cities (Central Committee 1986:96-7). In this directive cities and towns were defined more narrowly. Major modifications to the 1955 definition are as follows:

(1) Places with a population of more than 100,000 could remain as designated cities, but places with a population of fewer than 100,000 could retain the official city status only if they were provincial capitals, or important industrial or mining bases, or large scale goods and materials distributing centers, or important cities in border areas, where it was necessary for them to be under the leadership of the provincial government.

(2) Places could qualify as towns only if they had a minimum of 3,000 persons with 70 percent being non-agricultural, or if they had a population of 2,500 to 3,000 with more than 85 percent being non-agricultural. Commercial and handicraft centers with a population of less than 3,000 or non-agricultural population being less than 70 percent of the total population could be designated as towns if it was necessary for them to be under the leadership of the county-level government.

(3) The scope of the suburban area of a city should be reduced so that the agricultural population of the city would not be more than 20 percent of the total population of the city. Exceptions should be approved by the State Council.

1.3 1984 town definitions and 1986 city definitions

The third changes in town definition took place in 1984 (China, State Council 1984a). According to the new definition the following locations could be designated as towns:

(1) All seats of county-level governments.

(2) Townships with a total population of less than 20,000 and a non-agricultural population of more than 2,000 in the township government seat.

(3) Townships with a total population of more than 20,000 and the non-agricultural population in the township government seat being more than 10 percent of the total township population.

(4) Places in minority regions, sparsely populated remote areas, mountain areas, small industrial and mining areas, small ports, tourist points, and border ports with a non-agricultural population of less than 2,000, if necessary.

It was also stipulated that in areas where townships had been designated as towns, villages were to be put under the administration of towns.

Later in 1986 the State Council issued another document changing the city definition (China, State Council 1987:349-50). According to this document cities should be designated according to the following principles:

(1) A township with a non-agricultural population of at least 60,000 and an annual gross product of at least 200 million *Yuan* and that had already become a regional center could become a city. Important towns in minority and remote regions, important industrial, mining and scientific research bases, famous tourist areas, hubs of communications, and border ports with a non-agricultural population of less than 60,000 and an annual gross product of less than 200 million *Yuan* could be designated as cities if necessary.

(2) A county meeting the following conditions could be designated as a city: a total population of less than 500,000, a non-agricultural population of more than 100,000 in the town where the seat of the county government was situated, less than 40 percent of the permanent residents in that town being agricultural, and an annual gross product of at least 300 million *Yuan*. Villages and towns under the county's administration would be put under the city's administration.

(3) A county with a total population of more than 500,000, a non-agricultural population of more than 120,000 in the seat of the county government, and an annual gross product of more than 400 million *Yuan* could also be designated as a city.

(4) Counties with towns that were the seats of governments of autonomous prefectures (or leagues), although the non-agricultural population of these towns was less than 100,000 and the annual gross product was less

than 300 million *Yuan*, were eligible to be designated as cities if necessary.

The document also stipulated that a medium-sized city (one with urban districts) that had a non-agricultural population of more than 250,000 in the urban districts and an annual gross product of 1,000 million *Yuan* and that had become a regional political, economic, scientific and cultural center, exerting influence on and attraction to its surrounding counties, might implement the system of "city leading counties".

1.4 1993 city definitions

In 1993 the criteria for designating cities changed again (China, State Council 1993), while those for designating towns remain the same. The new criteria are as follows:

(1) Counties with a population density of more than 400 per square kilometer can be designated as cities if they meet the following conditions:

   (1.1) The town where the county government is situated has a non-agricultural population of more than 120,000, among them at least 80,000 being non-agricultural by household registration. The non-agricultural population of the whole county should be no less than 30 percent of the total, and no less than 150,000.

   (1.2) The county's gross output value of industry at the township level and above accounts for no less than 80 percent of the total gross output value of industry and agriculture, and is no less than 1,500,000,000 Yuan (at 1990 constant prices). The gross domestic product is more than 1,000,000,000 Yuan, with the value of the tertiary sector accounting for more than 20 percent; the local budgetary revenue is no less than 60,000,000 Yuan and the per capita revenue no less than 100 Yuan. A certain part of the revenue is turned over to the higher authorities.

   (1.3) Public facilities and infrastructure are fairly good. Among other things no less than 65 percent of the population uses running water; 60 percent of the roads are paved; and there is a good drainage system.

(2) Counties with a population density of between 100 and 400 per square kilometer can be designated as cities if they meet the following conditions:

    (2.1) The town where the county government is situated has a non-agricultural population of more than 100,000, among them at least 70,000 being non-agricultural by household registration. The non-agricultural population of the whole county should be no less than 25 percent of the total, and no less than 120,000.

    (2.2) The county's gross output value of industry at the township level and above accounts for no less than 70 percent of the total gross output value of industry and agriculture, and is no less than 1,200,000,000 Yuan (at 1990 constant prices). The gross domestic product is more than 800,000,000 Yuan, with the value of the tertiary sector accounting for more than 20 percent; the local budgetary revenue is no less than 50,000,000 Yuan and the per capita revenue no less than 80 Yuan. A certain part of the revenue is turned over to the higher authorities.

    (2.3) Public facilities and infrastructure are fairly good. Among other things no less than 60 percent of the population uses running water; 55 percent of the roads are paved; and there is a good drainage system.

(3) Counties with a population density of less than 100 can be designated as cities if they meet the following conditions:

    (3.1) The town where the county government is situated has a non-agricultural population of more than 80,000, among them at least 60,000 being non-agricultural by household registration. The non-agricultural population of the whole county should be no less than 20 percent of the total, and no less than 100,000.

    (3.2) The county's gross output value of industry at the township level and above accounts for no less than 60 percent of the total gross output value of industry and agriculture, and is no less than 800,000,000 Yuan (at 1990 constant prices). The gross domestic product is more than 600,000,000 Yuan, with the value of the tertiary sector accounting for more than 20 percent; the local budgetary revenue is no less than 40,000,000 Yuan and the per capita revenue no less than 60 Yuan. A certain part of the revenue is turned over to the higher authorities.

(3.3) Public facilities and infrastructure are fairly good. Among other things no less than 55 percent of the population uses running water; 50 percent of the roads are paved; and there is a good drainage system.

(4) The criteria for being designated as a city can be lowered if one of the following conditions is met:

(4.1) Places where a prefecture government is situated.

(4.2) Counties where the gross output value of industry at the township level and above is more than 4,000,000,000 Yuan; the gross domestic product value is no less than 2,500,000,000 Yuan; the local budgetary revenue is more than 100,000,000 Yuan, half of which is turned over to the higher authorities; the economy is developed and reasonably distributed.

(4.3) Important ports and trading ports along coasts, rivers and borders; and places where there is a national key project.

(4.4) Places with special political, military, and diplomatic needs.

When being designated as a city because of meeting one of the above conditions, the non-agricultural population of the seat of prefecture (or league, county) should be more than 60,000, among which at least 40,000 should have non-agricultural household registration.

(5) A few economically developed towns that have become the regional economic center can be designated as cities if necessary. The non-agricultural population should be no less than 100,000, among which 80,000 should have non-agricultural household registration. The local budgetary revenue per capita should be no less than 500 Yuan, at least 60 percent of which is turned over to the higher authorities. The gross output value of industry should account for more than 90 percent of the total gross output value.

(6) In principle, poverty-stricken counties receiving key support from the State, ministries and provincial governments, and counties receiving financial support will not be designated as cities.

(7) When designating cities the needs of urban systems and distribution should be met. There should be good geological and geographical conditions.

(8) After being designated as a city townships and towns will be under the administration of the city.

2. Different sources and series of urbanization data

There are basically two series of data on urbanization in China. One is based on the statistics provided by the public security bureau, the other is the census data. The former are usually published in the statistical yearbook edited by the statistical bureau, while the latter are published as census results.

2.1 Urbanization data from the statistical yearbook

Two types of data on urbanization can be found from the first sources:

2.1.1 Total population of cities and towns (TPCT)

This refers to the populations in the areas administered by designated cities and towns. It does not include the populations in the counties administered by a prefectural-level city, except for their populations in the designated towns.

2.1.2 Non-agricultural population of cities and towns (NAPCT)

This refers to the part of the total population of cities and towns which is non-agricultural by household registration.

2.2 Urbanization data from census

2.2.1 1953 census

As mentioned above there were no official definitions for cities and towns. The guideline in Fujian for the census was that all the populations living in the cities, towns administered by the county government, and important mining areas were counted as urban population. Populations living in the suburban area of cities were counted as rural population (Fu and Chen 1990:171-2).

2.2.2 1964 census

In this census the 1963 definitions were used. But only those in the total population of cities and towns who were non-agricultural by household registration were counted as urban population in this census (Fu and Chen 1990:172).

2.2.3 1982 census

The same definitions as the total population of cities and towns used in the annual statistics were used in this census.

2.2.4 1990 census and 1995 one percent population sample survey

In the 1990 census two criteria on urban population, which are also referred to as "the first criterion" and "the second criterion", were used (Population Census Office of Fujian Province 1992:1506-7).

Urban population based on the first criterion was the same as the total population of cities and towns used in the annual statistics.

City population based on the second criterion referred to the populations in the districts of cities (including suburban districts) and the populations in the street committees administered by cities without districts (i.e. county-level cities); town population based on the second criterion referred to the populations in the residents' committees of towns administered by the cities without districts, or of county towns.

Both criteria were also used in the 1995 one percent population sample survey.

REFERENCES

Arriaga, E., 1975. 'Selected measures of urbanization', in S. Goldstein and D. F. Sly (eds), *The Measurement of Urbanization and Projection of Urban Population*, pp. 19-87. Liège: Ordina Editions.

Beier, G. J., 1976. 'Can Third World cities cope?', *Population Bulletin* 31(4):1-36.

Brockerhoff, M. and E. Brennan, 1998. 'The poverty of cities in developing regions', *Population and Development Review* 24(1):75-114.

Brohman, J., 1996. *Popular Development: Rethinking the Theory and Practice of Development*. Cambridge MA: Blackwell.

Bronger, D., 1993. 'Urban systems in China and India — a comparison', in W. Taubmann (ed.), *Urban Problems and Urban Development in China*, pp. 33-76. Hamburg: Institutes für Asienkunde.

Brookfield, H., A. S. Hadi, and Z. Mahmud, 1991. *The City in the Village*. Singapore: Oxford University Press.

Button, K. J., 1976. *Urban Economics: Theory and Policy*. London and Basingstoke: The Macmillan Press.

Cao, Y., A. X. He, and M. Q. Lin, 1994. *Fuqing Shizhi (Annals of Fuqing Municipality)*. Xiamen: Xiamen University Press.

Central Committee of CCP and the State Council, 1984. Zhonggong zhongyang, guowuyuan zhuanfa nongmuyuyebu 'guanyu kaichuang shedui qiye xinjumian de baogao' de tongzhi (Circular of the Central Committee of the CCP and the State Council transmitting 'the report of the Ministry of Agriculture, Animal Husbandry, and Fishery on creating a new situation in commune and brigade enterprises'). Government document, Beijing.

Central Committee of CCP and the State Council, 1986. 'Directive of the Central Committee of the CCP and the State Council on adjusting the organization system of cities and towns and reducing suburban area of cities' (in Chinese), in Editorial Board (ed.), *Zhongguo Renkou Nianjian (1985) (Almanac of China's Population (1985))*, pp. 96-7. Beijing: China Social Science Press.

Central Employment Committee, 1986. 'Strategies and measures of the Central Employment Committee on solving the problem of rural surplus labor' (in

Chinese), in Editorial Board (ed.), *Zhongguo Renkou Nianjian (1985) (Almanac of China's Population (1985))*, pp.105-7. Beijing: China Social Science Press.

Chan, K. W., 1988. 'Rural-urban migration in China, 1950-1982: estimate and analysis', *Urban Geography* 9(1):53-84.

Chan, K. W., 1994. 'Urbanization and rural-urban migration in China since 1982', *Modern China* 20(3):243-81.

Chang, S. D., 1996. 'The floating population: an informal process of urbanization in China', *International Journal of Population Geography* 2(3):197-214.

Chang, S. D., M. Douglass, and W. B. Kim, 1989. Urbanization and urban policies in China: summary report. Paper presented at International Conference on China's Urbanization, East-West Population Institute, Honolulu, 23-27 January.

Chang, S. D. and R. Y. W. Kwok, 1990. 'The urbanization of rural China', in R.Y. W. Kwok, W. Parish, A. G. O. Yeh, and X. Q. Xu (eds), *Chinese Urban Reform: What Model Now?*, pp. 140-57. Armonk, NY: M. E. Sharpe.

Chen, F. T. and H. T. Pan, 1995. 'An analysis of the successful experience of the 100 million *Yuan* towns and townships in Fujian Province' (in Chinese), *Fujian Luntan (Fujian Forum)* 1:34-8.

Chen, H., 1996. 'Out-migration of rural labor and rural development in China' (in Chinese), *Renkou Yanjiu (Population Research)* 20(4):1-11.

Chen, J. Y. and D. C. Geng, 1993. *Zhongguo Nongye Laodongli Zhuanyi (China's Agricultural Labor Transfer)*. Beijing: People's Press.

Chen, J. Y. and J. Han, 1993. *Zhongguo Nongcun Gongyehua Daolu (China's Path to Industrialization)*. Beijing: China Social Science Publishing House.

Chen, J. Y. and B. L. Hu, 1994. 'China's three sector economic structure and the transfer of agricultural surplus labor' (in Chinese), *Jingji Yanjiu (Economic Research)* 4:14-22.

Chen, J. Y. and G. M. Huang (eds), 1991. *Fujiansheng Jingji Dili (The Economic Geography of Fujian Province)*. Beijing: Xinhua Publishing House.

Chen, M. and W. K. Zhuang (eds), 1994. *Jinjiang Shizhi (Annals of Jinjiang Municipality)*. Shanghai: Sanlian Publishing House, Shanghai Branch.

Chen, W., 1996. 'On China's urban development strategy' (in Chinese), *Dili Yanjiu (Geographical Research)* 15(3):16-22.

Chen, X. M., 1991. 'China's city hierarchy, urban policy and spatial development in the 1980s', *Urban Studies* 28(3):341-67.

Chen, Y. M., 1998. 'The new choice of rural laborers' (in Chinese), *HXWZ* (electronic journal), http://www.cnd.org:8018/HXWZ/cm9801c.hz8.html (13 May 1998).

China, Standing Committee of NPC, 1986. 'PRC regulations on household registration' (in Chinese), in Editorial Board (ed.), *Zhongguo Renkou Nianjian (1985) (Almanac of China's Population (1985))*, pp. 83-5. Beijing: China Social Science Press.

China, Standing Committee of NPC, 1990. 'Urban planning act of the People's Republic of China' (in Chinese), in Editorial Board (ed.), *Zhongguo Falu Nianjian (1990) (Almanac of China's Law (1990))*, pp. 176-7. Beijing: Office of *Almanac of China's Law*.

China, State Council, 1979. Guanyu fazhan shedui qieye luogan wenti de guiding (Regulations regarding some issues on the development of commune and brigade enterprises). Government document, Beijing.

China, State Council, 1981. Guowuyuan guanyu shedui qiye guanche guomin jingji tiao zheng fangzhen de luogan guiding (Some regulations of the State Council regarding the implementation of the strategy for readjusting national economy in commune and brigade enterprises). Government document, Beijing.

China, State Council, 1984a. 'Circular of the State Council approving the report of the Ministry of Civil Affairs concerning the adjustment of the criteria for establishing towns' (in Chinese), *Guowuyuan Gongbao (Bulletin of the State Council)*, No.30:1012-4.

China, State Council, 1984b. 'Circular from the State Council concerning the question of peasants entering towns for settlement' (in Chinese), *Guowuyuan Gongbao (Bulletin of the State Council)*, No.26:919-20.

China, State Council, 1986a. 'State Council's decision on establishing organization system of cities and towns' (in Chinese), in Editorial Board (ed.), *Zhongguo Renkou Nianjian (1985) (Almanac of China's Population (1985))*, p. 91. Beijing: China Social Science Press.

China, State Council, 1986b. 'State Council's stipulation on the criteria for urban-rural differentiation' (in Chinese), in Editorial Board (ed.), *Zhongguo Renkou Nianjian (1985) (Almanac of China's Population (1985))*, p. 92. Beijing: China Social Science Press.

China, State Council, 1986c. 'The directive of the State Council on preventing rural population from out-migrating blindly' (in Chinese), in Editorial Board (ed.), *Zhongguo Renkou Nianjian (1985) (Almanac of China's Population (1985))*, p. 108. Beijing: China Social Science Press.

China, State Council, 1987. 'Circular of the State Council approving and transmitting the report of the Ministry of Civil Affairs concerning the adjustment of the criteria for establishing cities and the conditions for city leading counties' (in Chinese), in Policy Research Office of the Ministry of Civil Affairs (ed.), *Minzheng Gongzuo Wenjian Xuanbian (Selected Documents on Civil Affairs)*, pp. 349-50. Beijing: Huaxia Publishing House.

China, State Council, 1989. 'Summary of the National Urban Planning Conference approved and transmitted by the State Council' (in Chinese), in Editorial Board (ed.), *Zhong Guo Chengshi Jianshe Nianjian (1986-1987) (Almanac of China's Urban Construction (1986-1987))*, pp. 14-7. Beijing: China Construction Industry Publishing House.

China, State Council, 1991. 'Circular of the State Council approving and transmitting the regulations of the Ministry of Public Security regarding household registration transfer' (in Chinese), in G. Weng (ed.), *Hukou Guanli Shouce (A Handbook on Household Registration Management)*. Shanghai: Shanghai Dictionary Publishing House.

China, State Council, 1993. Guowuyuan guanyu pizhuan minzhengbu quanyu tiaozheng sheshi biaozhun de baogao (Circular of the State Council approving the report of the Ministry of Civil Affairs concerning the adjustment of the criteria for establishing cities). Government document, Beijing.

China, State Council, 1996. Guowuyuan guanyu jiaqiang chengshi guihua gongzuo de tongzhi (Circular of the State Council on enhancing work on urban planning). Government document, Beijing.

China, State Statistical Bureau, 1986. *Zhongguo Tongji Nianjian (1986) (China Statistical Yearbook (1986))*. Beijing: China Statistical Publishing House.

China, State Statistical Bureau. 1988. *Zhongguo Tongji Nianjian (1988) (China Statistical Yearbook (1988))*. Beijing: China Statistical Publishing House.

China, State Statistical Bureau, 1991. *Zhongguo Tongji Nianjian (1991) (China Statistical Yearbook (1991))*. Beijing: China Statistical Publishing House.

China, State Statistical Bureau, 1994. *Zhongguo Tongji Nianjian (1994) (China Statistical Yearbook (1994))*. Beijing: China Statistical Publishing House.

China, State Statistical Bureau, 1996. *Zhongguo Tongji Nianjian (1996) (China Statistical Yearbook (1996))*. Beijing: China Statistical Publishing House.

China, State Statistical Bureau, Population and Employment Section, 1996. *Zhongguo Renkou Tongji Nianjian (1996) (China Population Statistics Yearbook (1996))*. Beijing: China Statistical Publishing House.

Chu, D. K.Y. and X. Z. Zheng, 1992. 'Fuzhou: capital of a frontier province', in Y. M. Yenug and X. W. Hu (eds), *China's Coastal Cities*, pp. 199-220. Honolulu: University of Hawaii Press.

Cui, G. H., Z. L. Hu, W. Z. Shen, Q. M. Jin, and T. X. Zheng, 1992. *Zhongguo Chengzhen Fazhan Yanjiu (A Study on China's Urban Development)*. Beijing: China Construction Industry Publishing House.

de Vries, J., 1984. *European Urbanization 1500-1800*. Cambridge MA: Harvard University Press.

de Vries, J., 1990. 'Problems in the measurement, description, and analysis of historical urbanization', in A. D. van der Woude, A. Hayami and J. de Vries (eds), *Urbanization in History: A Process of Dynamic Interaction*, pp. 43-60. Oxford: Clarendon Press.

Department of Land and Ocean Science, Nanjing University and Planning Department, Fuzhou Municipal Urban and Rural Construction Commission, 1992. Fuzhou chengshi zongti guihua tiaozheng jichu ziliao huibian (A collection of basic materials for the readjustment of Fuzhou overall urban planning). Government document, Fuzhou.

Douglass, M., 1991. 'Planning for environmental sustainability in the extended Jakarta metropolitan region', in N. Ginsburg, B. Koppel, and T. G. McGee (eds), *The Extended Metropolis: Settlement Transition in Asia*, pp. 239-73. Honolulu: University of Hawaii Press.

East Asia Analytical Unit, Department of Foreign Affairs and Trade, 1995. *Overseas Chinese Business Networks In Asia*. Canberra.

Ebanks, G. E. and C. Z. Cheng, 1990. 'China: a unique urbanization model', *Asia-Pacific Population Journal* 5(3):29-50.

Economic Information (17 December 1996), 1997. 'Urbanization: priority to development of towns', *China Population Today,* 14(1):20.

Editorial Department of 'Theory Study' of the Party School of Fujian Provincial Committee of CCP and Policy Research Office of Jinjiang Municipal Committee of CCP, 1994. *Jinjiang Mushi Yanjiu (Studies on the Jinjiang Model)*. Xiamen: Xiamen University Press.

Foreign Economic and Trade Commission of Fujian Province, 1998. Statistics on foreign direct investment by source countries (1979-1996) (in Chinese), http://www.fjfii.gov.cn/wzc/html/w-5-1-2 (9 May 1998).

Foreign Economic and Trade Commission of Fujian Province and Statistical Bu-
reau of Fujian Province, 1994. *Fujian Duiwai Jingji Shiwu Nian (Fifteen
Years of Fujian's Foreign Economy)*. Beijing: China Statistical Publishing
House.

Frank, A. G., 1969. *Capitalism and Underdevelopment in Latin America: Historical Studies of Chile*. New York: Monthly Review Press.

Friedmann, J., 1966. *Regional Development Policy: A Case Study of Venezuela*.
Cambridge MA: MIT Press.

Friedmann, J., 1972. 'A general theory of polarized development', in N. M. Hansen (ed.), *Growth Centers in Regional Economic Development*, pp. 82-107.
New York: The Free Press.

Friedmann, J. and M. Douglass, 1975. Agropolitan development: towards a new
strategy for regional planning in Asia. Prepared for Seminar on Industrialization Strategy and the Growth Pole Approach to Regional Planning and Development: the Asian Experience, sponsored by the United Nations Centre
for Regional Development, Nagoya, Japan, 4-13 November.

Fu, Z. D. and J. Y. Chen, 1990. *Zhongguo Renkou (Fujian Fence) (China's
Population (Fujian Volume))*. Beijing: China Financial and Economic Press.

Fuchs, R. J. and E. M. Pernia, 1987. 'External economic forces and national spa-
tial development: Japanese direct investment in Pacific Asia', in R. J. Fuchs,
G. W. Jones, and E. M. Pernia (eds), *Urbanization and Urban Policies in
Pacific Asia*, pp. 88-114. Boulder: Westview Press.

Fuchs, R. J. and E. M. Pernia, 1989. 'The influence of foreign direct investment
on spatial concentration', in F. J. Costa, A. K. Dutt, L. J. C. Ma and A. G.
Noble (eds), *Urbanization in Asia*, pp. 387-410. Honolulu: University of
Hawaii Press.

Fujian Daily, 1994. 'Fuzhou has become bigger' (in Chinese), *Fujian Ribao*, 17
August.

Fujian Daily, 1995. 'Warm congratulations on the third anniversary of the establishment of Jinjiang Municipality' (in Chinese), *Fujian Ribao*, 24 November.

Fujian Provincial Committee of CCP, 1991. Zhonggong fujian shengwei fujiansheng renmin zhenghu guanyu cujin xiangzhen qiye jixu jiankang fazhan de
ruogan guiding (Some regulations of Fujian Provincial Committee of the
CCP and Fujian Provincial Government on promoting continued and healthy
development of TVEs). Government document, Fuzhou.

Fujian Provincial Government, 1991. The resolution of Fujian Provincial People's Government regarding devolving authorities and simplifying proce-

dures for approving foreign investment projects (in Chinese), http://www.fjfii.gov.cn/wzc/html/w-2-2-12 (9 May 1998).

Fujian Provincial Urban and Rural Planning and Design Institute, 1995. Fuqing-shi chengshi zongti guihua jichu ziliao huibian (A collection of basic materials for Fuqing overall urban planning). Government document, Fuqing.

Fujian Today, 1998. 'New foreign investment is promoted and increases continuously in Fuqing' (in Chinese), *Fujian Today* (electronic journal), http://china-window.com/...day/cft80429.html#news-8, 15 July.

General Office of the Central Committee of CCP, 1995. Zhonggong Zhongyang bangongting, guowuyuan bangongting guanyu zhuanfa 'zhongyang shehui zhian zonghe zhili weiyuanhui guanyu jiaqiang liudong renkou guanli gong-zuo de yijian' de tongzhi (Circular of the General Office of the Central Committee of the CCP and the General Office of the State Council transmitting 'views of the Central Committee for the Comprehensive Administration of Public Security on enhancing the management of floating population'). Government document, Beijing.

General Office of Fuzhou Municipal Committee of CCP, 1996. Fuzhoushi jiaqiang liudong renkou guanli zanxing banfa (Temporary measures for enhancing the management of floating population). Government document, Fuzhou.

Gilbert, A. and J. Gugler, 1982. *Cities, Poverty, and Development: Urbanization in the Third World.* London: Oxford University Press.

Ginsburg, N., 1991. 'Preface', in N. Ginsburg, B. Koppel, and T. G. McGee (eds), *The Extended Metropolis: Settlement Transition in Asia*, pp. xiii-xviii. Honolulu: University of Hawaii Press.

Global News Digest, 1998. 'The life of the richest Chinese has become difficult since Suharto stepped down' (in Chinese). *Huanqiu Shibao*, 5 July.

Goldstein, S., 1990. 'Urbanization in China, 1982-1987: effects of migration and reclassification', *Population and Development Review* 16(4):673-701.

Goldstein, S. and D. F. Sly (eds), 1975. *The Measurement of Urbanization and Projection of Urban Population.* Liège: Ordina Editions.

Gu, S. Z., 1991. *Feinonghua Yu Chengzhenhua Yanjiu (Studies on Non-agriculturalization and Urbanization).* Hangzhou: Zhejian People's Press.

Guo, W. Q., M. J. Lin, S. C. Dong, and Y. W. Hong, 1994. *Dafuzhou Diqu Waixiangxing Jingji Fazhan Yu Touzi Huanjing Zonghe Yanjiu (A Comprehensive Study on Foreign-oriented Economic Development and Investment*

Environment in the Great Fuzhou Region). Beijing: China Science and Technology Publishing House.

Guo, Z. G. and G. S. Deng, 1995. 'On the real urbanization level of China' (in Chinese), *Renkou Yanjiu (Population Research)* 19(5):36-8.

Hackenberg, R. A., 1980. 'New patterns of urbanization in Southeast Asia: an assessment', *Population and Development Review* 6(3):391-419.

Hamer, A. M., 1987. 'Decentralized urban development: stylized facts and policy implications', in R. J. Fuchs, G. W. Jones, and E. M. Pernia (eds), *Urbanization and Urban Policies in Pacific Asia,* pp. 195-213. Boulder: Westview Press.

Hansen, N. M., 1981. 'Development from above: the centre-down development paradigm', in W. B. Stöhr and D. R. F. Taylor (eds), *Development from Above or Below? The Dialectics of Regional Planning in Developing Countries,* pp. 15-38. Chichester, NY: John Wiley and Sons.

Hauser, Philip M. 1987. 'Foreword', in R. J. Fuchs, G. W. Jones and E. M. Pernia (eds), *Urbanization and Urban Policies in Pacific Asia,* pp. xv-xvii. Boulder: Westview Press.

Heilig, G., 1997. 'Anthropogenic factor in land-use change in China', *Population and Development Review* 23(1):139-68.

Ho, S. P. S., 1979. 'Decentralized industrialization and rural development: evidence from Taiwan', *Economic Development and Cultural Change* 28(1):77-96.

Hu, A. G., 1997. 'Seeking a new soft landing: reducing high unemployment rate should be the first priority of macro-regulation' (in Chinese), *Liaowang (Outlook)* 31:12-3.

Hu, H. Y. and S. Y. Zhang, 1984. *Zhongguo Renkou Dili (Population Geography of China).* Shanghai: East China Normal University Press.

Hugo, G. J., 1980. 'New conceptual approaches to migration in the context of urbanization: a discussion based on the Indonesian experience', in P. A. Morrison (ed.), *Population Movements: Their Forms and Functions in Urbanization and Development,* pp. 69-113. Liège: Ordina Editions.

International Union for the Scientific Study of Population (IUSSP), 1982. *Multilingual Demographic Dictionary.* Liège: Ordina Editions.

Jones, G. W., 1983. Structural changes and prospects for urbanization in Asian countries. Papers of the East-West Population Institute, No. 88, Honolulu.

Jones, G. W., 1990. 'Structural economic change and its relationship to urbanization and population distribution policies', *Regional Development Dialogue* 11(1): 1-12.

Jones, G. W., 1991. 'Urbanization issues in the Asian-Pacific region', *Asian-Pacific Economic Literature* 5(2):5-33.

Jones, G. W., 1997. 'The thoroughgoing urbanisation of East and Southeast Asia', *Asia Pacific Viewpoint* 38(3):237-49.

Kelley, A. C. and J. G. Williamson, 1984. 'Population growth, industrial revolution, and the urban transition', *Population and Development Review* 10(3):419-41.

Khakee, A., 1996. 'Urban planning in China and Sweden in a comparative perspective', *Progress in Planning* 46(2):91-140.

Kim, W. B., 1989. Large cities and urban economy in China. Paper presented at international conference on China's urbanization, East-West Population Institute, Honolulu.

Kirkby, R. J. R., 1985. *Urbanisation in China: Town and Country in a Developing Economy 1949-2000 AD*. London: Croom Helm.

Kojima, R., 1995. 'Urbanization in China', *The Developing Economy* 33(2):121-54.

Koppel, B., 1991. 'The rural-urban dichotomy reexamined: beyond the ersatz debate?', in N. Ginsburg, B. Koppel and T. G. McGee (eds), *The Extended Metropolis: Settlement Transition in Asia*, pp. 47-70. Honolulu: University of Hawaii Press.

Kriedte, P., 1981. 'The origins, the agrarian context, and the conditions in the world market', in P. Kriedte, H. Medick and J. Schlumbohm, *Industrialization Before Industrialization*, pp. 12-37. Cambridge: Cambridge University Press and Paris: Editions de la Maison des Sciences de l'Homme.

Kriedte, P., J. Medick, and H. Schlumbohm, 1981. 'Introduction', in P. Kriedte, H. Medick and J. Schlumbohm, *Industrialization Before Industrialization*, pp. 1-11. Cambridge: Cambridge University Press and Paris: Editions de la Maison des Sciences de l'Homme.

Labor Bureau of Fujian Province, 1996. 'Some regulations on the management of the labor market in Fujian Province' (in Chinese), *Fujian Laodong (Fujian Labor)* 7:32-3.

Laquian, A., 1991. 'Urbanisation in China', in J. Y. Wang and T. H. Hull (eds), *Population and Development Planning in China*, pp. 235-63. Sydney: Allen & Unwin.

Laquian, A., 1996. 'The future of cities towards sustainable development' (in Chinese), *Chengshi Guihua (City Planning Review)* 20(4):28-31.

Lee, Y. S. F., 1989. 'Small towns and China's urbanization level', *China Quarterly* 120:771-86.

Lever-Tracy, C. and N. Tracy, 1993. 'The dragon and the rising sun: market integration and economic rivalry in east and southeast Asia', *Policy Organisation and Society* 6 (Summer):3-24.

Lewis, W. A., 1954. 'Economic development with unlimited supplies of labour', *Manchester School of Economics and Social Studies* 22(2):139-91.

Li, B. D. and Z. M. Wang, 1996. 'Inquiry into the problems in the revision of city overall plan' (in Chinese), *Chengshi Guihua (City Planning Review)* 20(4):9-13.

Li, J. B., 1997. 'The situation of temporary residents in Beijing and the countermeasures of municipal administration' (in Chinese), *Liaowang (Outlook)* 9:18-20.

Li, Q. X., J. A. Chen, and M. Yu, 1988. *Fujian Xiaochengzhen (Small Towns in Fujian)*. Fuzhou: Fujian Cartographic Publishing House.

Li, W. M., 1994. 'A comparative study on the familism in the organisation of small and medium-sized industries in Mainland China, Hong Kong and Taiwan' (in Chinese), *Zhongshan Daxue Xuebao (Journal of Zhongshan University)* 1:52-60.

Li, X. J., 1993. 'A summary for the seminar on comparative study of urbanization', in Editorial Board (ed.), *Zhongguo Jihua Shengyu Nianjian (1993) (China Family Planning Yearbook (1993))*, pp. 139-42. Beijing: Editorial Department of China Family Planning Yearbook.

Li, X. J., 1996. 'Locational behaviour of Hong Kong business investment in Mainland China' (in Chinese), *Dili Xuebao (Acta Geographica Sinica)* 51(3):213-22.

Liao, D. Q., 1995. 'China's urbanization road and rural reform and development' (in Chinese), *Zhongguo Shehui Kexue (Social Science of China)* 1:53-63.

Liao, S. Z., 1992. 'Promoting the development of Fujian's economy to a new level by accelerating the urbanization process' (in Chinese), *Fujian Luntan (Fujian Forum)* 6:32-6.

Lin, G. C. S., 1994. 'Changing theoretical perspectives on urbanisation in Asian developing countries', *Third World Planning Review* 16(1):1-23.

Lin, G. C. S. and Ma, L. J. C., 1994. 'The role of towns in Chinese regional development: the case of Guangdong Province', *International Regional Science Review* 17(1):75-97.

Linge, G. J. R. and D. K. Forbes, 1990. 'Appendix 1: definition of urban in the PRC', in G. J. R. Linge and D. K. Forbes (eds), *China's Spatial Economy*, pp. 193-8. Hong Kong: Oxford University Press.

Liu, G. H., 1993. The current situation of Fuzhou's floating population and the administrative counter-measures. Unpublished manuscript, Fuzhou.

Liu, R. S., 1993. *Fuzhou Chengxiang Jianshe Zhi (Annals of Urban and Rural Construction of Fuzhou Municipality)*. Beijing: China Construction Industry Publishing House.

Liu, S. X., Z. X. Wei, J. D. Fu, Z. M. Xu, and J. B. Wang, 1992. *Zhongguo Guoqing Congshu — Bai Xianshi Jingji Shehui Diaocha: Jinjiang Juan (China National Conditions Series — Social Economic Investigation in One Hundred Counties and Municipalities: Jinjiang Volume)*. Beijing: China Encyclopedia Publishing House.

Liu, Z., C. P. Wu, and Z. Z. Li, 1986. *Renkouxue Cidian (Dictionary of Demography)*. Beijing: People's Press.

Ma, L. J. C. and G. H. Cui, 1987. 'Administrative changes and urban population in China', *Annals of the Association of American Geographers* 77(3):373-95.

Ma, L. J. C. and C. S. Lin, 1993. 'Development of towns in China: a case study of Guangdong Province', *Population and Development Review* 19(3):583-606.

Mallee, H., 1995. 'China's household registration system under reform', *Development and Change* 26:1-29.

Mao, R. B., 1996. 'Be bold in reform to promote the healthy development of China's small towns' (in Chinese), *Jingji Yanjiu Cankao (Reference Materials for Economic Research)* 8-9:8-10.

McGee, T. G., 1971. *The Urbanization Process in the Third World*. London: G. Bell and Sons.

McGee, T. G., 1991. 'The emergence of Desakota regions in Asia: expanding a hypothesis', in N. Ginsburg, B. Koppel and T. G. McGee (eds), *The Extended Metropolis: Settlement Transition in Asia*, pp. 3-25. Honolulu: University of Hawaii Press.

Medick, H., 1981. 'The structures and function of population-development under the proto-industrial system', in P. Kriedte, H. Medick, and J. Schlumbohm,

Industrialization Before Industrialization, pp. 74-93. Cambridge: Cambridge University Press and Paris: Editions de la Maison des Sciences de l'Homme.

Mendels, F. F., 1972. 'Proto-industrialization: the first phase of the industrialization process', *Journal of Economic History* 32(1):241-61.

Mendels, F. F., 1981. 'Agriculture and peasant industry in eighteenth-century Flanders', in P. Kriedte, H. Medick, and J. Schlumbohm, *Industrialization Before Industrialization*, pp. 161-77. Cambridge: Cambridge University Press and Paris: Editions de la Maison des Sciences de l'Homme.

Montgomery, M. R., 1988. 'How large is too large? Implications of the city size literature for population policy and research', *Economic Development and Cultural Change* 36(4):691-720.

Ng, M. K. and F. L. Wu, 1995. 'A critique of the 1989 city planning act of the People's Republic of China: a western perspective', *Third World Planning Review* 17(3):279-93.

Office of Jinjiang Prefectural Committee of CCP, 1981. Jinjiang chendai gongshe sheyuan hezi banchang de diaocha (Investigation on collecting funds and establishing factories jointly by commune members in Chendai, Jinjiang). Government document, Jinjiang.

Omohundro, J., 1981. *Chinese Merchant Families in Iloilo*. Quezon City: Ateneo de Manila University Press and Athens, Ohio: Ohio University Press.

Panagariya, A., 1995. 'What can we learn from China's export strategy?', *Finance & Development*, June.

People's Daily, 1997. 'It is of great urgency to save the cultivated land', Editorial (in Chinese), *Renmin Ribao*, 19 May.

Pfister, N., 1997. On centres and suburbs: the changing spatial structure of Sydney, 1981 to 1991. Paper presented to Pacific Regional Science Conference Organisation 15th Meeting and Australian and New Zealand Regional Science Association 21st Meeting, Wellington, New Zealand, 8 to 12 December.

Planning Commission of Fujian Province, 1992. *Fujian Yanhai Diqu Guotu Kaifa Zhengzhi Zonghe Guihua (A Comprehensive Program for the Territorial Development and Readjustment in the Coastal Area of Fujian Province)*. Beijing: China Planning Publishing House.

Policy Research Institute of Fuzhou Municipal Committee of CCP, 1991. *Fuzhou Shimin Banshi Zhinan (A Guidebook for the Residents of Fuzhou in Handling affairs)*. Fuzhou: Haichao Photography Publishing House.

Population Census Office of Fujian Province, 1984. *Fujiansheng Disanci Renkou Pucha Ziliao Huibian (Tabulation on the 1982 Population Census of Fujian Province)*. Fuzhou.

Population Census Office of Fujian Province, 1990. *Fujiansheng Disici Renkou Pucha Shougong Huizong Ziliao (Tabulation on the 1990 Population Census of Fujian Province (Manual Tabulation))*. Beijing: China Statistical Publishing House.

Population Census Office of Fujian Province, 1992. *Fujiansheng 1990 Renkou Pucha Ziliao (Dianzi Jisuanji Huizong) (Tabulation on the 1990 Population Census of Fujian Province (Computer Tabulation))*. Beijing: China Statistical Publishing House.

Portes, A., 1997. 'Neoliberalism and the sociology of development: emerging trends and unanticipated facts', *Population and Development Review* 23(2):229-59.

Preston, S. H., 1979. 'Urban growth in developing countries: a demographic reappraisal ', *Population and Development Review* 5(2):195-215.

Qiu, S., 1995. *Jinjiang Jingshen Tansuo (Exploring Jinjiang Spirit)*. Beijing: People's Press.

Ranis, G. and J. C. H. Fei, 1961. 'A theory of economic development', *American Economic Review* 11(4):533-65.

Ranis, G. and F. Stewart, 1993. 'Rural nonagricultural activities in development: theory and application', *Journal of Development Economics* 40(1):74-100.

Renaud, B., 1981. *National Urbanization Policy in Developing Countries*. New York: Oxford University Press.

Richardson, H. W., 1980. 'National urban development strategies in developing countries', *Urban Studies* 18(3):267-83.

Rondinelli, D. A., 1978. *Urbanization and Rural Development: A Spatial Policy for Equitable Growth*. New York: Praeger Publishers.

Rondinelli, D. A., 1980. 'Balanced urbanization, regional integration and development planning in Asia', *Ekistics* 47(284):331-9.

Rondinelli, D. A., 1983. *Secondary Cities in Developing Countries: Policies for Diffusing Urbanization*. Beverly Hills: Sage.

Shannon, T. R., 1989. *An Introduction to the World-System Perspective*. Boulder: Westview Press.

Sit, V. F. S. and S. L. Wong, 1989. *Small and Medium Industries in an Export-Oriented Economy: The Case of Hong Kong*. Hong Kong: Centre of Asia Studies, University of Hong Kong.

Sit, V. F. S. and C. Yang, 1997. 'Foreign-investment-induced exo-urbanisation in the Pearl River Delta, China', *Urban Studies* 34(4):647-77.

Skeldon, R., 1990. *Population Mobility in Developing Countries: A Reinterpretation*. London: Belhaven Press.

Skeldon, R., 1997. 'Rural-to-urban migration and its implications for poverty alleviation', *Asia-Pacific Population Journal* 12(1):3-16.

Smith C. A., 1985. 'Theories and measures of urban primacy: a critique', in M. Timberlake (ed.), *Urbanization in the World-Economy*, pp. 87-117. Orlando: Academic Press.

Sorenson, T., 1997. Interfacing regional development theory and practice. Presidential address delivered to Pacific Regional Science Conference Organisation 15th Meeting and Australian and New Zealand Regional Science Association 21st Meeting, Wellington, New Zealand, 8 to 12 December.

Speare, A., P. K. C. Liu, and C. L. Tsay, 1988. *Urbanization and Development: The Rural-Urban Transition in Taiwan*. Boulder: Westview Press.

State Commission on Economic Reform, Research Group on China's Small Towns, 1996. 'System changes in the process of China's small town growth' (in Chinese), *Jingji Yanjiu Cankao (Reference Materials for Economic Research)*, 8-9:3-6.

Statistical Bureau of Fujian Province, 1989. *Fujian Fenjin De Sishi Nian (Forty Years' Great Progress in Fujian)*. Beijing: China Statistical Publishing House.

Statistical Bureau of Fujian Province, 1990. *Fujian Tongji Nianjian (1990) (Fujian Statistical Yearbook (1990))*. Beijing: China Statistical Publishing House.

Statistical Bureau of Fujian Province, 1991. *Fujian Tongji Nianjian (1991) (Fujian Statistical Yearbook (1991))*. Beijing: China Statistical Publishing House.

Statistical Bureau of Fujian Province, 1992. *Fujian Tongji Nianjian (1992) (Fujian Statistical Yearbook (1992))*. Beijing: China Statistical Publishing House.

Statistical Bureau of Fujian Province, 1993. *Fujian Tongji Nianjian (1993) (Fujian Statistical Yearbook (1993))*. Beijing: China Statistical Publishing House.

Statistical Bureau of Fujian Province, 1994. *Fujian Tongji Nianjian (1994) (Fujian Statistical Yearbook (1994))*. Beijing: China Statistical Publishing House.

Statistical Bureau of Fujian Province, 1995. *Fujian Tongji Nianjian (1995) (Fujian Statistical Yearbook (1995))*. Beijing: China Statistical Publishing House.

Statistical Bureau of Fujian Province, 1996. *Fujian Tongji Nianjian (1996) (Fujian Statistical Yearbook (1996))*. Beijing: China Statistical Publishing House.

Statistical Bureau of Fujian Province and Public Security Bureau of Fujian Province, 1989. *Fujiansheng Renkou Tongji Ziliao Huibian (1949-1988) (A collection of Population Statistics of Fujian Province (1949-1988))*. Beijing: China Statistical Publishing House.

Statistical Bureau of Fuqing Municipality, 1991. *Fuqing tongji nianjian (1990) (Fuqing statistical yearbook (1990))*. Unofficially published government statistics, Fuqing.

Statistical Bureau of Fuqing Municipality, 1995. *Fuqing tongji nianjian (1995) (Fuqing statistical yearbook (1995))*. Unofficially published government statistics, Fuqing.

Statistical Bureau of Fuzhou Suburban District, 1993. *Fuzhou jiaoqu guomin jingji tongji ziliao (1992) (The statistical material on the national economy in Fuzhou suburban district (1992))*. Unofficially published government statistics, Fuzhou.

Statistical Bureau of Jinjiang Municipality, 1995. *Jinjiangshi guomin jingji tongji ziliao (1994) (The statistical material on the national economy in Jinjiang Municipality (1994))*. Unofficially published government statistics, Jinjiang.

Stöhr, W. B., 1981. 'Development from below: The bottom-up and periphery-inward development paradigm', in W. B. Stöhr and D. R. F. Taylor (eds), *Development from Above or Below? The Dialectics of Regional Planning in Developing Countries*, pp. 39-72. Chichester: John Wiley and Sons.

Stöhr, W. B. and D. R. F. Taylor, 1981. 'Introduction', in W. B. Stöhr and D. R. F. Taylor (eds), *Development from Above or Below? The Dialectics of Regional Planning in Developing Countries*, pp. 1-14. Chichester: John Wiley and Sons.

Sun, J. Z., Y. X. Yuan, J. N. Li, S. L. Zhao, M. Z. Li, X. X. Zhang, and L. T. Feng, 1996. *Bashi Niandai Zhongguo Renkou Biandong Fenxi (Analyses on China's Population Changes in the 1980s)*. Beijing: China Financial and Economic Publishing House.

Tang, W. S., 1995. Urbanization in China's Fujian Province since 1978. Occasional Paper No.43, Hong Kong: Institute of Asia-Pacific Studies, Chinese University of Hong Kong. Hong Kong.

Tang, X. X., 1991. *Fujian Jingji Zonghe Kaifa Lun (On Fujian's Comprehensive Economic Development)*. Fuzhou: Fujian Science and Technology Publishing House.

Tao, R., 1995. 'On the development potential of large cities and the selection of population policies: China's policies on the development of large cities viewed from the debate on "overurbanization"' (in Chinese), *Zhongguo Renkou Kexue (Chinese Journal of Population Science)* 5:40-7.

Taylor, J. R. and J. Banister, 1991. 'Surplus rural labor in the People's Republic of China', in G. Veeck (ed.), *The Uneven Landscape: Geographic Studies in Post-Reform China*, pp. 87-119. Baton Rouge LA: Geoscience Publications, Department of Geography and Anthropology, Louisiana State University.

Tian, X. Y., 1989. 'Studies on the problem of China's urban population criteria' (in Chinese), *Renkou Yu Jingji (Population and Economics)* 1:3-6

Todaro, M. P., 1969. 'A model of labor migration and urban unemployment in less developed countries', *American Economic Review* 58(1):138-48.

Todaro, M. P., 1981. *City Bias and Rural Neglect: The Dilemma of Urban Development*. New York: Population Council.

Tracy, N., 1996. The overseas Chinese and China: the critical linkage. Unpublished manuscript.

Tsai, H. H., 1987. 'Population decentralization policies: the experience of Taiwan', in R. J. Fuchs, G. W. Jones and E. M. Pernia (eds), *Urbanization and Urban Policies in Pacific Asia*, pp. 214-29. Boulder: Westview Press.

United Nations, Department for Economic and Social Affairs, 1974. *Methods for Projections of Urban and Rural Population*. ST/ESA/SER.A/55. New York.

United Nations, 1980. *Patterns of Urban and Rural Population Growth*. New York.

United Nations, 1993. *State of Urbanization in Asia and Pacific*. New York.

United Nations, Department for Economic and Social Information and Policy Analysis, Population Division, 1995. *World Urbanization Prospects: The 1994 Revision*. ST/ESA/SER.A/150. New York.

United Nations, Department for Economic and Social Affairs, Population Division, 1998. *World Urbanization Prospects: The 1996 Revision*. ST/ESA/SER.A/170. New York.

Wallerstein, I., 1974. *The Modern World-System: Capitalist Agriculture and the Origins of the European World-Economy in the Sixteenth Century.* New York: Academic Press.

Wallerstein, I., 1976. 'A world-system perspective on the social sciences', *British Journal of Sociology* 27(3):343-52.

Wang, G. W., 1993. 'Greater China and the Chinese overseas', *China Quarterly* 136:926-48.

Wang, L. Y., 1996. 'On the management of China's urban temporary residents under the conditions of socialist market economy' (in Chinese), *Renkou Yanjiu (Population Research)* 20(4):12-9.

Wang, S. J., 1995. 'On the growth of China's large cities at the current stage' (in Chinese), *Zhongguo Renkou Kexue (Chinese Journal of Population Science)* 6:17-23.

Wang, S. J. and Z. G. Zhou, 1993. 'The investigation on invisible urbanization in the rural areas and the estimate on its level' (in Chinese), *Renkou Yu Jingji (Population and Economics)* 1:16-24.

Weber, A. F., 1968. *The Growth of Cities in the Nineteenth Century*, third printing. Ithaca, NY: Cornell University Press.

Wei, J. S., 1990. 'Trends in population growth in China's towns during the eighties, and town population in-migration and its decisive factors: a historic convergence of two types of demographic change', *Chinese Journal of Population Science* 2(4):317-29.

Williamson, J. G., 1988. 'Migration and urbanization', in H. Chenery and T. N. Srinivasan (eds), *Handbook of Development Economics, Volume 1*, pp. 425-63. Amsterdam: Elsevier Science Publishers.

Wong, K. C., 1997. Entrepreneurship of ethnic Chinese business community in Southeast Asia since the mid-19th century. Paper presented at Chinese Southern Diaspora Workshop, Australian National University, Canberra, 11 July.

Wong, S. L., 1985. 'The Chinese family firm: a model', *British Journal of Sociology* 36(1):58-72.

Wong, S. L., 1988. 'The applicability of Asian family values to other sociocultural settings', in P. L. Berger and H. H. M. Hsiao (eds), *In Search of an East Asian Development Model*, pp. 134-54. New Brunswick and Oxford: Transaction Books.

World Bank, 1994. *World Development Report, 1993.* New York: Oxford University Press.

Wu, T., 1994. *Jinjiang Huaqiaozhi (Annals of Jinjiang Overseas Chinese)*. Shanghai: Shanghai People's Press.

Wu, T., Y. B. Ke, L. Jiang, and Z. L. Chen (eds), 1994. *Kua Shiji De Zhongguo Renkou: Fujian Juan (The Population of China towards the 21st Century: Fujian Volume)*. Beijing: China Statistical Publishing House.

Xin, Z. P., 1996. 'The essentials of international city theories: with reference to the development of China's international cities' (in Chinese), *Chengshi Wenti (Urban Issues)* 3:8-13

Xing, W. X., L. S. Zhuang, and K. L. Wei, 1990. *Fujian Chengzhen Fazhan Yu Buju (The Development and Distribution of Cities and Towns in Fujian Province)*. Fuzhou: Fujian Science and Technology Publishing House.

Xu, M. Q. and Y. Z. Wang, 1992. *Jinjiang Ren (Jinjiang People)*. Beijing: China Literary and Art Workers Association Publishing Company.

Xu, X. Q. and S. M. Li, 1990. 'China's open door policy and urbanization in the Pearl River Delta region', *International Journal of Urban and Regional Research*, 14(1):49-69.

Xu, X. R. (ed.), 1996. *Jinjiang jiaotong yunshu zhi (Annals of communications and transportations of Jinjiang)*. Unpublished manuscript.

Yan, X. P., 1996. *Fujiansheng Duiwai Jingmao Nianjian (Almanac of Foreign Economic Relation and Trade of Fujian Province)*. Beijing: China Books Publishing House.

Yan, Z. M., 1989. 'On the criteria for dividing China's rural-urban population and the problem of China's urban scale hierarchy' (in Chinese), *Renkou Yu Jingji (Population and Economics)* 2:50-5.

Yeh, A. G. O. and X. Q. Xu, 1996. 'Globalization and the urban system in China', in F. C. Lo and Y. M. Yeung (eds), *Emerging World Cities and Pacific Asia*, pp. 219-67. Tokyo: United Nations University Press.

Yin, R. K., 1984. *Case Study Research: Design and Methods*. Beverly Hills: Sage Publications.

Young, E., 1994. 'Internal migration', in D. Lucas and P. Meyer (eds), *Beginning Population Studies (Second Edition)*, pp. 91-100. Canberra: National Centre for Development Studies, Australian National University.

Yu, D. P., 1995. Thoughts on the reasonable measurement of regional urbanization levels (in Chinese), *Renkou Yu Jingji (Population and Economics)* 5:39-42.

Yu, H. J. and Y. M. Ning, 1983. *Chengshi Dili Gailun (An Introduction to Urban Geography)*. Hefei: Anhui Science and Technology Publishing House.

Zhang, B. Z., 1995. *Zhongguo Chengshihua Daolu Qiusuo (Exploring China's Urbanization road)*. Haerbing: Heilongjiang People's Press.

Zhang, R. Y. and Z. L. Lu, 1986. *Fujian Diqu Jingji (Fujian Regional Economy)*. Fuzhou: Fujian People's Press.

Zhang, Y., 1997. 'Implementing vigorously and reliably the pilot plan regarding the reform of the household registration system in small towns and cities' (in Chinese), *Renmin Ribao (People's Daily)*, 24 October.

Zhao, S. K., C. Lin, Y. S. Liu, and Z. Q. Zeng, 1996. *Fuzhou Nianjian (1996) (Fuzhou Yearbook (1996))*. Beijing: China Statistical Publishing House.

Zhao, Z. W., 1992. Household and kinship in recent and very recent Chinese history: theory and practice of co-residence in three Chinese villages in Beijing area. Unpublished Ph. D thesis, Cambridge University, Cambridge.

Zheng, J. M., 1996. Fujian Tudi Kechixu Liyong Yanjiu (A study on Fujian's sustainable land use). Unpublished Ph.D. thesis, East China Normal University, Shanghai.

Zhong, F. G., 1995. 'An analysis of population urbanization in the Pearl River Delta—a strongly foreign-oriented economic region' (in Chinese), *Renkou Yu Jingji (Population and Economics)* 2:3-9.

Zhong, F. G., 1997. China's urbanization: transition since 1949. Paper presented at IUSSP 23rd General Conference, Beijing, 11-17 October.

Zhou, Y. X., 1988. 'Definition of urban places and statistical standards of urban population in China: problems and solutions', *Asian Geographer* 7(1):12-28.

Zhou, Y. X., 1989. The urban statistical units of China: problems and proposal. Paper presented at International Conference on China's Urbanization, East-West Population Institute, Honolulu, 23-27 January.

Zhou, Y. X., 1991. 'The metropolitan interlocking region in China: a preliminary hypothesis', in N. Ginsburg, B. Koppel and T. G. McGee (eds), *The Extended Metropolis: Settlement Transition in Asia*, pp. 47-70. Honolulu: University of Hawaii Press.

Zhou, Y. X., 1993. 'Some new trends of China's urbanization in the 1980s: with reference to the proportion of urban population in China's fourth population census' (in Chinese), in Y. M. Yeung (ed.), *Zhongguo Chengshi Yu Quyu Fazhan: Zhanwang Ershiyi Shiji (China's Urban and Regional Development: Looking into the 21st Century)*, pp. 105-32. Hong Kong: Hong Kong Institute of Asia-Pacific Studies, Chinese University of Hong Kong.

Zhou, Y. X. and Y. L. Shi, 1995. 'Towards establishing the concept of physical urban area in China' (in Chinese), *Dili Xuebao (Acta Geographica Sinica)* 50(4):289-301.

Zhu, B. S., 1997. 'The duration of stay and displacement of the floating population in the urban area: a case study of Shanghai Municipality', in China Population Association (ed.), *Twenty-Third IUSSP General Population Conference: Symposium on Demography of China*, pp. 215-20, Beijing.

Zhu, Y., 1991. 'Some comparisons between the urbanization in developed countries and that in developing countries and their implications' (in Chinese), *Renkou Yanjiu (Population Research)* 5:46-9.

Zhu, Y., 1992. 'Promoting the urbanization process of Fujian on the basis of co-ordinated development of large, middle and small cities' (in Chinese), *Fujian Luntan (Fujian Forum)* 9:32-4.

Zhu, Y., 1994a. 'Fujian's population migration since the 1980s' (in Chinese), *Fujian Shifan Daxue Xuebao (Journal of Fujian Normal University)* 1:17-23.

Zhu, Y., 1994b. 'Population distribution and urbanization' (in Chinese), in Wu et al. (eds), *Kua Shiji De Zhongguo Renkou: Fujian Juan (The Population of China towards the 21st Century: Fujian Volume)*, pp. 180-202. Beijing: China Statistical Publishing House.

Zhu Y., 1997. 'The fertility transition in the areas with well-developed township and village enterprises: a comparison of two models' (in Chinese), *Renkou Yu Jingji (Population and Economics)* 2:53-6.

Zhu, Z., 1991. *Renkou Dili Xue (Population Geography)*. Beijing: China People's University Press.

Zhuang, R. X., 1996. 'Enhancing the planning and construction of development zones and fostering the growth pole of regional economy'(in Chinese), *Fujian Duiwai Jingmao (Fujian Foreign Trade and Economy)* 1:31-3.

INDEX